W9-AAX-399

" A practical book filled with great examples and tips from successful publishers. The authors understand what it's like to work with little money and too much to do. It is great for training others or answering your own questions..."

—John Griffin, President, Magazine Group, *National Geographic*

" With competition for readers' time and money so fierce these days, this book offers invaluable advice for creating print and online publications that will grab an audience—and stir them to action—without overspending your budget. It is *so* practical, filled with great examples and backed up with the personal experience of the authors."

—Jay Harris, President & Publisher, *Mother Jones* magazine

" A practical, example-filled resource from two publishing experts who've been there, done that. This kind of experience-based advice is priceless if you're trying to launch or sustain a publishing effort on a tight budget."

—Holly Brady, Director, Stanford Publishing Courses

" If you just happen to be crazy or dedicated enough to want to launch a message-driven print magazine in the 21st century, you're going to need all the help you can get. Lucky for you, Cheryl Woodard and Lucia Hwang have done a tremendous job assembling most of the information you'll need to get going."

—David Loeb, Publisher, *Bay Nature* magazine

" I wish this book had been available when I was starting out as an editor 14 years ago. What makes it such a practical resource for nonprofits on a limited budget are the very specific tools and tips covering all aspects of newsletter and magazine publishing ..."

—Stephanie Roth, Editor, *Grassroots Fundraising Journal*

" Whether it's budgeting, scheduling, art direction, or rights management, nonprofit publishing is all in the details. This comprehensive guide covers—in an informative and lively way—everything you'll need to manage your publication from concept to finished product."
—**Timothy Lyster, Publisher,** *The Nonprofit Quarterly*

" As I read this manuscript, I could only wish it had been written 35 years earlier, when I began to work on a nonprofit magazine start-up with a bunch of equally naive colleagues. Oh, the pain and heartache we would have been spared .... Do not lift a finger to start a nonprofit publishing venture before reading every page of this book."
—**Mark Dowie, Former Publisher & Editor,** *Mother Jones* **magazine**

" The authors really understand what it's like to work in a nonprofit, with no money *and* too much to do. They explain how to prioritize, how to deal with office politics—and how to create effective publications on a shoestring."
—**Jeff Perlstein, Executive Director, Media Alliance**

" If your nonprofit is publishing or thinking of publishing, this is your bible! Thorough, practical, and well researched, the book offers technical advice and real-world examples."
—**Tom Peterson, Senior VP of Communications & Marketing, Heifer International**

always up to date

The law changes, but Nolo is on top of it! We offer several
ways to make sure you and your Nolo products are up to date:

1 **Nolo's Legal Updater**
We'll send you an email whenever a new edition of this book is
published! Sign up at **www.nolo.com/legalupdater**.

2 **Updates @ Nolo.com**
Check **www.nolo.com/update** to find recent changes
in the law that affect the current edition of your book.

3 **Nolo Customer Service**
To make sure that this edition of the book is the most
recent one, call us at **800-728-3555** and ask one of
our friendly customer service representatives.
Or find out at **www.nolo.com**.

please note

We believe accurate, plain-English legal information should help you solve many of your own legal problems. But this text is not a substitute for personalized advice from a knowledgeable lawyer. If you want the help of a trained professional—and we'll always point out situations in which we think that's a good idea—consult an attorney licensed to practice in your state.

1st edition

Every Nonprofit's Guide to Publishing

by Cheryl Woodward and Lucia Hwang

070.59
W

FIRST EDITION	JUNE 2007
Editor	BARBARA KATE REPA
Cover Design	SUSAN WIGHT
Book Design	SUSAN PUTNEY
Production	JESSICA STERLING
Index	BAYSIDE INDEXING
Proofreading	JOE SADUSKY
Printing	CONSOLIDATED PRINTERS, INC

Woodard, Cheryl.
    Every nonprofit's guide to publishing : creating newsletters, magazines &
websites people will read / by Cheryl Woodard and Lucia Hwang.
        p. cm.
    ISBN-13: 978-1-4133-0658-3 (pbk.)
    ISBN-10: 1-4133-0658-6 (pbk.)
1. Nonprofit organizations--Publishing. 2. Internet publishing. 3.
Nonprofit organizations--Public relations. 4. Social marketing. I. Hwang,
Lucia. II. Title.
HD62.6.W66 2007
070.5'94--dc22   2006039255

Copyright © 2007 by Nolo
ALL RIGHTS RESERVED. PRINTED IN THE USA.

No part of this publication may be reproduced, stored in a retrieval system, or transmitted in any form or by any
means, electronic, mechanical, photocopying, recording, or otherwise without prior written permission.
Reproduction prohibitions do not apply to the forms contained in this product when reproduced for personal use.

Quantity sales: For information on bulk purchases or corporate premium sales, please contact the Special Sales
Department. For academic sales or textbook adoptions, ask for Academic Sales. Call 800-955-4775 or write to
Nolo, 950 Parker Street, Berkeley, CA 94710.

About the Authors

Tonya Perme

Cheryl Woodard is a full-time publishing business consultant. She writes business plans for new publications, helps existing publications improve revenues or efficiency, and coaches individuals through the ups and downs of their publishing efforts. Woodard has a BA in Economics from the University of California, Berkeley and is a cofounder of *PC Magazine, PC World,* and *MacWorld.* She is the author of *Starting and Running a Successful Newsletter or Magazine,* also published by Nolo.

Lucia Hwang is an award-winning investigative reporter and feature writer. Since 2004, she has worked as the editor for the magazine of a nonprofit association. Hwang has been a staff and freelance writer for a wide variety of publications—from daily newspapers to alternative city weeklies to magazines—and has also taught investigative reporting and news writing. She is a graduate of the University of California, Berkeley and the Columbia University Graduate School of Journalism.

Acknowledgments

Much thanks to editor Barbara Kate Repa for doing what she does.

Thanks to Jake Flaherty and Jonathan Wieder for deconstructing the art of publication design.

Thanks to the folks at California Lawyer for first showing me how magazines go together.

Thanks to my parents, Eugene and Theresa Hwang, who put up only a minor fuss upon learning that their eldest daughter wanted to write for a living.

And thanks to all people everywhere who still love to read.

—Lucia Hwang

Dedications

Cheryl Woodard dedicates this book to her dad, Reverend GH (Jack) Woodard, for teaching her to read h-o-n-e-y at the breakfast table one day—and many other useful things after that.

Lucia Hwang dedicates this book to her husband, Brent, who steadfastly supported the career of a penniless reporter for all the years it took to learn this stuff.

Foreword

In researching this book, we studied the newsletters, magazines, and websites of large and small nonprofits, ranging from *National Geographic* to a local theater group.

We also relied on our own experiences in the publishing industry. Author Lucia Hwang is a journalist and magazine writer who currently edits a nonprofit association's magazine. Working virtually by herself, Hwang produces ten issues per year of the magazine with the help of a part-time freelance designer and a group of freelance writers, and we find that her situation is a common one among nonprofit magazine editors. Author Cheryl Woodard is a cofounder of *PC Magazine*, *PC World*, and *Macworld*, currently working as a full-time publishing business consultant helping clients increase their publishing efficiency and effectiveness. Woodard is also the author of *Starting and Running a Successful Newsletter or Magazine* (Nolo). In the decade since that book was first published, Cheryl has been advising large and small publications at a range of organizations.

During our combined years in publishing, we have observed the industry from every angle, especially noting how commercial media companies are drastically cutting back on their investment in good journalism. Most of the stories readers want to read about compelling social issues are never assigned to reporters at commercial newsletters, magazines, and websites. The excuse is that the issues are too complicated. Or investigating the story would cost too much or take too much time. Or advertisers might be offended.

Nonprofit publications struggle valiantly to fill that void and serve the common good. Yet, even though nonprofit publications outnumber the commercial ones by a factor of ten, there is very little public praise or recognition for them. Therefore, we have selected some of our favorite nonprofit publications to highlight as examples in this book as a way to support them and provide some extra exposure for the good work that they do.

We encourage you to find your own examples and use them for inspiration. The resources chapter lists many different sources for finding good publications or websites. In fact, the best way to quickly learn the publishing business is to study how other organizations are doing it. Better yet, ask other publishers and editors for advice. You will find that nonprofit publishing people are friendly and eager to help.

Welcome to publishing.

About This Book

This book takes you inside the publishing business so that you can adopt strategies used by professional publishers to create their magazines, newsletters, and websites. It covers every step, from conceiving a new story idea to finding out whether readers like what they're reading. The insights in these pages are drawn from interviews with dozens of editors at nonprofit organizations of every size, people who know how to function like a big-time publisher without actually being one.

Every chapter contains tips about how to modify or adapt standard publishing industry practices to meet the unique needs of your own organization, whatever its resources.

Finding Your Own Way

Publishers come in different sizes and shapes. Motivated do-it-yourselfers can find inexpensive tools and publish on a shoestring. Others spend millions of dollars to operate with glossy professional images on every page and the finest writers given months to research their stories, reaching millions of readers every month. Despite their differences, publishers at every spending level follow the same general procedures: assigning stories, adding images, and meeting deadlines. In other words, you don't have to have access to bottomless coffers to produce fine print and Web publications that effectively communicate your organization's messages to the public.

In fact, it's talent, not money, that makes the best publications so good. And you can find publishing talent everywhere. Volunteers can be trained to take great photographs or write inspiring articles. Outside freelancers can be hired for ad-hoc assignments such as sprucing up your newsletter's design or adding features to your website. Staffers can learn to meet a printing deadline, negotiate a consulting contract, or sell some ads.

Communication is key to creating publications that make you proud while at the same time fulfilling their purpose and keeping within your budget. This book focuses a great deal on communicating by helping you establish guidelines, schedules, and budgets that bring people together to support your publishing efforts. This kind of communication keeps every key contributor—writers, staff, board members, printers, and website hosting services—informed and on the same page.

The book also provides forms and instructions for adapting standard publishing industry methods, such as editorial calendars and production schedules, to the unique needs of your organization. Examples are included in every chapter representing organizations of every size and purpose. You can adopt the industry's best practices, even in the humblest of circumstances, and radically reduce your stress levels while improving the quality of your work.

Nonprofit publishers face a number of additional unique challenges—and this book provides help to meet them all. It shows you how to:

- craft a mission statement that spells out how you plan to balance your readers' taste for independent news articles and your organization's legitimate need for self-promotion (see Chapter 1)

- set up an editorial process that shields you and your writers from overly meddlesome staff and board members, while getting the very same people to share information efficiently (see Chapter 2)

- create budgeting documents to help assess whether the organization is getting value for the money it spends on publishing (see Chapter 3)

- tap into software and Internet services that can help you get a first-rate website up and running for a modest investment (see Chapter 8)

- adopt rules and policies that help you raise serious money from advertisers and sponsors without jeopardizing your nonprofit status with the IRS or violating ethical standards (see Chapter 10), and

- use simple, affordable feedback mechanisms to determine if you're doing a good job when there are few others around you to offer constructive criticism and feedback (see Chapter 11).

Fulfilling a Mission

At the end of the day, every nonprofit publisher must fulfill some purpose beyond simply getting out the next issue or website update. The larger goals may include retaining members, raising revenue, boosting donations, encouraging members to be more active in the organization, connecting members with one another or with your organization and its work, raising awareness of your programs, and providing continuing education services to members.

This book helps you translate those bigger goals into your publishing plans. It will help you decide what to publish, how much to spend, and how to track the results.

As described below, the chapters cover every aspect of the publishing story.

- **Figuring out what material to publish.** Chapter 1 is about defining your goals and the editorial mission for each publication or website that you manage. This mission statement can be shared with donors, freelance writers, staff, and others who contribute to your success. And it simplifies the process of acquiring and organizing all of your content.

- **Managing the production process.** Chapter 2 covers basic workflow and scheduling for print publications and websites and explains the techniques publishers use to keep on track.

- **Drawing up a reasonable budget.** Starting with the biggest items first, Chapter 3 describes how much you should plan to spend for your newsletters, magazines, and websites; what staffing is common at comparable publications; and how to make your own spending choices.

- **Finding and hiring talented people to help.** Chapter 4 explains what kind of experience and background to look for and cultivate and where you can find people to help with the publishing effort, including freelancers. Recruiting a strong editorial advisory board is also covered in that chapter.

- **Creating consistently compelling content.** Chapter 5 reveals the secrets to developing strong story ideas, assigning stories, reporting and writing, editing, packaging and developing editorial voice, covers, and where to turn for sources of inspiration.

- **Designing eye-catching print or website pages.** Chapter 6 explains how to incorporate great design into your publications to grab and hold readers, even if you don't have professional designers on staff. It also describes how to commission artwork, work with freelance designers and artists, and stretch your art dollars.

- **Finding the best printer for your needs.** Chapter 7 is a printing tutorial. It covers the whole process of printing magazines and newsletters, from finding appropriate printers to getting the finest quality and value from them.

- **Producing a website and other Web publications.** Chapter 8 is a survey of the programs and services publishers can use to produce a website with all the latest features, from blogs to live chats. It also offers tips for producing and sending other types of Internet communications, such as email newsletters and alerts.

- **Distributing your publication.** Chapter 9 includes important information about how to earn significant postage discounts from the U.S. Postal Service. Marketing, pricing, and other subscription-related tasks are covered there, too.

- **Advertising and other income sources.** Chapter 10 covers how to find advertisers and manage the sales process, plus how to avoid triggering the unrelated business tax income if your sales are successful.

- **Soliciting feedback.** The mysteries of getting readers to tell you what they think and using that feedback to improve the publication are detailed in Chapter 11. Feedback also helps to justify and resolve investment questions.

- **Taking advantage of available resources.** Books, websites, magazines, organizations, consultants, peer groups, and other information sources are listed in Chapter 12. ●

Table of Contents

11   Connecting to Readers

12   Resources

Appendix: How to Use the CD-ROM

Index

1

Getting Started

Every publication serves two masters: the organization that pays the publishing bills and the people who read it. This chapter will help you create a publication that meets both of their needs.

First, it reviews the most common reasons nonprofit organizations launch newsletters, magazines, and online publications. Next, it discusses your publication's purpose, focusing entirely on how it will meet your organization's needs. It then explains how to meet your readers' needs through establishing the publication's editorial mission. It offers practical advice about how to balance the interests of your nonprofit and the publication's readers—and ends with some tips for troubleshooting common problems.

Balancing Priorities

While it may seem easy to define a publication's purpose and mission, expect some disagreement—especially if the publishing venture is new or represents a change from the way things have been done in the past. Publications often generate new and unexpected confusion within a nonprofit or churn up longstanding controversies within it.

Often, no one on staff has any editing or publishing experience, but everybody has ideas about what should be published in the new newsletter, magazine, or website. Some ideas will be wonderful. And some will be completely inappropriate—such as the one from the board member who wants to put his grandson's video project on your alumni association website. Or the major donor who wants to advertise her Hummer dealership in your ecology club newsletter.

Money can be another source of confusion and dissension. Program managers may resent the money earmarked for a flashy website rather than for their programs, and board members may have unreasonable hopes about generating donations or ad revenues with a new magazine.

And, not knowing any better, everyone may expect to create a first-class product on a third-class budget, with no extra staff and no extra time allowed for planning sensibly.

You will never completely avoid conflict, but you can reduce much of it by taking the time to thoroughly discuss and define both a purpose and an editorial mission for every new magazine, newsletter, or online publication. (See "Crafting Your Mission Statement," below, for details about communicating ideas within the organization.) This step will help manage everyone's expectations, and also help fend off inappropriate suggestions down the road, by developing and communicating your plans before the publishing begins. And if you are reevaluating an established publication—looking for a new direction or greater impact—then writing the purpose and mission statements anew can lead to fresh ideas and help resolve dissension. (See "Troubleshooting Editorial Mission Problems," below, for more about revamping a conflicted publishing project.)

The Publication's Purpose

The first essential task is to decide what purpose a publication will serve for its organizational master, your nonprofit, and how it will contribute to those goals. Think in terms of outcomes that you hope will result after making the effort to publish: more donations, happier volunteers, greater success in your efforts to educate or empower people. The road to successful publishing starts with a clear sense of where you want to go and why.

Often, the purpose of a nonprofit's publication is obvious and unequivocal: The board of directors wants to attract younger members by sending out an email newsletter, for example, or the organization's new director who has venture capital roots hopes to attract big donors through a slick magazine. But sometimes the purpose is less clear—and in those situations, it is wise to gather input from a group of those involved to get a consensus before going forward. (See "Crafting Your Mission Statement," below, for details.)

There are a number of reasons nonprofit organizations typically decide to publish a magazine, newsletter, or website—ranging from getting new members to targeting underserved ones. Often, a publication serves a number of purposes.

Recruiting and Retaining Members

Publications can be extremely effective in recruiting and retaining members for consumer associations, arts organizations, and hobby or professional groups. Skimming through nonprofit member publications, you will usually find membership issues highlighted through photographs of organization activities, articles promoting the benefits of belonging, and information about how to participate. In addition, by providing useful information about the nonprofit's cherished causes, such publications can become prized benefits on their own. In fact, organizations commonly list their print publications, electronic newsletters, and members-only Web features as primary membership benefits.

While the technique is not generally available for newsletters or not relevant for online publications, some nonprofits use their magazines to recruit members by distributing them widely on newsstands and in bookstores.

EXAMPLE: The National Audubon Society produces a lavish, award-winning magazine, *Audubon*, to inspire new readers to join one of the 500 local chapters of the Society and help protect wildlife. Published bimonthly, the magazine is a public expression of the group's mission and activities. Every issue is filled with inspiring nature photographs, articles about how to participate in the Society's work around the world, and thoughtful information about environmental issues.

Not every member publication needs to be lavishly produced to attract the attention of potential members. It is most important for the publication to reflect the mission and voice of your organization.

EXAMPLE: The magazine *Coop America Quarterly* has a humble, down-to-business appearance befitting the organization's mission, which is harnessing economic power to create a socially just and environmentally sustainable society. The publication's editors convey the value of belonging to the organization by packing each 40-page issue with practical advice on sustainable living and responsible investing. People looking for an alternative to the high-consumption values they find in other magazines are attracted to the low-impact values expressed in the *Quarterly*, and the magazine draws in lots of new members at "green living" conventions and other venues where it is displayed.

Creating a Sense of Community

Some people are compelled to join a particular nonprofit organization because they crave a connection to people with whom they work or live. This is true for some unions and rural cooperatives that exist because of a shared type of work or location.

In addition to making new people feel welcome, these organizations can use their publications to remind existing members how they benefit from belonging to the organization and encourage them to remain involved.

EXAMPLE: *Kentucky Living* is a monthly magazine that reaches 500,000 members of the state's rural electric cooperatives. It is distributed exclusively to people who already belong to a cooperative, and there is no attempt to use the magazine to recruit outside readers or new members. Instead, the magazine's sole purpose is to "create a community of people who take pride in thinking of themselves as Kentuckians and as knowledgeable electric coop members to improve their quality of life." The design is humble to deliberately send members a message that their money is not being used for lavish publication expenses—and the content is helpful rather than confrontational. The editors steer clear of divisive politics, for example, and focus instead on profiles of local people and articles about energy efficiency. Ads are welcomed, particularly from local companies and coop members.

Educating About Issues

Many nonprofit publications are designed to "change the world" by arming individuals with information that empowers them to make thoughtful choices. The newsstands are filled with examples in the fields of environmental protection, health care, public affairs, culture, and social justice.

The goal of these publications is to reach as many like-minded people as possible and provide readers with unique and compelling information about the nonprofit's cause. To reach the widest possible audience, organizations with a cause to promote often decide to publish in several formats at once: websites, blogs, podcasts, electronic newsletters, and print publications. And every publishing effort is designed to reflect the mission and the expectations of the audience—using environmentally friendly soy inks for an ecology magazine, for example, or online audio clips and blogs for one about political issues.

EXAMPLE: *Mother Jones* magazine publishes revelatory journalism that seeks to "inform and inspire a more just and democratic world." Designed to reach the widest possible audience, the magazine is distributed in bookstores and to about 200,000 paid subscribers. Each bimonthly issue averages 90 pages in print with additional material simultaneously published online. The magazine is also available on microfilm, on CD-ROM, and electronically, and the organization also recently launched a radio program, podcasts, and blogs. When the editors take up an issue such as global warming or campaign finance reform, they are also able to engage readers in a two-way conversation through online forums.

But a big-scale approach to news may not be reasonable for every cause-related publication. Many smaller nonprofits choose to focus on communicating in depth with a smaller number of people—a strategy that does not require many resources. Nonprofits can have tremendous impact by concentrating on a small, tightly defined audience and then providing wonderful journalism packaged in much humbler clothing.

EXAMPLE: The Ecology Center of Berkeley, California, publishes *Terrain* magazine four times per year. Its mission is to educate and inform a dedicated community of environmental activists living in the San Francisco area—people who have been working on environmental issues for many years. To save costs, each issue is limited to 40 pages produced on the least expensive paper, with minimal use of color and other expensive design elements. Instead of spending money on fancy packaging or technology, the *Terrain* editors focus the nonprofit's small budget on acquiring great reporting from a large stable of talented local writers.

Activating Readers

Having assembled an audience of like-minded people, many organizations use a publication to call them into action on specific issues. Through a newsletter, a magazine, a website, or emails, readers can be recruited to write letters, sign petitions, donate money, vote, volunteer, or attend conferences. The editorial style of these communications is focused and specific—telling targeted individuals what they're being asked to do and why and providing an easy way to respond.

EXAMPLE: By covering political and education issues in its main newsletter, *California Teacher*, the California Federation of Teachers tries to motivate its readership to advocate for the teaching profession, whether it's for more respect, better funding, or defeating political measures seen as damaging to students and teachers. The newsletter is one of the union's main methods for communicating with and activating its 120,000 members. For example, its articles explain why the organization endorses candidates and ballot measures. It has asked readers to donate money to causes to help teacher colleagues in other parts of the country. And it encourages readers to attend upcoming conferences and meetings of the organization's leadership by listing a calendar of events in every issue.

> ⓘ **CAUTION**
>
> **Lobbying restrictions.** Some 501(c) nonprofits either cannot take any stances on political initiatives or offices or must severely limit their spending on political activities. Unions and some other organizations are given special leeway, but many nonprofits are legally restricted in lobbying. Be sure you know the rules for your organization before you start publishing. (See Chapter 5, "Lobbying Restrictions May Limit Your Content," for more details.)

Boosting Contributions

Often, the best future contributors to an organization are the people who have made a donation in the past. Recognizing this, many nonprofits publish newsletters or magazines just for their donors and volunteers, or have sections or entire websites that only people fitting these categories can access.

These publications focus on communicating the work the organization is doing for an important cause and highlight why that work is important. Sometimes citing academic experts, independent journalists, or government officials, these publications often take pains to educate readers about the overall state of the problem and the remedies their nonprofit is developing. Such publications are often filled with appeals for additional support and photographs of the people who benefit from it. It's also a common practice to profile and praise volunteers so that other people are inspired to do the same.

> **EXAMPLE:** *World Ark* magazine is a donor publication published by the Heifer Project, a group that strives to end world hunger through sustainable agriculture programs. Anyone who gives $25 to Heifer automatically receives a year's subscription to *World Ark*. Each issue profiles successful Heifer projects and explains the organization's different programs around the world. Photographs show the faces of people Heifer is helping and the Heifer volunteers who are helping them. The magazine puts Heifer's work in context by running excerpts from popular books, for example, or statisti-

cal information about poverty—so that readers also learn something. The magazine has been so successful at raising new donations from past contributors that Heifer recently was able to increase its frequency from four to six issues per year and the number of pages in every issue from 36 to 48.

Targeting Underserved Readers

Many nonprofits serve communities of people who have been overlooked by other information providers, even though their need for information may be very great. Parents of disabled children, for example, may find that consumer-focused publishers essentially ignore them. In these cases, publishing could become the main activity of a nonprofit organization that is looking to fill those information gaps.

These nonprofit publications typically draw on community experts who can provide practical information—for example, a magazine for recent immigrants could feature advice from immigration lawyers. Often these publications also combine expert advice with first-hand stories contributed by people within the community. Funding is generally covered by grants and donations rather than advertising or paid subscriptions. And such nonprofits sometimes have to find creative ways to distribute their publications to the right people, because the commercial distribution channels, such as newsstands, won't work.

EXAMPLE: The nonprofit La Leche League encourages breastfeeding and was formed 60 years ago by a group of mothers to combat a rash of new advertising and magazine articles sponsored by the baby food industry pushing bottle feeding and commercial baby formulas. The women started publishing newsletters, books, and magazines to provide accurate, non-commercial advice and information to new mothers. They distribute *New Beginnings* magazine through nursing coaches and pediatrician's offices. And parent-to-parent articles are a major focus of *New Beginnings*: On average, readers contribute about half of the content of the magazine. Editors pose several new questions in each issue asking how parents would handle a specific situation and then post the responses in subsequent issues. Experts provide another 25% of the content either in original feature stories or through book excerpts. The League devotes the remaining pages, about 25% of the total non-ad pages, to recognizing donors and promoting the League and its activities.

When Not to Publish

Not every organization needs to produce a periodical print or online publication.

If your nonprofit is still tiny, staffed mainly with volunteers who are busy providing direct services to the community and fulfilling the basic mission of the organization, perhaps it's not yet worth the drain on time, resources, and staff to publish. Or perhaps your nonprofit does not have a built-in or wide readership that might justify a regular publication, such as an organization devoted to providing summer camp to grade school girls that's primarily funded by one foundation. In that case, it might make more sense to produce an annual report for financial supporters and parents of camp participants.

In other instances, the information needs of your sector may already be met by an existing publication or website. Rather than publishing your own publication, perhaps you would better advance your cause by referring your members to these sources.

The Publication's Editorial Mission

The editorial mission is a succinct description of what your publication will do for its readers. Often, publishers share the mission statement with others as a quick means of explaining what the articles are designed to accomplish. For example, you can include the editorial mission statement in your advertising sales literature, in your budgeting documents, and in the guidelines you give to prospective writers.

The mission statement also helps people within the organization remain clear about why the publication is being produced, from the perspective of its readers. Some sample statements are provided later in this chapter.

Your mission statement should be in writing and should also answer these questions: Who will read this publication? What does it need to say to them? And what information would be most valued by those readers? As explained in this section, answering these questions requires defining the target audience and giving thought to what the content will provide. The process for crafting your editorial mission and who should be involved in it are discussed later in the chapter.

A well-defined editorial mission helps people support a publication, while an ill-defined one inevitably leads to confusion and dissent. For example, writers can submit appropriate articles if they fully understand who's going to read them and why. And communicating those essential details ahead of time practically guarantees that you'll have to do less rewriting and editing down the line. Likewise, staffers and board members are less inclined to suggest off-target story ideas if they understand the publication's promise to its readers.

A solid editorial mission can also help your publication set clear priorities for its work and resources. For example, if you are developing a new website for your publication and overwhelmed by which features to include on your limited budget, the editorial mission will remind you of your focus.

People sometimes spend weeks or months wrestling over the problem of crystallizing a new publication's editorial mission or reinventing the mission for an existing publication—and many would prefer to just publish the thing and figure out the mission later. But the exercise is necessary to keep the publication focused.

Defining Your Target Audience

Nonprofit organizations commonly communicate with many different people: members, foundations, private donors, legislators, media, and the general public. But no single publication can meet the different information needs of every group.

You can help avoid overlap, and also make sure that every key reader is being served, by addressing every individual newsletter, magazine, or website to a specific audience. Many nonprofits develop a different publication for each audience: perhaps a magazine for donors; separate newsletters for volunteers, media contacts, and staff; and a website for the public. Each of these publications would need a mission statement of its own.

Even though a mission statement normally does not include any information about reader behavior, organizations generally do try to define specific behavior they hope their publications will inspire in readers. After all, everything nonprofits publish has some mission beyond simply publishing—such as getting people to join, donate, volunteer, or vote.

Considering those intended results while writing the mission statement can help focus the many editorial choices that arise later on. For example, if your fundraising department hopes to persuade current donors to include the organization in an estate plan, then your donor magazine could rightly provide financial planning information, including how to reduce estate taxes through charitable giving, and profiles of people who have willed you money.

At this early planning stage, it's also a good idea to begin collecting any information you can find about the audiences you plan to reach. Many organizations spend time and money conducting research with key audiences before designing a new publication. (See Chapter 11 for more detail on conducting surveys.) Generally, surveyors ask for standard demographic information, such as age, income, and education. They also commonly ask about activities related to the organization's programs and gather any available feedback showing what the audience already knows about the organization.

Those at the nonprofit who are planning the publication then try to address any information gaps they find among the members of key audiences. For example, if the local nature conservancy plans to promote bird-watching tours through a new magazine, the editors could survey prospective readers about their traveling habits and experiences. Learning that most future readers do travel frequently, but not to watch birds, the editors would know to feature first-timers in the new magazine and to tailor articles to the information needs of newcomers: how people spend their time on bird-watching tours, how much they spend, what people wear, where they sleep, and so forth.

Developing Content Ideas

For many new publications, the editorial mission does not really come into focus until there is a specific plan for what content will be included. So it's often a good idea to draw up some content ideas that will help everyone understand that general plan. At this mission-writing stage, you are not actually recruiting writers or assigning articles, but just generally making some notes about the following:

- **potential contributors**—naming writers or commentators readers would likely find interesting or authoritative

- **topics**—the subjects that you want to cover, including any crucial issues in the field that should be addressed most urgently

- **taboos**—whether any topics would be inappropriate for the publication, based on the organization's overall mission, and

- **potential sources**—including whether there are any other print publications or websites that might help supplement the information you plan to publish.

Sharing your thoughts about content can help ward off loads of conflict down the road. For example, when a board member or staff person has helped you come up with ideas for suitable content, that same person will find it difficult later on to bump readers aside in favor of their own self-promotion interests. In the best of circumstances, these content discussions can serve to educate everyone about how a publication must balance the needs of its two masters. (See "Crafting Your Mission Statement," below, for more tips about communicating your plans.)

The finished editorial mission statement becomes a foundation for specific editorial planning that will define what topics you plan to cover, which writers would be the best ones to use, and how you will fill up a year's worth of pages with content that matches your mission. At the end of your considerations about content, you should be able to define a kind of "job description" for the new project—an editorial mission statement.

Sample Editorial Mission Statements

The final statement you write should be a sentence or two in length, as illustrated by the examples of strong editorial mission statements below.

- *American Educator* describes itself as "the professional journal of the American Federation of Teachers, published for classroom teachers and other education professionals from preschool through university." Its mission statement explains that: "The magazine concentrates on significant ideas and practices in education, civics, and the condition of children in America and around the world."

- *Dollars and Sense: The Magazine of Economic Justice*, published by the nonprofit Economic Affairs Bureau, has the following editorial mission statement: "We explain the workings of the U.S. and international economies, and provide left perspectives on current economic affairs. Our audience is a mix of activists, organizers, academics, unionists, and other socially concerned people."

Notice the absence of adjectives in these examples. Novice publishers often want to describe the style of a publication: "witty, graphic, hard-hitting, timely, handsome." But such terms don't actually help people understand what a publication is about. Instead, stick to nouns, such as "ideas," "perspectives," "practices," "information," and "advice."

Also notice that these statements tell readers what will *not* appear in these publications. For example, *American Educator* does not try to help teachers with personal finances, health issues, or travel plans; it is strictly about their work as educators. If a mortgage company someday suggested it would advertise in *American Educator* if the magazine included some personal finance articles, the editors could point to their concept statement and say, "Sorry, but financial advice is not the mission for this publication."

The Glimpse Foundation: One Organization, Many Missions

The overall mission of the nonprofit Glimpse Foundation is "to foster cross-cultural understanding and exchange, particularly between the United States and the rest of the world, by providing forums for sharing the experiences of young adults living and studying abroad." The foundation has several different publications, each with its own unique purpose and publishing plan.

"Glimpse Abroad," the website, is the central project of the foundation's editorial team, because its youthful audience is very Internet-oriented. The site's mission is described this way: "Glimpse Abroad represents an online community of young adults devoted to cross-cultural learning and exchange. It features first person, cultural-experience pieces written by study abroad students, volunteers, international students, and others living abroad. Relying on narrative story lines and rich sensory detail, these articles capture readers' attention and concern by making the world personal."

Glimpse Quarterly, the print magazine, is designed to increase traffic at the website and build exposure for the organization by distributing copies to people with a likely interest through selected bookstores and college classrooms. Through advertising, the print magazine also generates a small amount of revenue that supports other programs. The magazine's mission statement reads: "*Glimpse Quarterly* is an international news, travel, and culture magazine that features compelling narratives written by youth living abroad, on themes ranging from quarry divers in France to taxicabs in Kyrgyzstan to genocide in Central Africa. With depth, breadth, and intimacy, we tackle the international issues that no one talks about and delve into the daily cultural realities that no one sees."

"Freshly Squeezed," one of Glimpse's free monthly email newsletters, is designed to draw readers onto the website in between issues of the print magazine. Its mission statement reads: "Each edition of 'Freshly Squeezed' presents our Editor's Picks, which contain the best of newly added Glimpse content."

"The Word" is Glimpse's free monthly email newsletter for international educators and travel program organizers who can promote their programs to Glimpse's student audience by encouraging their current participants to write for "Glimpse Abroad." Its mission statement reads: "Educators and program providers can stay informed of contribution opportunities for their participants by spreading 'The Word,' our content recruiting newsletter."

> ⊙ **TIP**
> **Finding examples of mission statements.** You can find sample mission statements by looking at the materials other nonprofit organizations use to recruit writers or sell ads in their publications. Some will also describe a publication's mission when using it to sell subscriptions or memberships. Check their websites.

Crafting Your Mission Statement

You can begin developing a publishing purpose and an editorial mission statement by drafting one and then gathering feedback. Or start off by convening or asking people to first answer these big-picture questions. Either way, you should bring everyone together to hash out the final mission. Everyone in your organization who is likely to be involved with the publishing project should be invited to discuss the publication's purpose and help formulate its mission statement. As mentioned, the more people are encouraged to participate in this early stage, the more likely they will support the publication later on.

For example, if the finance director has the power to approve or reject your publishing budget, give her a chance to tell what tangible results she thinks the new website should produce. And if the program managers are expecting the new magazine to cover their programs, or the director is hoping that his views will feature prominently in every issue of the newsletter, you will benefit from learning about those ideas before you start publishing.

This is the best way to keep people from secretly constructing unreasonable hopes or fears that might erode their support later on. You don't have to agree with everything people say. But encouraging their candor about their expectations for the publication provides important opportunities.

Addressing expectations. You can address and potentially refute unrealistic expectations only if you know about them. For example, if the finance director wants you to produce $1 million in website revenues but spend only 50 cents producing it, you have the chance to explain the true costs and revenues of Internet publishing.

Likewise, if you learn that the program managers are jealous about how much newsletter coverage is given to each other's programs, you can ask them to work out an equitable plan among themselves, without putting you into the role of arbitrator.

In addition, people will have conflicting expectations, and it's unwise to move forward without addressing them.

Dealing with money matters. Money is also a common source of conflict and confusion. Some people will want a slick magazine or a website filled with bells and whistles; but other people will have different ideas about how to spend the organization's resources. It's much wiser to air these debates ahead of time—and hopefully, arrive at some consensus—rather than live with an ongoing feud about why the website is or is not doing such-and-such or why the magazine is so humble.

Meeting readers' needs. There is often political scuffling about how to best serve readers. Everyone in your organization has a stake in each of your publications, and this is the time to help people understand that readers have a stake in the publications, too. So when pondering your publication's future, ask people to focus on how readers will benefit. These conversations will yield huge benefits if everyone understands from the beginning that you must give readers their due in your publications—or nobody will be willing to read them.

Here are some additional tips for the process.

- **Allow enough time for deliberations.** Concepts gain clarity after this buffeting process, so do not skip over it.

- **Add details.** If people can't agree on a theoretical list of ideas, give them something specific to chew on, such as a list of the topics you hope to cover in the first year or the specific organizational benefits you hope to achieve.

- **Look for role models.** Study what other organizations have done for inspiration and guidance.

- **Get help if you can afford it.** Nonprofits often hire a consultant to help hash out the mission and develop a specific editorial plan.

• **Take the time to get it right.** Don't stop the process until you have general consensus about a specific mission statement for your publication.

<table>
<tr><td>(!)</td><td>**CAUTION**</td></tr>
</table>

Reevaluating your mission. Organizations evolve—and your publication's editorial mission may need to grow with it. Sometimes the work of the organization changes. Sometimes the demographics of the organization's members change, becoming a younger or older or more ethnically diverse constituency. Sometimes the composition of the organization's staff and board leadership changes and the new group is more willing or less willing to experiment or take risks in the publication. And sometimes it becomes clear that the publication's current editorial mission is just not attracting readers. In these situations, you may need to reevaluate and revise your editorial mission.

Troubleshooting Editorial Mission Problems

Even after developing an editorial mission statement that captures the spirit of the publication and gives you a goal to strive toward, complications can arise. People can forget about the mission they've agreed to support and turn into busybodies who ask you to include material clearly outside of the previous agreement. Or a mission can grow stale and seem irrelevant if the audience's needs change over time.

And ideas that seemed straightforward in the planning stages can sometimes turn out to be more complicated when you try to execute them. For instance, when a publication serves as the public voice of a large, complex organization, it must address challenging, complicated issues—without offending too many board members, donors, members, employees, or readers. And if a nonprofit with clout takes a contentious political stance, its publications will likely become the focal point of that controversy.

Even tiny organizations can drift away from the balanced, mission-driven publishing work they set out to accomplish. For example, when an association's membership is falling off, a natural instinct is to pump more self-promotional content into its publications. But there is no better way to drive members away than by substituting the here's-what-you-want-to-know articles with too much here's-how-great-we-are content.

Generally, the best way to handle problems that develop is to go back through the process described in this chapter—bringing people together to review and, if necessary, to revise the editorial mission statement for each struggling publication. And, as described below, there are some remedies you might try to control specific types of damage.

Undermining the Editorial Mission

There may be a small group of influential board members, some staff members, or even readers who start criticizing the direction of your publication. Watch for this distress signal and address it quickly and openly. Keep in mind that dissent can and should be used constructively, whether it's to improve the editorial mission or reaffirm the organization's commitment to it.

One signal of dissent may be email messages complaining or commenting about the publication that somehow bypass publication staff and get sent to higher-ups. Another sign may be that a subsection of the organization, such as the board, holds meetings or makes plans for the publication without consulting the staff members who work on it.

A good step in dealing with the problem of people undermining the publication's editorial mission is to call on the support of your organization. Touch base with your supervisor or others at your organization who oversee communications, whether it's a senior staff person or a committee of board members, and discuss the need to address the problem.

In the best of worlds, the members of management within your organization understand and fully back your editorial mission. If not, take this opportunity to remind them about your purpose and how you work to achieve it. If you were able to solicit and secure the buy-in of these stakeholders when the editorial mission was developed, you're merely asking them to stand by their original convictions. Hopefully, these people, especially if they are peers of or have the same level of influence as the critics, will assume the role of quelling the criticism.

If you need to handle the critics yourself, bring along the highest-level backer of the majority position that you can, and together remind them of the editorial mission of the publication. Emphasize how it was developed and the reasons the contested choices were made—and why those choices are helping the organization.

Critics who never backed the editorial mission, and still don't, often pose an ongoing challenge. Basically, they never accepted that they got outvoted. You may never persuade them to accept your position, but you can mitigate their influence. The main thing you can do is point out, diplomatically but firmly, that they are a minority viewpoint and that the publication must fulfill the desires of the larger organization by honoring its editorial mission. If pushed, someone from your organization may be willing to go as far as telling the critic that continuing to undermine the editorial mission is disruptive and won't be tolerated.

You can also take a different tack and buy yourself periods of calm by occasionally meeting with your publication's harshest critics. Often they just need a chance to vent their frustrations and feel as if they have influence over the organization. Having lunch together and letting them talk may quiet them down somewhat, as they would feel that they have already given direct input to or have regular access to the ears of the publication staff. Shutting some people out will only make them agitate harder.

EXAMPLE: One former editor of a weekly paper for members of a food cooperative remembers how powerful committee members constantly complained that the paper was not running enough direct news about the organization and was venturing into topics beyond its proper scope. The editor never disagreed with the critics but, instead, pointed out all the recent articles about the coop in the paper and described his need to satisfy readers' interests, too. The critics would rumble but back off for the time being. "We tried to be really nice, and explain to these people that if we show the wider readership that we're interested in the issues they're interested in, we're more likely in the long run to get them interested in joining the coop," he said. By never directly disagreeing or contradicting them, he was able to hold these critics at bay and continue the type of news coverage the nonprofit needed.

Urging Self-Promotion

The tendency of an individual or small group to fixate on self-promotion probably sounds all too familiar to anyone who has been in charge of a nonprofit publication. A board member or staff person emails you and strongly suggests that you write a prominent feature story about one of your organization's longtime programs—cc'ing a slew of folks in upper management about the idea. Unfortunately, there's really nothing new to report and the pitch sounds either boring or too obviously like an advertisement.

Consider the difference between copy that you'd read in a brochure, which is usually meant to sell you something, and copy that you'd read in a newspaper or magazine, which is usually meant to inform you. People tend not to read brochures unless they're in the market for some product or service—and even when they do, it's usually with an attitude of skepticism and suspicion. If you fill your publication with too much self-promotional "sales" copy, you'll only foster these negative feelings and ultimately alienate readers.

That's not to say, however, that the publication of a nonprofit can never mention what it does. A nonprofit's publication should have some coverage of the organization's activities. Just remember that not everything the organization does is a news story and that overplaying or overblowing this kind of material comes off to readers as insincere.

Think of creative ways to package this type of self-promotional information. For example, highlight your nonprofit's activities with an events calendar. Introduce staff members to readers by doing "quick-hit" profiles that give just a basic biographical sketch and then focus on one aspect of the person's role at the nonprofit, such as the most recent work accomplishment. Or spotlight one of your nonprofit's programs by publishing just one illuminating photo with a thoughtful caption, instead of writing a story that intimates the program is newsworthy when it's not.

But to achieve the proper balance with content mix, you'll have to learn how to handle a real stinker of a situation when someone pushes inappropriate suggestions. Sometimes it works best to carefully listen to and thank the person for the idea but not act on it.

Another alternative, which takes more effort but probably works better in the long run, is to try and educate your colleagues about what makes a good story and the basic journalistic tenets of newsworthiness. Here, again, it's important to refer back to your editorial mission. Give examples of stories that fit well with your mission. Discuss your concern that a story that does not present any news could turn off readers—or worse, alienate them. Encourage your colleagues to come back with story ideas that offer relevant news or would excite readers. Hopefully, this bit of education will make them think twice about future suggestions.

As the publication's staff, though, it's always a good idea to step into the other person's shoes and take a moment to consider his or her idea. Maybe a general feature story about the program would be extremely boring, but the topic may merit a chat with the program manager to see if an interesting and better story lurks within the larger idea.

Covering Controversy

One of the biggest challenges for many nonprofit publications is how to handle content that will generate controversy, whether it's among staff, funders, members, your industry sector, or the general public. Controversial topics tend to fall into one of the following categories: subjects that are about your nonprofit's internal or external problems or make your organization look bad, subjects that challenge readers' or your donors' prevailing viewpoints, and subjects that question your nonprofit's dominant paradigm or "sacred cows."

While not all organizations can avoid controversy, and some actually promote a "controlled" type of controversy by soliciting lively letters to the editor or hosting website forums in which members can debate topics, the vast majority of nonprofits shun such content.

There's no one approach to handling these situations. And there may be no solution to the controversy, either. Some events or topics will always cause conflict among your publication's or nonprofit's constituencies.

Once again, you can get some help out of this hot water by referring to your publication's editorial mission and asking whether the content in question furthers its intended goals. Sometimes your organization may have to make a hard decision about placing certain constituencies above others. For example, perhaps an article you want to publish would enlighten readers but kill your chances of funding with an important foundation. When forced to evaluate which option would be worse, or better, it may help to involve your nonprofit's management, the board of directors, and your editorial advisory board, if you have one. (See Chapter 4 for details on forming and working wth editorial boards.)

When it comes to reporting about the organization's own problems, refer to whatever general communications policies your nonprofit may already have in place or any that specifically concern the controversy at hand. While nonprofit publications rarely discuss such issues in their pages, your organization might decide it is helpful to acknowledge the conflict and publish some kind of note encouraging readers to get in touch if they are concerned or want more information. If you have the resources and the controversy seems potentially explosive, your nonprofit may also consult a public relations firm for help.

Content that challenges the viewpoints held by readers, funders, and the organization in a constructive way that helps them develop a stronger and more nuanced understanding of the nonprofit mission should be given as much free rein as possible. Usually, editors find that readers are much more open to content that makes them think twice than the organization is comfortable publishing. The trick is in overcoming staff fears or assumptions about what's appropriate.

You have a better chance of shepherding through this kind of content if you involve the organization's gatekeepers early in the process and if you have some advocates, such as board members or representatives from your editorial advisory board, arguing on your behalf. Approach management early about your intentions and discuss your reasons for exploring the topic. Explain how it will help, not hurt, the organization. Keep members of management apprised of the story's development. Hopefully, if the organization's leadership is included in the content development process, they will be less likely to quash it. After a controversial story runs, be sure to forward any complimentary feedback from readers, or at least reinforce to the organization that the sky did not fall.

Outgrowing Your Editorial Mission

If your organization has expanded or changed significantly in its work since you drafted your publication's editorial mission, it may be time to reevaluate and revise it.

You may also have reached a point where you feel your mission is not working and you need a new vision. If you can't seem to muster much feedback from readers or when readers and even organization staff admit they do not read the publication, it may be time for a major overhaul. If members start calling or writing and asking to be taken off the mailing list, or don't renew their subscriptions, that's another red flag.

EXAMPLE: For decades, one college alumni group has been publishing a magazine as a recruitment tool and benefit for members. In recent years, new graduates of the college have been joining the alumni association at about half the rate that earlier generations had joined. A new communications manager identified the problem: The association's magazine and website featured baby boomers who looked more like the parents of recent grads than the grads themselves. Nobody planned to exclude the younger generations, but the group's board members, editors, and staff—mostly baby boomers themselves—had simply lost the younger perspective. Articles focused on the activities of these much older alums, and advertisements hawked estate planning services and retirement communities. A new editor was hired and charged with addressing the problem. He succeeded by recruiting a new generation of writers, redesigning the magazine, launching a series of email newsletters on early career topics rather than retirement, and revitalizing the association's website. Within a couple of years, the college's newest graduates started joining the alumni association in greater numbers.

Managing the Publishing Process

I f you are new to publishing or have experience only with some parts of it, this chapter will help you understand the steps involved, from start to finish. Regardless of what type of publication you are producing, whether it's in print or online, all share some commonalities in how they are put together to form a finished product.

This chapter also discusses the various steps required to move content in a timely and orderly fashion—and provides you with tangible ways to manage the process.

An Overview of the Publishing Process

Think about your publishing activities in these main categories and in this order: editorial, design, production, and distribution. For publications that carry advertising, add a sales category that runs concurrently with editorial.

If your publication has a small staff, one person or maybe only a couple of people will be handling all these steps. At larger publications, departments are organized and named around these functions. (Staffing is discussed in Chapter 4.)

In addition to hiring staff, publishers use schedules and budgets to help function smoothly. This book provides budgeting worksheets and blank scheduling templates that can help you streamline the process, eliminate serious mistakes, and reduce the overall stress of producing new issues or website updates day after day and month after month.

Finally, a successful publisher must assemble a suite of helpful computer programs and link them together to efficiently and flawlessly carry every article from the writer's fingertips to the reader's eyes. Once those systems are in place and your staff is trained to use them, the publishing process can be very easy to manage. But without them, you'll find yourselves struggling to complete each issue.

Editorial

This step includes generating ideas for content, soliciting it, and shaping the words into a final form. It involves people who write for the publication—which can include the publication's staff, freelance writers, and the nonprofit's staff or board members—along with those who edit that text, turning it into the most suitable presentation for your readers.

When the editors are through with their finished product, which most often will be words in an electronic file, it is ready to be designed to fill the publication's pages. There are a number of scheduling and planning forms that help keep these important initial steps on track. (See "Creating Calendars and Schedules," below, for details.)

Sales

If you opt to include advertising in your publication or on your website, a sales staff will contact individuals and companies that seem to be a good fit for your readership, negotiate a contract that defines ad sizes and prices, collect the advertising from the advertiser or its agency, and make sure it's in the right form and format to be printed. Such sales may be made by an inside sales staff or outsourced to freelancers or a sales company. (Forms and programs to help manage the sales process are described in Chapter 10.)

Design

This step determines how the content in your publication will be presented visually to best attract readers. Someone will be charged with obtaining artwork that complements the articles and with arranging how the print or Web pages look. This step often involves designers and freelance photographers and illustrators. But at small nonprofits, this function is often handled by an editor who doubles as designer, the graphic designer on staff of the larger group, or a contract designer hired from the outside.

(The process of finding good freelance artists and negotiating with them is detailed in Chapter 4, and the process of acquiring artwork from them is described in Chapter 6, which also includes a description of page design software. And if the pages are destined for a website, the additional programs that might be used to get them up and running are described in Chapter 8.)

Production

Before the publication actually gets sent to the printer or posted on the Internet, it also goes through a quality control phase during which everyone takes a final pass through the issue or planned posting to make sure that a photo doesn't accidentally appear with the wrong caption or that all the links on a Web page jump to the right place. This can involve making a mock issue or dummy of the publication or posting a preview version of the issue to a protected area of the website for internal testing. (This quality control step is detailed in Chapter 6.)

Once all the pages are free of errors, the publication enters the true production phase. For a print publication, your files from page design software are transformed into files that will control how the printing presses generate the physical paper object. (See Chapter 7 for complete details on the printing process.)

For an online publication, your graphic files must be converted into a format that Web browser programs can read, and those browser-friendly files must be uploaded onto a website hosting computer. (See Chapter 8 for more on producing a website.)

Printers and Web vendors will supply their own proofreading dummy copies after converting your graphic files into their computer systems. You can check their proofs against your own final dummy to find and correct any mistakes that may have slipped during the conversion process. (Printer proofs are covered in Chapter 7 and Web proofs are covered in Chapter 8.)

Distribution

The final step is to get your publication to readers. If yours is a print publication, this involves the U.S. Postal Service, a mailing house, a newsstand distributor if you are carried on the news racks, or your circulation or subscriptions department if you have one.

For emails and websites, this step will involve your publication's web-master or your nonprofit's Web manager, and likely coordination with any outside vendors that you might use to manage your Web content and advertising. (Subscriber names and postal or email addresses are captured and maintained in large database programs that are described in Chapter 9, along with details on distributing your printed periodicals and emails.)

Managing the Process

Now that you know more about the general publishing process, you're ready to learn about the specific steps that need to happen, when they should happen, and how best to oversee the entire publishing process.

Amazing content does little good if a writer fails to turn a story in on time or the person designing your publication has artwork, but no copy because the copy editor is still poring through the manuscript. Files must be shipped to the printer by the deadline date, new editions should be posted to the website when promised, and fresh issues have to be delivered on time to the newsstand distributor. Slipping up in any of these areas can mean not only loss of reputation among readers, but extra printing costs or lost advertising, and even penalties to pay.

Workflow

If you've ever thrown a joint party with friends, you know it would be foolish to simply depend on each person to contribute what's needed without any discussion beforehand. Some degree of planning and scheduling is necessary to ensure you will have all the components of a successful bash. Perhaps one person is in charge of the decorations and agrees to arrive an hour early to set up. Another might be responsible for the beverages. Without planning, your party could end up with all desserts and no entrées, or tons of food but no plates or utensils.

The same goes for a publication. To produce any given issue, a host of tasks—usually performed by several people—must be completed in the right order and on time. Articles must be conceived, assigned, reported and written, edited, and proofread. Artwork and photography must be brainstormed, researched, assigned or purchased, and incorporated into the design of the pages. If you carry advertising, all the business transactions involved in that must be finalized and the ad must be integrated into the publication. As the content is being made final, the printer and mail house must be contacted, paper ordered, mailing lists compiled, and postage readied for a print publication.

Websites share these steps in developing and readying content but go through their own production process of specifying and transferring content and advertising onto the appropriate servers that feed the website and testing the site to make sure everything is working before it goes live for the world to see.

Workflow Calendars: So Much More Than Tracking Dates

Workflow calendars—which are often created with some kind of spreadsheet program and look like a grid or table with the publication's components along one axis and deadlines along another—help keep you on top of tasks and deadlines and enable you to plan work activities.

For example, you may be rushing about to meet your deadline in shipping a current issue to the printer, but when you glance at the calendar, you may also see that the cover story for the next issue is due from the writer in a week. This may prompt you to take 15 minutes to call the writer to check in on whether the story is progressing and to plant the reminder that you're expecting the piece.

That 15-minute call could save you hours, days, or even weeks of frustration and panic down the line compared to if you had not made it. If you weren't aware of your workflow, hadn't had a handy document to consult, and hadn't known it was time to call the struggling writer, you might not have learned any of this until it was too late to keep the story on schedule. (See "Creating Calendars and Schedules," below, for a sample and more detail on this.)

Your thinking can't be isolated to the current issue you're working on, either. Even while you are finalizing one issue, your mind must project into the future. Articles may be waiting to be edited, you may be assigning stories two or even three issues ahead, and you may be thinking of concepts for future cover images and stories. Putting out a publication of any kind is a constant like juggling act.

ess goes smoothly, it's important to v is simply a breakdown of the logical nce you understand what needs to nd who makes it happen, you can s and schedules.

anage the production process, you you'll be managing. That requires u intend to provide.

ly plan in one-year increments— think ahead more than a year. nization will be celebrating its 10th al series throughout its anniversary lishments over the past decade. That vance planning when selecting and antage.

Most of the time, however, it works fine to plan your publications for the year to come and then do more detailed planning issue by issue. Annual planning usually involves creating a schedule that gives an overview of main target dates for sending the publication to the printer and also for when it will be distributed to readers or go live on your website and creating an editorial calendar describing any special focus topics for each issue.

Some planning is usually essential, since advertisers often seek a publication's editorial calendar so they can choose how to spend the dollars they have allotted for advertising. And your publication's ad salespeople use the editorial calendar to pitch likely advertisers. (See

White Plains Public Library
Renewal Receipt
TeleCirc: 6V4 41865
Circulation Dept: 422-1400

Date due: 8/5/2017/23:59
Title: Every nonprofit's guide to publishing
Author: Woodard, Cheryl,
Item ID: 31544100032309

Visit us on the web at
www.whiteplainslibrary.org

Chapter 10 for details on including ads in your publication and working with advertisers if you do.)

Planning usually involves setting timelines and deadlines and describing expected content for two or even three consecutive issues. This ensures that:

- You have an outline to help act as a blueprint for the current issue.
- Activities and assignments that need to be rolling for the next issue are underway.
- Ideas for future issues are starting to be discussed.

Creating Calendars and Schedules

The main ways that publications keep their publishing plans on track are by using schedules and calendars, both of which can be adjusted to accommodate simple or complex operations.

Some schedules are common to the entire publication, such as the annual list of dates when each issue is supposed to hit readers' mailboxes or go live on the Internet. Some schedules are department-specific, such as the schedule editors use to track content, the schedule production staff uses to coordinate all the different department deadlines, or the schedule that sales staff uses to know when to quit selling ad space and start collecting the material that will make up the ads. A department-specific schedule might give only cursory deadlines for other tasks that need to be done but break down departments' own tasks into minute steps. At small publications, all of these schedules may fit neatly on a single document.

At the very least, however, most publications have schedules that outline activities and deadlines over an entire year, and then schedules that outline activities and deadlines issue by issue.

Annual Publication Schedules

All publications should have handy an annual publication schedule that provides an overview of the entire year's key dates and deadlines. The most logical way to create an annual publication schedule is to reverse engineer the timeline.

Depending on whether your publication is quarterly, bimonthly, monthly, or published more frequently, decide the date by which you want all your readers to receive each issue. Or if you sell your publication on the newsstand, know the date by which the company that gets your magazine to the racks needs to receive it.

Next, write down in detail all the steps and vendors your publication passes through after leaving your hands. Then assess what amount of time those involved will need to do their jobs and how many days you should allow for each step to take place. For print publications, talk with your printer about how long the print run will take; then talk with your distributor and determine how many days to allow for the issue to reach readers in the mail or on the news rack. For a website, confer with whoever engineers your site to see how long it will take to upload files and test the site before you take it live. In this manner, work backward through the steps and note for each issue the date the task should be started and completed.

It's a good idea to budget in extra days at each step to give some margin of error and cushioning in case something goes wrong. Be sure to consider holidays and weekends.

EXAMPLE: If distributors need each issue by the 15th of each month, don't start from the 15th. Assume you'll need to get the issue to them by the 11th or 12th.

After you've completed this, you should have a table outlining key publishing deadlines for the entire year: when you need to deliver your electronic files to the printer or get your files to the Web manager to upload; when you should expect to see the final version of what your readers or viewers will see; when your publication should hit readers' mailboxes, newsstands, or the Internet. Make special note of the date you need to ship each issue to the printer or get files to the Web manager; you will be using that as a launch point to create your issue-by-issue schedules.

Editorial Calendars

Another useful type of annual schedule is the editorial calendar. Editorial calendars spell out, issue by issue, any special topics or content that you plan to feature in the year to come. They are most common and necessary for publications that publish monthly or more frequently, less common for publications that are produced quarterly or less frequently.

As mentioned, advertisers use editorial calendars to help plan their advertising strategy and spending. Knowing the focus of each issue helps them target their advertising to the ones with readers most receptive to their product or service.

EXAMPLE: A magazine about the environment might focus on the safety of drinking water in one issue, the future of alternative fuel vehicles the next, development along coastlines the one after, the top-five most influential environmentalists in the issue after that, and so on. An electric car company provided with your editorial calendar can plan to advertise in the issue spotlighting alternative-fuel vehicles.

Freelance writers also seek out editorial calendars because knowing which topics your publication plans to focus on, and when, helps them formulate appropriate story ideas and pitch them to you at the right time. And staff members also use the calendars to become informed about what articles they should be writing or assigning.

To create the calendar, your publication's staff and other interested people, such as an editorial advisory board, should first meet and map out the subject areas you intend to focus on during the upcoming year. (See Chapter 4 for more on selecting and working with editorial boards.) It's generally a good idea to convene in mid-autumn so you have time to compile your ideas and incorporate them into planning for the next calendar year.

Most publications pick areas for editorial focus by noting hot topics or trends in their field, as well as perennial subjects that their readers may expect them to cover. They then decide at what point in the year those topics would be most relevant.

EXAMPLE: If your nonprofit focuses on nature, the stories in your publication will naturally coincide with the seasons. Spring is often a time for publications to consider "birth" or "renewal" stories. Summer is when many readers take vacations. Fall marks the time that both kids and adults head back to school. And winter is when people generally celebrate the biggest holidays and reflect on family themes. Of course, these are just conventions that your publication could choose to follow or might decide to break from, to great effect.

When you know what topics will be covered in which issue, compile the list and seed in the important deadlines by which you must receive article pitches and advertisers must buy space.

Deadline dates are often set well in advance of the actual issue release date. You may choose to budget in an even longer buffer. For the purpose of developing content, this gives you plenty of lead time to entertain story submissions and still generate and assign articles to fill holes in coverage.

And since many companies and individuals map out their advertising buys a year at a time, the calendar will give them plenty of notice and increase your chances of attracting advertising. Your sales staff will also be able to better prepare plans to target advertisers.

Sample Editorial Calendar

Below is a sample editorial calendar for a bimonthly university alumni publication. Reflecting the year's ebb and flow, the topic of "volunteerism" is scheduled for the new year to coincide with when readers may have set new year's resolutions to be more active in the community. "Educational tours and travel" is scheduled for spring, when readers are most likely to be making their summer vacation plans. "The worth of a college degree" is scheduled right around the time that students are submitting their college applications.

TIP

When advertisers may help you focus. If your publication carries a substantial amount of advertising, you may choose your editorial focus based on the different categories of advertisers and when readers would be most likely to make those purchases.

Editorial Calendar for Arch University's Alumni Publication			
Issue	Topic focus	Deadline for editorial pitches	Deadline for advertising
January/February	Volunteerism	October 1	November 1
March/April	Studying abroad	December 1	January 1
May/June	Educational tours and travel	February 1	March 1
July/August	20 most influential alumni	April 1	May 1
September/ October	Returning students	June 1	July 1
November/ December	The worth of a college degree	August 1	September 1

Since the editorial calendar is a document that will be distributed to people spending money or seeking work with your organization, be sure to present it in a professional and attractive layout. At the least, make sure it is clear and easy to read at a glance. Usually, a simple table format works well.

CD-ROM

A template for creating an editorial calendar similar to the one above is available on the CD-ROM included with this book. You will simply have to add the specifics of your publication's issue, topic focus, and deadlines.

TIP

Track unusual deadlines. In addition to creating an editorial calendar, it may be helpful to gather a separate listing of any important content to publish in any given issue. For example, some organizations are obligated by law or charter to disseminate certain information to their members or funders and use their publications as the main venue to do that. Some organizations may conduct mail-in elections and distribute ballots through their publications. And the U.S. Postal Service requires all periodicals to annually publish ownership and management information and their circulation numbers in a particular issue of the publication. (See Chapter 9 for more detail on this and other postal regulations.)

Issue Schedules

Once you have a good picture of what your publication year will look like, you can incorporate that information into a production schedule for each issue or website update. This is the document that will keep you on task and on time when you publish.

The schedule is for your benefit, so if you occasionally need to bend the timelines to accommodate a timely topic or trend for your readers, be flexible.

TIP

Coordinate all advertising. If your publication accepts advertising, make sure that you, or the people responsible for coordinating ads within your nonprofit, create a schedule that guides advertising functions and integrates with editorial deadlines.

The schedule that the editorial department uses should summarize the entire lineup and order of what you'll be publishing in one convenient spot: the sections, departments, features, columns—and the dates each must be completed.

As a format, shown in the sample below, you could use a one-page grid or table that clearly displays the following information in rows that can be read across columns containing the following information:

- the content "slug"—that is, the brief descriptive phrase of the story
- the editor assigning the piece
- the date the story was assigned
- the name of the writer from whom the piece is due
- the number of pages allowed for the story; if read vertically, this column will produce the total pages of content, which can help you determine the size of the issue
- the date the story is expected to be turned in, perhaps followed by a blank column for you to fill in the actual date the story is turned in
- the date the story is due to the art department, followed by the date it's delivered
- the date the story is due to copyediting, followed by the actual dates, and
- the expected date the entire piece will be reviewed as complete.

Additional dates you might track if you have a print publication:

- the date you deliver files to the printer
- the date you receive proofs, or bluelines
- the date the publication goes on press, and
- the date the publication should be mailed.

Additional dates you might if you have a website:

- the date you deliver files to your Web manager, and
- the date you expect to review and test the Web pages before you make them live on your website.

As shown in the example below, when making an Issue Schedule, create columns with due dates for each step of your editorial process and also note other steps that would be useful to help you plan the details of the publication. For example, you might want to include a column stating the date you'd like to have the story assigned to a writer. The schedule should evolve or be tailored to help your publication, so if you observe that you customarily fall behind in one phase, maybe you could better manage that time by further breaking down the steps and responsibilities involved. If you find certain categories don't really need to be tracked or processes change to make them extraneous, delete them.

To actually set deadline dates, refer to the annual publication schedule you drew up earlier and identify the date by which you must send your publication to the printer or have it ready to be posted on the Web. Again, working backwards and consulting with the others involved, determine how much time would be ideal, or typical, to allot for each task to successfully complete it. As before, build in extra days to buffer against unexpected problems and delays. Fill in those dates and circulate the schedule among other relevant staff members to make sure that the timelines are realistic for them, too.

Create a schedule for the issue or Web posting you are currently working on, the one you will be working on next, and perhaps even the one after that. The farther into the future the publishing date, the more ambiguous the content lineup will be. Distribute copies of these schedules to everyone who works on the publication, and post the schedule in a prominent place for all to consult.

The grid below is a schedule to be used by the editorial department of a bimonthly alumni magazine. It contains quite a bit of detail about individual stories and due dates, and more general information about the stages of the publishing process after the material gets handed off to the people who handle production functions.

TIP

Stagger your deadlines to avoid bottlenecks. If you publish a regular column or material that predictably appears in every issue, set earlier dates for receiving that content so that deadlines are staggered and don't all hit at the same time. That way, you can get some items squared away first, and as crunch time approaches near key deadlines, you can devote more attention to the articles or sections that really are time-sensitive or may have arrived late.

Issue Schedule for Arch University's Alumni Publication

Issue date: January/February   **Editorial calendar focus:** Volunteerism

Deadline to mail house, or live on Internet: 12/20

Deadline to review printer's proofs (bluelines) of issue: 12/1

Deadline to ship the issue to printer or deliver files to Web manager: 11/27

Deadline to sign off on all materials: 11/20

Materials due from advertisers: 10/31

Story/Section	Story assigned by	Story assigned	Story due from	# of pages	Due to editor	To editor	Rough manuscript to art/designer
Cover: Volunteer of the year				1		(Fill in actual date here)	
Table of contents				1			
Letters to the editor/ masthead				1			
News briefs							
Slug: Campus news roundup	Editorial staff		Editor A	2	10/1		10/3
Slug: New Nobel Prize Winner	Editor A		Freelance writer A	1	10/1		10/3
Slug: Lawsuits over student fees	Editorial staff		Editor B	2	10/1		10/3
Total news briefs pages				5			
Departments							
Column 1	Editor A		Columnist A	1	9/22		9/24
Column 2	Editor B		Guest Columnist B	1	9/22		9/24
Total dept pages				2			
Feature well							
Slug: 10 outstanding alumni volunteers	Editor A		Staff writer A	6	9/26		9/28
Slug: Essay on individual volunteerism vs. social policy	Editor A		Freelance writer B	3	9/26		9/28
Slug: Mental health issues among students	Editor B		Freelance writer C	4	9/26		9/28
Total features pages				13			
Total editorial pages				23			
Total advertising pages			Sales dept	9			
TOTAL PAGES IN ISSUE				32			

Due to copyediting	To copy	Final copy due to art/ designer	To art/ designer	Final layout from designer	From designer	Ready to print or post	To print or post
	(Fill in actual date here)		(Fill in actual date here)		(Fill in actual date here)		(Fill in actual date here)
10/24		10/27		11/10		11/17	
10/24		10/27		11/10		11/17	
10/24		10/27		11/10		11/17	
10/12		10/15		10/30		11/17	
10/12		10/15		10/30		11/17	
10/17		10/22		11/5		11/17	
10/17		10/22		11/5		11/17	
10/17		10/22		11/5		11/17	

Newsletters that don't publish as many pages or online publications that post weekly may have no need for such a detailed issue-by-issue schedule. In those cases, maybe an annual publication schedule augmented with key dates, such as the deadline for content, copy editing, art or design, and sending to the printer or the Web manager, may be enough. The point is to create guiding documents that help your publication do whatever it needs to stay on schedule.

CD-ROM

A template for creating an issue schedule similar to the one above is available on the CD-ROM included with this book. You will simply have to add the specifics of your publication's issue, topic focus, and deadlines.

Enforcing Deadlines

The number one way that novice publishers waste money is by missing production deadlines. As soon as you miss a deadline, your printer or website vendor can start tacking on late fees and rush charges. Missed deadlines and late copy also stresses the art and production staff's capacity to make up for lost time, which may lead to chronic resentment and frustration among them. And the quality of your publication will invariably suffer as a result. Typos and other errors will get overlooked. Page layouts may be boring, with scanty and unimaginative artwork and photos, because the designer will not have enough time to experiment with the pages or properly research photos.

Writers and editors are not the only ones who miss deadlines, unfortunately. In fact, advertisers can become the worst offenders by falling into a habit of routinely sending new art after the production deadline is passed. This can be a tough habit to break once your advertisers grow accustomed to it, but it can add thousands of dollars to your printing bills every year if it becomes a common practice.

Any way you look at it, you must develop a culture that respects deadlines.

Ideally, if you develop the production schedule in cooperation with your colleagues, everyone will take the deadlines seriously. But it's naïve to think this will automatically happen without some extra effort and attention. It's typically the job of the managing editor to check in with each department to find out whether the flow of copy is conforming to the schedule and to crack the whip if it's not. But if your publication does not have a managing editor, the editor must fill this role, or the role could be assigned to a staff member who is detail-oriented, communicates clearly, and excels at coordinating editorial functions.

This gatekeeper should regularly check in with all the people responsible for working on the publication and offer friendly, and sometimes not-so-friendly, reminders about deadlines in person, by phone, or by email. The best managers do not scare or scold but simply work with the people involved to deliver what's needed and set clear expectations.

TIP

That train has left the station. Some publishers find that the best way to condition everybody to respect deadlines is simply not to wait for latecomers. That is, without blame or recrimination, simply send the issue out on time. For example, rather than scrambling to fill a hole when an article comes in too late, some editors routinely stash away extra stories they can move up to bump and replace a late one. Any freelancer who does not deliver on time does not get new assignments. And advertisers who submit artwork after the production deadline must pay a late fee or run their overdue ads in the next issue instead of the current one.

Making a Budget

Few people relish the task of budgeting. But having a thoughtful budget and maintaining it in good shape clears the way for a happier worklife—and a more prosperous publication—down the road. And if you set up the budgeting process correctly from the outset, it will provide information you can use to manage your publishing resources effectively; meet government reporting requirements; and make persuasive presentations about your publishing activities to donors, managers, and board members.

This chapter covers the basics you'll need to know to establish a budget for every publication your nonprofit produces, whether you work in concert with accounting people on staff or are responsible for your publication's budgeting on your own.

All nonprofit organizations face unique reporting and accountability requirements that the IRS imposes. And in turn, foundations, public grant makers, and private donors often use IRS information to assess how an organization is spending money. So an organization's tax accounting habits can have a huge influence on its fundraising activities. This chapter also describes the controlling IRS rules and donor evaluation standards so that you can set up your budgets to satisfy them.

Finally, some of these internal and external reporting requirements generate extra record-keeping demands—and you will get guidance here on dealing with that, too.

Consulting With Accounting Advisers

Established nonprofit organizations are usually staffed with plenty of accounting professionals who are responsible for managing budgets, filing taxes, and supplying financial information to board members and donors. This section offers suggestions about how to communicate effectively with them.

But new or small organizations often have to make do without in-house accounting experts. For do-it-yourselfers, this section explains how to find good software and the best outside help when needed.

In-house Accounting Departments

In larger nonprofits, editors and publications managers can generally depend on the organization's accounting staff to handle nearly everything related to their budgeting needs.

But there are some areas that require special accounting attention once a nonprofit takes on the task of putting out a publication—and your in-house experts may not have had experience with them. For example, because of IRS regulations on income from advertising sales, nonprofit publications must record and report advertising sales income for every issue of every publication, instead of lumping all the issues and publications together. (See Chapter 10 for more on advertising in general, and "Customizing Your Chart of Accounts," below, for a summary of the key IRS requirements.)

Ask someone in the accounting department to skim through this book as a refresher on accounting issues unique to nonprofit publications. That may be all that's needed to ensure your group is up to speed. But in addition, you may choose to assign one liaison who works on your publication to take charge of communicating with the accounting department about budgeting and other financial issues. Ideally, that person will function as a two-way communicator: learning what the accounting department needs and advising staff there about what the people who work on the publications are doing. (Tips for handling these communication issues are covered in "Using Budgets to Prove Performance," below.)

Certified Public Accountants and Auditors

A certified public accountant (CPA) helps an organization file the required tax returns and comply with tax laws that might jeopardize its status as a nonprofit, tax-exempt organization. Most nonprofits consult with a CPA when the organization is initially formed, and then at least once a year after that.

An auditor conducts the annual financial audit that is required by the bylaws of many nonprofit organizations. Many states also require an audit for nonprofits receiving contributions over a specified amount—the amount varies from state to state—or for nonprofits that hire a paid fundraiser. Contact your state's Secretary of State or Office of the Attorney General for specific auditing rules in your state.

Sometimes the auditor is the same person as the CPA, but sometimes a different CPA is hired to do the audit. Normally, the board of directors hires the auditor rather than the nonprofit's staff, and the audit report is directed to the board. Other than having your numbers in order, your only involvement with the audit will likely be to answer a few questions if particulars about the publication's finances need to be clarified. For example, the auditor may need to know how your organization allocates membership dues for publications, or how much advertising revenue came in from your electronic newsletter. Answers to the auditor's most common questions nearly always come from information readily at hand in your day-to-day accounting activities, as long as you set up the accounting systems recommended here.

TIP

Where to find experienced help. Look for a CPA or auditor with a track record in the nonprofit world. Get references and check them before making any hiring decision. Fortunately, many CPA firms offer free or low-cost accounting and auditing services to nonprofits.

And there are a number of groups you can contact for more information and possible leads, including:

- Accountants for the Public Interest, at www.geocities.com/api_woods/api/apihome.html, and
- Clearinghouse for Volunteer Accounting Services, at www.cvas-usa.org.

In addition, the website at www.idealist.org, a clearinghouse for consultants who work with nonprofits, publishes articles and FAQs for nonprofits seeking outside experts.

Finally, the website at www.compasspoint.org publishes general information about managing nonprofit organizations, including some excellent articles about budgets, tax returns, and audits.

Basic Budgeting and Accounting Terms

You can easily master a few basic accounting terms—enough to hold a meaningful conversation about your publication's budget with an auditor or accountant—without having to become an accounting expert.

- **Assets** include money in a bank account or real estate, as well as activities that generate future economic benefits, such as a donor's pledge to cover all of your website expenses or an advertiser's yet-to-be-paid invoice for last month's newsletter sponsorship. Items counted as assets include cash and cash equivalents such as a bank certificate of deposit or savings bond, investments, contribution pledges, receivables, inventories, property, and prepaid expenses.

- **Liabilities** include obligations to pay money or provide goods and services in the future, such as unpaid bills. For example, if a donor gives $100,000 to your organization so that you can publish a series of pamphlets or develop new content for your website, the $100,000 remains a liability until the pamphlets or Web pages are completed. Other liabilities are debts and unpaid bills, which are called accounts payable in accounting lingo. Liabilities also include deferred income, which refers to money someone pays before you earn it. For example, when a subscriber pays for a year's worth of newsletters in January, your accountant does not record the subscription income until each newsletter issue is delivered to the reader. Meanwhile, the January payment is counted as deferred income.

- **Revenues** include cash contributions and other kinds of financial support the organization receives. There are two kinds of revenue for a nonprofit: fee-for-services income and contributions. Dues or subscriptions that pay for a publication, advertising income, and other publishing receipts are counted as fee-for-service revenue. Donations, including donated services, are counted as contributions. For example, if a website developer volunteers to redesign your website, the work will count as a noncash contribution to the organization.

- **Expenses** include all the money that you spend carrying out the work of your organization or producing products such as newsletters. Nonprofit organizations classify their expenses by function, as described later in this chapter.

- **Gains and losses** include transactions that are not directly related to the organization's core activities, such as stock market investments or the sale of real estate.

Source: Adapted from *Not-for-Profit Accounting Made Easy,* by Warren Ruppel (Wiley).

Using Accounting Software

Accounting software, used in some form by most nonprofits from tiny institutions to big ones, makes smooth budgeting possible—much like a good email program makes it easy to maintain your address book, send attachments, and file messages for future reference. Choosing the right accounting software is usually the first step in developing your budgeting system.

Most big nonprofits have accounting staff and systems already in place. For these larger organizations, accounting for publications is a matter of fine-tuning the established system. (See "Customizing Your Chart of Accounts," below, for more on this.) But startups and smaller nonprofits will need some help in structuring their budgeting procedures and deciding which software to use. (See "Popular Nonprofit Accounting Programs," below, for details about available choices.)

TIP

Get advice from your financial pro. Ask your bookkeeper, auditor, or CPA to identify accounting programs that other nonprofit clients are using. If one of your financial advisers uses a particular software program, then he or she may be willing to show you how to use it correctly and make it easier for the two of you to work together.

Every program automates basic nonprofit accounting tasks such as creating reports and tracking revenues and expenses. But neither the programs used by large nonprofit organization nor the standalone software used by small ones has been designed specifically to handle publications. This section explains how to extract information from standard accounting systems that will help you manage the unique reporting requirements of publications and develop a publishing budget.

Popular Nonprofit Accounting Programs

Nonprofit organizations have accounting issues that are different from those faced by commercial enterprises. Instead of being judged by the profits they earn, nonprofits are often valued by the social good they provide. And because of this extra dimension, nonprofit accounting is a bit more complicated than commercial accounting. Fortunately, there are software programs available that satisfy these unique accounting demands.

QuickBooks Premier Nonprofit Edition (Intuit) is available for $400. This program, a version of the popular QuickBooks programs for small business management, is suitable for any organization that is not required to file IRS Form 990—the income statement filed by nonprofit organizations. For example, any nonprofit that earns less than $25,000 per year in donations is not required to file an income statement, and many very small or very new organizations do not file one. (See "IRS Reporting Requirements," below, for more about Form 990.) Because QuickBooks is so widely used, you can readily find many freelance bookkeepers and accounting consultants who are familiar with it—a plus if you plan to outsource these functions. There are also companies, community colleges, and business groups offering QuickBooks training programs—live, on video, or on the Internet. And Intuit provides plenty of free information at www.quickbooks.intuit.com, including a directory of accounting professionals to help you set up and use the software.

NonProfitBooks (BtoPCommerce) offers a number of programs with features that are not available in basic business accounting programs such as QuickBooks. These programs expand and customize the basic software to accommodate nonprofit tasks, but you must buy either QuickBooks or Microsoft Small Business to use NonProfitBooks. For example, the NonProfitbooks accounting module can track multiple budgets, automatically sharing expenses among them—something you cannot do in QuickBooks. And the NonProfitBooks Office module adds a database to track donors, donations, and program outcomes. These packages cost from $400 to $1,200, depending on the level of sophistication you need, plus whatever you paid for QuickBooks or Microsoft Small Business. And for additional fees, the company offers training and consulting services to nonprofits. This would be a good choice for an organization that is large enough to file IRS forms and track lots of different programs, but small enough to need outside accounting help from consultants or professional accountants. More information is online at www.nonprofitbooks.com.

Popular Nonprofit Accounting Programs, continued
Blackbaud is an accounting software company focused on the nonprofit sector, offering products suitable to bigger organizations. Its programs were developed to conform to IRS reporting requirements imposed on those who make grants. They run without any other program such as QuickBooks and also provide functions not covered by QuickBooks, such as a program to manage Web-based fundraising activities. This option would be suitable for larger nonprofit organizations, including those operating several programs or multiple publications and websites. Go to www. blackbaud.com for more information.

Establishing a Chart of Accounts

Accountants organize spending and revenue activities that are tracked and monitored on a Chart of Accounts (COA), which is a list of all assets, liabilities, revenue, and expenses assigned to each activity. As you set up a new accounting program or begin a new activity such as publishing in an organization that already has established accounting systems, the organization's COA will need to be created or amended. Sometimes your accountant will handle this detail. But this section explains how you can create one on your own, should you be charged with the task.

There will be one account number in the COA for specific expense items such as salaries, office supplies, and travel expenses and then, within that activity account, a unique number for each of your programs. As you spend money or earn money from dues or grants, each dollar coming in and going out is attached to one of these account numbers. Some examples are given below. In each of them, you will see an expense or revenue number indicated in the first four numbers, followed by a program account number in the last four numbers.

4010-2355 Individual donations (4010) – from a website (2355)

5450-2355 Earned revenue (5450) – from advertising on the website (2355)

8190-2355 Freelance writing expenses (8190) – for the website (2355)

To ensure that your organization's COA properly and automatically records your publishing activities, it is good to be aware of what categories are identified in the COA and discuss them with your accountant.

Customizing Your Chart of Accounts

To meet IRS regulations, U.S. Postal Service requirements, and the information needs of some foundations and grantors, a nonprofit's COA must be customized to accommodate publications as described below. If you sell no ads in your publications, and your organization does not receive Nonprofit Standard or Periodicals postage discounts, then this customization may not be necessary. (See Chapter 9 for more on these discounts.)

Tracking variable and fixed publishing expenses. A variable expense is money spent producing each online posting or newsletter issue. For example, freelance writing fees for one month's posting to your website depend on how many articles were commissioned and how much you paid each freelancer. To record variable expenses, organizations assign a unique account number to every issue of a publication. (See "Calculating Taxable Income," below, for a detailed explanation and sample COA.) Fixed expenses such as staff salaries do not change from one issue to the next because an editor's salary stays the same no matter how many website pages or newsletter articles he or she produces during the year. Fixed expenses are not normally charged to any particular issue and do not get issue-related coding in the COA.

Customizing Your Chart of Accounts, cont'd.

Tracking each publication individually. IRS regulations require nonprofits to report their income and expenses for each publication separately. (For specifics, see "IRS Reporting Requirements," below.) The simplest way to satisfy this requirement is to assign a unique project code in your organization's COA for every publication: one for your email newsletter, one for your magazine, one for your website.

Allocating publishing expenses. Most organizations use a formula to determine what share of their publishing costs should be charged to fundraising, overhead, or programs. A publication designed to educate high school kids about career options, and totally funded through grants or donations, might be treated as a program. One that is designed exclusively to raise money from donors might be charged completely to the fundraising department. And one created for communicating with members might charge 100% of publishing expenses to overhead.

Many organizations use unique program numbers for each function. For example, an organization might use the number one for all fundraising expenses, two for programs, and three for overhead. If the website's primary function is collecting donations, then it would be considered a fundraising activity and it would have a program code starting with the number one. But if the website basically provides information as a service to members, then it would likely be considered a management activity, and it would have a program code starting with the number three. (See "Communicating Results to Outsiders," below, for more on this.)

Budgeting Tips for Publications

Once the budget basics—advisers, software, and a Chart of Accounts—are in place, then you can begin to estimate your expenses and create a budget for your publication.

Unfortunately, there isn't one single budget format that will serve every type of publication. The budgeting worksheet offered in this chapter is a starting ground, but it's likely that you'll need to make adjustments based on the particulars of your organization and your publications. This section offers some general tips to help you create an effective publication budget of your own.

Focus on the Most Expensive Items First

You'll have different budget problems with every publication type, but you can always make budgeting easier by focusing on the largest expenses first, then lumping the smaller ones together. For example, salaries, benefits, and other compensation-related fixed expenses are often the largest budget items for an organization that hires an editor to create newsletters, magazines, or websites. (Chapter 4 discusses editorial and advertising sales salaries and commissions; refer to that information for estimating these staffing expenses.)

After staff costs, the largest expenses for most magazines and printed newsletters are printing, paper, and postage. A website spends most of its money paying programmers to generate Web-based tools or content-related features of the site and promoting traffic. (Chapter 7 will help you estimate printing expenses. Chapter 8 will help with projecting website expenses. And Chapter 9 covers postage.)

Understand What Drives Variable Expenses

For print publications, the total variable expense is driven by four key decisions, all discussed in greater detail throughout this book:

- the number of issues you print in a year
- the number of pages in each issue
- the production quality of each issue—such as paper choices, use of color, and design specifications, and
- the number of copies you distribute.

You can stay on top of your budget by learning how decisions about frequency, issue size, quality, and distribution drive those costs. If you need to reassess or cut spending, you will know exactly which decisions to change.

For electronic publications, including emails and websites, content programming is often the most expensive item, followed closely by marketing or traffic-building efforts. For example, adding a blog to your website involves the one-time cost of programming the blogging capacity into your site, plus the ongoing cost of paying someone to write the blog if you don't do it yourself. You can easily track which blogs and other articles draw the most traffic and then fine-tune future budgets to focus on expanding the most popular features first.

 RESOURCE
Some online services automate the feedback process for you. For example, Groundspring.org processes online donations for nonprofit clients. Its software records how every donation was generated—which magazine article, which Web page, which email. You only have to learn and use the coding system that comes free with the service to automate the tracking process.

Establish Priorities

Publishing decisions usually involve choosing between various ways to spend the available resources.

For example, if you know that using a lighter-weight paper cuts printing and postage expenses by 30% per issue, then you could spend 30% more paying for experienced journalists to write articles for your magazine. You might need to determine what's more important to your organization: the expensive look and feel of each copy, or the quality of writing inside. That's the kind of trade-off you can make intelligently when you know how your decisions are driving your costs. And different organizations will justifiably come out differently on these trade-offs. The point is to know where you can make a difference by breaking down the total publishing task into separate decisions.

Use the editorial guidelines you developed in Chapter 2 as a discussion point for making these trade-off decisions. And then use your budget to highlight or communicate the resulting choices so that people within your organization understand the financial ramifications.

Review and Revise

The budgeting process normally takes several months and a number of versions before it takes a final form. This is because your thinking will likely change as you gather new information.

> **EXAMPLE:** After doing its budgeting research, one organization discovered that it would have to pay more than expected to hire an experienced editor to create one email newsletter. It also discovered that the actual costs of sending email newsletters would be much lower than planned—and that sponsors would be willing to pay handsomely to advertise in the e-letters. That fresh information led to a revised publishing plan: The organization agreed to hire a full-time, well-paid editor for electronic newsletter, but asked that person to produce three sponsored publications instead of just one—and then used the extra sponsorship revenue to pay the higher salary.

RESOURCE

A number of books cover the budgeting process for nonprofits in detail, but like most general books, they don't address the specifics of budgeting for publications. Each book contains greater detail about several of the topics mentioned here: working with a CPA, audits, developing a Chart of Accounts. A few examples include:

- *Bookkeeping Basics: What Every Nonprofit Bookkeeper Needs to Know*, by Debra L. Ruegg and Lisa M. Venkatrathnam (Amherst H. Wilder Foundation)
- *Bookkeeping for Nonprofits: A Step-by-Step Guide to Nonprofit Accounting*, by Murray Dropkin and James Halpin (Jossey-Bass), and
- *Not-for-Profit Accounting Made Easy*, by Warren Ruppel (Wiley).

Using Budgets to Prove Performance

No matter how well you edit and design your publication, some people within your organization will judge it based exclusively on whether it brings in financial benefits. If your publication does not, you may be put in the position of proving that its cost is justified in some other way.

Unfortunately, most publications cost more to produce than they earn in income from readers and advertisers. In other words, they will not look good by the simple measure of money. Fortunately, you can usually elevate the conversation beyond money and win more support for the publications within your organization and even among outside donors and contributors if you take the trouble to capture and report other, measurable publishing results—an increase in membership renewals, for example, or a boost in attendance at meetings.

This strategic approach to budgeting links spending to forward-looking performance goals so that your organization can get a fair return on its publishing expenditures. And it also allows you to expand your publications when they meet or exceed their goals—and to cut back or eliminate them when performance disappoints. If you want to adopt this strategic approach to budgeting, then gather both financial and nonfinancial information—and use it to make your case.

For example, if membership and revenues are falling, a nonprofit will likely consider cutting spending on magazines and newsletters going to members unless it can determine how the publications help to stave off additional membership losses. But the only way to make that connection is by routinely collecting information linking them together.

Here is how to start.

- **Define success.** Consider the mission of your publishing efforts, and then take time to define information that will measure whether each publication is achieving its purpose, such as an increase in membership renewals, boosted donations from existing donors, or expanded contact with prospective members. (See Chapter 1 for more detail on composing and communicating your mission.) Remember to include nonfinancial activities that might increase the health or visibility of your organization, such as the number of letters written to your editors, the number of hits on your website, attendance at annual meetings, or hours of service donated by volunteers.

Profile of a Publishing Score Card

A community theater group, Leo's Lighthouse Theater, is planning to spend $24,000 annually writing and printing a monthly newsletter, *Leo's Lights*, to promote attendance at performances. The group has two goals for the newsletter. First, it hopes to boost ticket sales and increase income. Second, and more important, it hopes to lure more males to attend its performances.

The theater's director decided to make a before-and-after measurement of this second concern, male attendance. For three months before publishing the first newsletter issue, volunteers stood at the doors counting people who entered the theater. The group determined that 3,302 (or 78%) of the 4,233 people coming to that season's plays were women, and roughly 931 (or 22%) were men.

After publishing the newsletter for a year, the counting exercise was repeated and the second time, the group estimated that male attendees had increased to 1,509 and total audience numbers had increased by 15% to 4,868. Total revenues from ticket sales increased by $78,000.

The nonprofit's publishing scorecard after a year is represented below.

Publishing Scorecard for *Leo's Lights*

Total newsletter publishing expense	$24,000
Total increase in audience (4,868 minus 4,233)	635
Newsletter cost per new attendee, all genders	$37.80
Number of new male attendees	578
Newsletter cost per new male attendee	$41.52

This newsletter was a success in generating more revenue than it cost to produce, but more important, it yielded a significant number of men who might become long-term theater patrons.

- **Track performance.** Assign someone to measure nonfinancial activities: logging letters as they come in, collecting data about volunteer time from program managers, and any other tangible response to the publication. You cannot depend on the accounting department to record most of these outcomes, which do not directly affect accounting concerns such as audits and taxes.

- **Link performance to spending.** Match those strategic outcomes—increased member renewal rates, higher website traffic numbers, boosted volunteer hours—by putting them together onto a single spreadsheet page or "score card" for each publication. (The budget worksheet later in this chapter shows some examples. Chapter 11 describes other ways to measure and document outcomes.) If you compare measurable outcomes to expenses over time, you will eventually learn what performance results are reasonable—for example, that each issue of your email newsletter can generate 5,000 new hits to your website or a 10% lift in membership renewals.

Meeting Internal Requirements

Most organizations will give your publication an "A" in Financial Prudence if you simply spend what you promised to spend and if that spending lines up with historical expectations.

Basing current spending levels and publishing outcomes on past experiences seems fair, but only if everything else is the same—and only if the past budget and spending was reasonable from the beginning. At many nonprofits, neither assumption is actually true. For example, many organizations want to publish more exciting content on their websites because of the Internet's popularity with younger audiences. But Web expenses are hard to predict, and nobody has extensive experience budgeting for them to use as guidance. Consequently, lots of editors are asked to generate great Web content without adding any staff or funding to their budgets—a frustrating and unrealistic situation for everyone.

Another problem is that managers develop a "comfort zone" with a specific level of spending, often as a result of the political struggles within the organization. For example, people may agree over the years that their member publications should consume only a certain percentage of the total budget, because anything more would have to come from some other department's pocket.

Often the only way to break through these kinds of roadblocks is to make a direct link between publishing outcomes and spending. For example, you might want to figure out whether your organization can generate less-expensive membership renewals through the website and e-letters managed by your communications department or through the traditional printed direct mail campaigns managed by the membership group. The answer is simple to calculate: Divide total spending by renewals generated and see which costs less. Even if the facts and figures are on your side, internal politics may not guarantee that managers will agree to divert funds from the membership department to the website. But at least you will be able to present a reasoned and documented argument for doing so.

Sometimes you can also break a spending logjam by proving that new spending will bring in more than enough new revenue to justify it.

EXAMPLE: When one new editor took over the quarterly donor magazine for a large, national charity, she figured out that the magazine, which cost about $1.45 per copy to publish, was generating new donations averaging about $2.60 per copy–a calculation nobody had ever made before. The editor persuaded her managers to increase the frequency of the magazine and also to increase the issue size. Magazine spending rose to $1.95 per copy in the first year under her new plan, but happily, donations rose to more than $4 per copy.

Communicating Results to Outsiders

Even after the dust settles from internal budget battles, most nonprofits still have to answer to outside forces. If you closely track and report income and spending activities, you will have persuasive facts and figures when it comes time to explain your publishing mission to outsiders.

For example, the IRS, which grants or withholds tax-exempt status, also monitors how nonprofits are spending their money to ensure that tax-exempt funds are used to benefit the public. The IRS requires every nonprofit that collects more than $25,000 in donations in one year to file an annual report, Form 990, which also documents how the donated funds were spent. One part of the form divides spending into three spending categories: programs, management or overhead, and fundraising. This breakout is also commonly reported in an organization's annual audit—a document read closely by some foundations, government agencies, and major donors. (For more on From 990's reporting mandates, see "IRS Reporting Requirements," below.)

Program spending is defined as money spent directly on an organization's charitable activities and programs. Management covers administrative activities—such as accounting, marketing, and staff management. Fundraising includes all spending that is directly linked to raising money from donors, such as the cost of consultants, direct mail campaigns, and events. As discussed earlier, making sure that your publishing Chart of Accounts accurately reflects how you view your publishing mission is an important factor. If fundraising is the primary mission of your website, then its expenses should be reported to the IRS under that functional category. But if your website is designed to educate the public about some important health or social issue—such as how to deal with cancer or how to be an engaged citizen—then its expenses should be counted as program spending in your Chart of Accounts and reported as such to the IRS. If a publication serves a number of different purposes, accounting for them can be shared, as described below.

In addition to the IRS, several watchdog organizations also monitor nonprofit spending on behalf of the general public and private philanthropists. (See "Heed the Nonprofit Performance Watchdogs," below.) Most of these groups analyze information reported on IRS Form 990 to determine whether or not individual nonprofits are behaving responsibly from a financial viewpoint. In particular, they look at the breakdown of expenses among programs, fundraising, and overhead functions. For example, the Better Business Bureau publishes a series of financial standards for nonprofit organizations that are summarized below and described on its website at www.give.org. And other watchdog organizations also publish their own standards for financial performance.

From an outside contributor's viewpoint, the more your organization spends on programs, the better. After all, donors want their funds to reach the hurricane victims or the hungry children, rather than being used to publish a fancy, self-congratulatory magazine celebrating your staff or volunteers. Based on that logic, the Better Business Bureau recommends that every nonprofit should spend at least 65% of its total expenses on programs. This ratio is one of the most-watched performance indicators for nonprofits—and many larger charitable organizations try to exceed it, spending 75% or 80% of their total expenditures on programs.

Some analysts argue that the 65% to 80% spending goal is too restrictive, particularly for the small and new nonprofits that rarely meet it. After all, spending too little on administration and fundraising may diminish the long-term sustainability of a brand-new organization. But donors like it, and therefore, the spending standard is probably here to stay.

By every spending standard, publications are commonly lumped into management or fundraising categories, not charged as a program. The trouble is that most publications lose money. Therefore, even a modest newsletter has the potential to drive overhead or fundraising expenses way north of 35% and downgrade your good standing with the watchdogs and rating services. Smaller, local organizations may operate under the radar of these watchdog groups, but any large national charity must consider these spending guidelines in the budgeting process.

The obvious remedy is to define all your publication spending as a program function within your Chart of Accounts so that publishing costs do not fall into the 35% management and fundraising bucket.

Categorizing your publications as programs is the best option for many nonprofits, particularly when the publications directly serve the public by providing fresh information about public issues or news of import to the general public.

Heed the Nonprofit Performance Watchdogs

If your organization files IRS Form 990 and relies heavily on support from well-established foundations, then you should know how these groups will rate it. The performance watchdogs are the ones to watch.

The most comprehensive resource for information about financial standards is the National Center for Charitable Statistics at the Urban Institute at www.nccsdataweb.urban.org, because this site offers research reports, news articles, and advice for nonprofit managers in addition to offering rating services. Start there if you need to quickly learn how these standards might affect your organization.

You can also see whether your organization has already been rated by checking the sites listed below. But note that all of the data is taken from IRS Form 990; if you don't file that form, then you won't be rated.

The prime nonprofit watchdog organizations include:

- The American Institute of Philanthropy, at www.charitywatch.org
- The Wise Giving Alliance of the Better Business Bureau, at www.give.org
- The Guidestar database, at www.guidestar.org, and
- Charity Navigator, at www.charitynavigator.org.

EXAMPLE: The Glimpse Foundation, which aims to promote global aware-ness, classifies its print magazine, website, and electronic newsletters as program expenses because almost all of the content is educational.

EXAMPLE: The Foundation for National Progress, which promotes civic engagement by providing investigative reporting and news, also classifies all of its publishing activities—including *Mother Jones* magazine and its related website and newsletters—as programs.

But this option simply isn't available for everyone. In particular, mem-bership organizations generally classify their publications as management expenses, because their main purpose is to communicate with staff or members, not the public. And publications serving the donors of a public charity generally define publications as fundraising activities.

Another option is to allocate your publishing costs among all three functions using some objective measure to determine the allocation. For example, if your 90-page magazine devotes 16 pages to fundraising, six pages to member news, and 68 pages to educational feature articles, then it would be appropriate to split the publishing costs as: 18% to fundraising, 7% to overhead, and 75% to programs. But be careful. If your characterization of your publication doesn't match reality, the IRS and watchdog groups may challenge it.

TIP

Check specific accounting guidelines for government contracts. Government agencies have their own systems for classifying publishing expenses by function that is separate from IRS Form 990. In most cases, local, state, or federal government funding agencies will automatically classify your publication as an overhead expense. However, you can argue for a different accounting if that classification threatens to reduce your grant or government funding. Ask the agency for instructions about obtaining an exception if your publication serves a specific program function, such as education.

IRS Reporting Requirements

The IRS requires every public charity and private foundation to file annual tax returns, but there are many exceptions to this rule. For example, most faith-based organizations, including religious schools, are not required to file income tax returns.

Any public charity that earned less than $25,000 in donations during the year is not required to file. For this reason alone, many very small or brand-new organizations do not need to file tax returns.

If your nonprofit has applied for a tax exemption but the IRS has not yet ruled on your application, then you are not required to file a return until the ruling on it comes through.

On the other hand, groups that engage in substantial political activity, particularly those organized under section 527 of the Internal Revenue Code, are required to report contributions and disbursements so that their support and operations are in the public domain in advance of elections. (See Chapter 5, "Lobbying Restrictions May Limit Your Content," for related details.) And every private foundation, regardless of income, is required to file a return.

> **CAUTION**
>
> **Ad revenues trigger tax-filing requirements.** You must file a tax return if you earned any money from what the IRS calls "unrelated business" activities, including advertising sales, even if your organization is not otherwise required to file tax returns. For this reason, some nonprofit organizations do not accept advertising in their publications or on their websites. (Chapter 10 covers the pros and cons of advertising in detail. Also, review "Unrelated Business Income," below, for details on the tax question.)

Qualifying nonprofits must file Form 990, "Return of Organization Exempt From Income Tax," or Form 990-EZ, "Short Form Return of Organization Exempt From Income Tax," for some qualifying nonprofits with gross receipts of less than $100,000 and total assets of less than $250,000. If you have any doubt about whether your organization should file income tax returns, check with an accountant or review the IRS instructions for Form 990 and 990-EZ, which are posted at the IRS website at www.irs.gov/instructions/i990-ez/index.html. You can also study how other nonprofit organizations have completed the form by going to the website at www.guidestar.org, which includes a database of recently filed IRS 990 returns from many public charities and foundations.

> **CD-ROM**
>
> Copies of Form 990 and Form 990-EZ, along with the instructions the IRS provides to complete them, are included on the CD-ROM that accompanies this book.

Unrelated Business Income

The Unrelated Business Income Tax, or UBIT, is designed to keep nonprofit groups that are exempt from paying income taxes from competing unfairly with commercial businesses that *do* pay those taxes.

According to the IRS, unrelated business income is "income from a trade or business, regularly carried on, that is not substantially related to the charitable, educational, or other purpose that is the basis of the organization's income tax exemption." For example, if your community theater group were to open a professional catering business to raise money, its catering profits would be considered unrelated business income. Similarly, advertising profits are nearly always considered unrelated business income.

But several activities are specifically excluded, even if they generate a lot of cash, including:

- services that are only available to members or clients—such as a school cafeteria
- sales of donated goods—such as those at a hospital's thrift shop, and
- activities carried out exclusively by volunteers—such as a soccer club bake sale.

There is a question in Part VI of IRS Form 990 that asks, "Did the organization have unrelated business gross income of $1,000 or more during the year covered by this return?" If you answer yes to that question, then you are required to submit a report of that income. (See Chapter 10 for more detail on UBIT as it relates to advertising.)

You may need your accounting system to track unrelated business income because if you have several publications that carry ads, the IRS requires you to keep a separate accounting of each one. That's the main reason you need to create separate account numbers for every publication. (The chart explained in "Calculating Taxable Income," below, gives an example.)

RESOURCE
Unified Financial Reporting System for Not-for-Profit Organizations, by Russy D. Sumariwalla, Wilson C. Levis, Russy D. Sumariwalla, and Wilson C. Levis (Jossey-Bass).

Using the Right Numbers: The Unified Chart of Accounts

The National Center for Charitable Statistics, along with a handful of other nonprofit support organizations, developed a Unified Chart of Accounts (UCOA) so that nonprofits can quickly and reliably translate their financial statements into the categories used by the IRS, federal Office of Management and Budget, and most foundations and grant organizations. You can find information about the UCOA at http://nccsdataweb.urban.org/FAQ/index.php?category=77.

According to its creators, "The UCOA unifies the reporting requirements of various federal, state, and nonprofit monitoring agencies into one system. It will help nonprofits 'cross-walk' all of their financial reporting requirements, including Form 990, into one system. The secondary goal of the UCOA is to establish uniform terminology within and between nonprofit organizations and funding agencies."

The nonprofit accounting software recommended earlier in this chapter incorporates UCOA formats, but some larger nonprofit organizations may be using software developed before the UCOA was created. If this is your situation, you may want to consider rearranging an existing Chart of Accounts to match the UCOA, which is becoming an industry standard.

Calculating Taxable Income

In determining taxable profits, the IRS wants to know how much revenue you generate through an unrelated business activity, such as advertising, and how much you spend overall to produce the product—

for example, how much you spend to produce the publication or website that carried ads.

There is no tax liability if there is no net income from the activity—that is, if spending exceeds revenue. This is another reason for carefully tracking every individual direct and variable publishing expense, using the Chart of Accounts as a reference.

You can deduct 100% of direct ad sales costs from advertising revenues. Direct advertising sales costs include commissions, travel expenses, and salaries and benefits of sales staff. You can also deduct the ad-related portion of your variable publishing costs, such as printing and postage expenses, according to the advertising share of your publication.

> **EXAMPLE:** If your eight-page newsletter has two ad pages, you can include 25% of your variable costs in the expenses that you deduct from advertising revenues before any income tax is due. (Variable costs are explained in "Variable Expenses," below.)

Break out your advertising revenue according to the individual advertisers, because the IRS distinguishes between ads from members and ads from outside companies. Ads from your members or your own programs may be so closely related to your mission that the IRS will not include them as unrelated business income. But ads from outside companies will certainly be classified as unrelated business income. It's necessary, then, to use one unique account number for ad revenue from outside companies or organizations, a different number to record ads for your own programs, and a third number for ads from members.

TIP

Be sure to get the right COA. Show your accountant or bookkeeper the IRS guidelines regarding taxable advertising revenues (included in Chapter 10), and also provide your CPA with the COA information in this chapter. Ask the person who is responsible for setting up the Chart of Accounts for each publication's advertising revenues to follow these guidelines.

Account numbers that meet IRS reporting requirements and use the UCOA might look like those in the chart below. In the UCOA, revenue from advertising is generally classified using a number between 5450 and 5459. In keeping with that, the example uses 5450 to represent all advertising revenue from members and 5451 to indicate advertising revenue from outside companies.

Next, a different project code is assigned to distinguish each of the organization's publishing projects: 010 for the member magazine, 020 for the website, and 030 for electronic newsletters.

Finally, the example uses a unique number, generally stated as a date, to indicate each issue of each publication. This allows you to track the expenses and income of each issue as discussed earlier in the chapter.

RESOURCE

The IRS hosts an online exemption workshop. The Internal Revenue Service hosts a Web-based version of its Exempt Organizations Workshop covering tax compliance issues confronted by small and mid-sized tax-exempt organizations. The free online workshop, "Stay Exempt—Tax Basics for 501(c)(3)s," consists of five interactive modules on tax compliance topics for exempt organizations:

- **Tax-Exempt Status.** How can you keep your 501(c)(3) exempt?
- **Unrelated Business Income.** Does your organization generate taxable income?
- **Employment Issues.** How should you treat your workers for tax purposes?
- **Form 990.** Would you like to file an error-free return?, and
- **Required Disclosures.** To whom do you have to show your records?

The training program is available at www.stayexempt.org.

Sample Accounting Codes
Description of the Revenu_
Revenue from ads sold to members (5_ magazine (010) for the November 20_
Revenue from website ads (020) so_ during the month of January 2008 (0801)
Revenue from ads sold to outside companies (5451) sμ ing the electronic newsletter (030) for November 2008 (081_

Postal Service Requirements

SKIP AHEAD

The information in this section applies only to publications that are mailed. If you are publishing online only, you can skip it and go on to "Creating a Publishing Budget," below.

All publishers pay higher postage rates for ad pages than for all other types of content. There is a United States Postal Service (USPS) formula for calculating the advertising share of each issue based on its weight and the percentage of ad pages it contains. This distinction between ad and other pages creates the accounting burden discussed in this section. In addition, some nonprofit organizations receive significant postage discounts by following USPS mailing restrictions—sending copies only to paid members, for example. (See Chapter 9 for the rules about all available postal permits.) These restrictions also create accounting issues addressed in this section.

Before sending any magazines or newsletters into the postal system, you must estimate and report the postage charges for that issue, based on its ad content and the terms of your postage discount permit. The USPS will help you with these estimates, and you can also simplify the process by setting up your Chart of Accounts to distinguish between

...enses related to member copies versus nonmember copies, or any other distinctions that arise under the terms of your particular postal permit. (The postal forms that publishers use to apply for specific postal permits are included on the CD-ROM that accompanies this book and are discussed in detail in Chapter 9.)

To accommodate the postal reporting requirements regarding advertising and nonadvertising pages, you must capture page counts for every issue that you mail. Publishers generally collect page counts either in an advertising sales management database that they create for themselves using a database program such as Excel or FoxPro, or by using another advertising sales management program. (The budgeting worksheet in this chapter, below, also demonstrates this concept. See Chapter 10 for more on specific ad sales management programs.)

CAUTION

Uncle Sam is watching you. The USPS occasionally checks to be sure that a publisher is correctly estimating and reporting postage charges. Having all of the right information within your Chart of Accounts and your advertising sales management program will help you respond to one of these postal audits, if you ever face one.

The following table illustrates how an organization might assign COA account numbers to accommodate the postal requirements discussed here. First, following UCOA guidelines, the sample has assigned the overall category 8400 to all variable expenses related to publishing—and postage is always counted as a variable expense. Next, the specific codes 8401 and 8402 are used to distinguish between member and nonmember postage expenses. Then, the sample uses the same codes developed earlier for advertising revenue to identify each publishing product: 010 for the member magazine, 020 for the website, and 030 for electronic newsletters. Since there are no postage expenses for the website or electronic newsletters, there should be no expenses coded 8401-020 or 8401-030. Finally, the sample uses the same dating system to record each individual issue of the magazine or website update.

Sample Accounting Codes for Postage Expenses	
Description of the Expenses	Account Codes Assigned (Expense-Project-Date)
Postage for copies mailed to members (8401) of the member magazine (010) dated October 2008 (0810)	8401-010-0810
Postage for sample copies mailed to nonmembers (8402) of the member magazine (010) for October 2008 (0810)	8402-010-0810

Creating a Publishing Budget

Most accounting software programs include budgeting worksheets to help you plan for publishing expenses. The trouble is, many publishing expenses are easier to understand and plan in nonaccounting terms. For example, changing the number of pages in a magazine can dramatically increase or reduce its printing and postage costs—but accounting systems don't usually record or budget for underlying expense drivers such as page counts. You will find it hard to make a decent budget in QuickBooks or any other accounting program if you don't first plan ahead for the details underlying many of your publishing expenses.

The publishing budget worksheet included here is designed to help you plan and manage all the nonfinancial publishing decisions discussed earlier in this chapter: how many pages you publish, how many copies you print, how many ads you sell. The worksheet helps you translate those decisions into dollars and cents by calculating how the budget changes as you refine your ideas. After polishing your thoughts by scanning this worksheet, you can put the resulting budget into your accounting system.

CROSS-REFERENCE

Some of the publishing decisions needed for completing this worksheet are discussed later in this book. You would be wise to hold off on completing the worksheet until you finish reading the chapters about hiring people (Chapter 4), planning content (Chapter 5), printing (Chapter 7), Web publishing (Chapter 8), postage options (Chapter 9), and selling ads (Chapter 10). These chapters will help you make the decisions that go into a final publishing budget and plan.

If you have already started publishing, then you may find it easier to use the worksheet presented here immediately. You can gather the necessary information from your current publishing activities and use the worksheet to predict spending under different scenarios. For example, if you've been publishing a quarterly newsletter, you can use the worksheet to estimate the financial impact of moving to six or eight issues per year instead of four. In this way, the worksheet will allow you to change the underlying assumptions behind your current spending and project a new budget based on new assumption.

If you are starting from scratch and have no previous publishing budgets to draw upon, you can use the worksheet to collect information as you gather it over the course of your planning process: salaries from the recruitment and hiring process, printing costs from negotiations with printers, postage from the USPS. And if you change your mind about basic assumptions—such as how many issues to produce per year, for example, or how many copies to print—then the worksheet will help you estimate the financial implications.

CD-ROM

The Budget Worksheet discussed here is included in spreadsheet format on the CD-ROM that accompanies this book.

Each of the major sections of the worksheet—Staffing and Other Fixed Costs, Publishing Assumptions, Variable Expenses, Revenue, and Net Publishing Income—is discussed below, followed by a completed sample of the section of the worksheet that was discussed.

Staffing and Other Fixed Costs

This section explains budgeting costs for employees of your organization, not contractors or freelance contributors, which are discussed in a later section.

Job titles and salaries. Edit the job titles or add different ones to the worksheet template if you plan to hire more employees. Most nonprofits hire at least one editor on staff. Do not include outside freelancers or contractors in this section, which should include only people who become regular part-time or full-time employees of your organization.

Payroll taxes and benefits. After deciding who will be hired and for what salary, you must include any benefits that your nonprofit pays, such as pension contributions, insurance coverage, and vacation pay. Also include the employer's share of any payroll taxes that are required by law in your state. Ask an accounting professional to help you project these benefits costs based on what your organization offers to its employees.

Other overhead. Finally, include any expenses that employees will incur just by becoming employees, such as phone charges, office supplies, computers, and software. If there are particularly large or controversial items needed for your budget—for instance, if you wish to buy different computers for these employees from what people use in other parts of the organization—then add extra lines to highlight those expenses.

CROSS-REFERENCE

Chapter 4 discusses hiring people, both as employees and as freelancers. After reading it, you should be able to complete the first budgeting step: Staffing and Other Fixed Costs.

Nonprofit Publishing Budget Worksheet

STAFFING AND OTHER FIXED COSTS				
		January	February	March
Job Titles and Salaries	**Annual Salary** (Divide annual salary by 12 for monthly amount)			
Editor	$85,000	$ 7,083	$ 7,083	$ 7,083
Associate Editor	$60,000	$ 5,000	$ 5,000	$ 5,000
Webmaster	$60,000	$ 5,000	$ 5,000	$ 5,000
Ad Sales Manager	$45,000	$ 3,750	$ 3,750	$ 3,750
Subtotal of salary expenses		$20,833	$20,833	$20,833
Payroll Taxes and Benefits	**% of salary** (Multiply % by salary expense)			
Social Security and Medicare taxes	8%	$ 1,667	$ 1,667	$ 1,667
Medical insurance benefits	15%	$ 3,125	$ 3,125	$ 3,125
Retirement plan matching benefit	5%	$ 1,042	$ 1,042	$ 1,042
Subtotal of taxes and benefits		$ 5,833	$ 5,833	$ 5,833
Other Overhead	(Enter monthly estimates)			
Travel expenses		$ 1,500	$ 1,500	$ 1,500
Phone		$ 900	$ 900	$ 900
Rent		$ 850	$ 850	$ 850
Supplies		$ 250	$ 250	$ 250
Computers		$ 400	$ 400	$ 400
Marketing		$ 1,200	$ 1,200	$ 1,200
All other office expenses		$ 700	$ 700	$ 700
Subtotal of overhead		$ 5,800	$ 5,800	$ 5,800
Subtotal of staff and fixed costs		$32,467	$32,467	$32,467

Publishing Assumptions

As noted earlier, many decisions about your publication, such as the print run and issue size, will not appear in accounting programs. For a website, you will decide how many pages of content there will be and how often new content will be posted. Use the budget worksheet to record your decisions about those items.

You might get needed guidance for making these decisions by paying attention to what other nonprofit organizations are publishing. (You can also look at "Lessons Learned From a Publishing Survey," below, for benchmarks of publishing habits among small, medium, and large nonprofit organizations.)

TIP

The importance of staying flexible. Some of your most basic publishing assumptions are likely to change as you learn more about the process, or after you review the whole plan with decision makers at your organization. For example, you may start out planning to publish 12 issues per year of your newsletter, but after weighing the newsletter effort against other projects, you may decide to cut back to a quarterly print newsletter and spend your remaining resources developing website content. Use the second budget section to capture and update those decisions as you work on them.

Frequency. The worksheet also requires you to indicate the number of issues that will be published in each month and the number of times website content will be updated. In the sample section of the worksheet filled out below, there is a bimonthly print magazine and a website updated every business day. The worksheet shows a 1 in January and March to indicate the print magazine, and a 20 in every month to represent the website updates. Use whatever numbers accurately reflect how often new content will be produced in your publications.

Number of pages. Print publications are usually roughly the same size from issue to issue because organizations decide how many pages they can afford to produce in a year and then stick closely to that number. Adding more pages to the issue size increases the burden on editors and also affects postage and other variable costs. One staff editor can usually handle no more than about 200 pages of content per year, depending on how much work he or she puts in for every page. (Chapters 4 and 5 address these editing issues.)

Websites also tend to have a consistent format throughout the year, with a regular number of articles and features that you must add or revise each time the site is updated. For the budget, estimate how many pages of new or revised content you will publish with each update so that you can determine how much work will be involved.

Print distribution. For every month that you are planning to publish a printed magazine or newsletter, estimate the total number of copies you will distribute. The sample worksheet offers a list of possible ways to distribute: to members, prospective members, conference attendees, and others. But your budget should conform to your distribution plan. (See Chapter 9 for a complete explanation of this plan.)

Website visitor counts. When budgeting for an electronic newsletter or website, estimate how many people will visit the site each month or receive each issue of the newsletter. For example, if you offer a new e-newsletter to members, the number of people who subscribe is likely to build up over time. These numbers are relevant to sponsors and advertisers, and they're also valuable for your own marketing efforts because they show how many people you are reaching.

Advertising. The worksheet lists several different kinds of advertising pages that might appear in a print magazine or newsletter. You can change this section to match your organization's decisions about accepting ads. (Chapter 10 covers advertising sales in detail.)

TIP

Copy good ideas from other publications. A quick way to help decide what kind of ads might fit into your publication or website is to look at other nonprofits for examples. If you find a newsletter with a tidy, attractive classified ads section, for example, you can use that one as a model for budgeting yours: How many listings appear on a page? What does the publication charge per listing?

In a later section of the worksheet, you will see the advertising income that results from the choices made in this section. Notice that in this section, ad pages are subtracted from the total number of pages in the issue to indicate how many editorial pages you will produce. Some organizations limit the number or percentage of ad pages in their publications because of restrictions that the USPS imposes on their permit class, or for other reasons.

The worksheet automatically calculates the percentage of ad pages to total pages. In the example given, there are 15 ad pages in each 70-page issue, or about 21% ads. The worksheet is also set up to calculate how many editorial pages will be in the issues after ad pages are subtracted from the total.

The worksheet separates print ads from online ads. There are separate lines for entering how many banner and text ad units will be running on the website every month. (These topics are covered in more detail in Chapter 10.) Revenue from these online ads is calculated later in the worksheet.

CROSS-REFERENCE

You will be working to decide the budgeting items listed in the Publishing Assumptions part of the budget as you read through the entire book, including items such as how often to produce your newsletter or magazine or how many pages of content to post at your website. This section of the budget also captures your expectations about advertising sales—that is, how many pages or online ads you expect to sell. That subject is detailed in Chapter 10.

Nonprofit Publishing Budget Worksheet, continued

PUBLISHING ASSUMPTIONS			
	January	February	March
Frequency			
Issues published this month	1		1
Web update performed	20	20	20
Number of Pages			
Pages in magazine issues	68		68
Web pages per update	12	12	12
Subtotal of number of pages published	**80**	**12**	**80**
Print Distribution (Indicate the number of copies that will go through each channel)			
Number of member copies	15,000		15,000
Samples to prospective members	1,500		1,500
Conference copies	300		300
Inventory copies	500		500
Ad sales promotion copies	300		300
Newsstand or retail copies			
Subtotal of number of copies distributed	17,600		17,600
Print Order (Distribution plus 10% spoilage)	19,360		19,360
Website Visitor Counts			
Number of website visitors per month	1,100	1,200	1,450
Number of email names used	11,000	11,000	11,000
Advertising - Print			
Classified ads from members			
Number of listings	32		40
Listings per page	16		16
Subtotal of classified ad pages	2		2.5
Small business ads from outside companies			
Number of ads	18		18
Ads per page	9		9
Subtotal of small business ad pages	2		2
Display ads from internal programs			
Number of pages	3		2.5

Nonprofit Publishing Budget Worksheet, continued

PUBLISHING ASSUMPTIONS, continued			
	January	February	March
Display ads from outside companies			
Number of pages	9		11
Subtotal of display ad pages	12	0	13.5
Total number of print ad pages	16	0	18
Editorial pages produced for print			
Total issue pages (from above)	68	0	68
Minus ad pages (from above)	16	0	18
Equals print editorial pages	52	0	50
Ad ratio (percent of issues given to ads)	24%		26%
Total number of content pages produced (print plus online)	64	12	62
Advertising - Online			
Number of banner ads	2	3	2
Number of text ads	5	5	9
Subtotal of online ad units	7	8	11

Variable Expenses

Once you have made key decisions about your publication, such as how big it will be and how often it will be published, you can begin estimating the publishing costs in detail.

This section of the worksheet calculates variable publishing expenses so that the budget will change automatically if you change any of the assumptions established in the previous section. For example, if you add more pages to the magazine, the freelance content costs would increase automatically.

This works because of the budgeting assumptions created here. For example, a printer can tell you how much it will cost to print a single copy of your newsletter or magazine. After you enter this number, the worksheet takes over and estimates the total printing bill based on the number of copies entered earlier. If you change the print run, the printing budget will automatically change, too. Likewise, if you negotiate a better price with a printer, you could update the worksheet and recalculate the printing budget.

Content-related costs. Proofreaders, illustrators, and other freelance contributors are often paid by the word or by the page. That practice makes it relatively easy to estimate what you will have to spend per page of writing or photography. For example, if a typical page on your website includes one 400-word article and a writer is paid 75 cents per word, then the page will cost $300 in writers' fees.

On the worksheet, these per-page prices are entered into a box in the second column, and the costs for each issue are calculated automatically, based on the number of editorial pages produced. Notice that since advertisers are responsible for producing the content of their ad pages, the worksheet does not include advertising pages in these content estimations.

When staff editors handle nearly all of the content work—for example, if they do their own copyediting and shoot their own photographs— then there would not be any per-page expenses in this section of the worksheet. In this section, include only amounts paid to outsiders.

Print manufacturing. The "prepress charges" noted on the worksheet include technical adjustments made to your publication files that prepare them for printing. (That process is described in Chapter 7.)

Some organizations handle these adjustments internally and do not pay for outside prepress services, but if you are planning to use an outside vendor, then you would estimate the costs in this section of the worksheet. Typically, publications pay a prepress vendor a certain amount per page—for both ad and editorial pages—and the worksheet is set up to calculate these costs per issue page.

Printing bills are complicated, especially for magazines. There are many individual decisions—such as the choice of paper, how much color is used, and how the issues are bound—that affect the total printing bill. Printers can provide detailed cost projections for any variation you request. (The subject is covered in Chapter 7.) For this worksheet, the printing costs are based on average prices paid for 70-page magazines in these quantities. Entering this per-copy printing cost in the box on this worksheet has automatically produced a total printing budget for each issue based on the number of copies entered earlier on the worksheet.

Website production costs. Many organizations pay a monthly or annual fee to outsource their Web functions. Others handle the work in-house and do not charge anything to the publications department. The organization in the sample pays $7,500 per year to an outside Web hosting service. (Chapter 8 includes detailed information about websites.)

Distribution. The term "Circulation Fulfillment" refers to a company that will maintain a database of your member or subscriber names, generating mailing labels from the database every time an issue is mailed or emailed to readers, and keeping track of those members who must be reminded to renew or pay for their memberships. (See Chapter 9 for a detailed discussion.)

Many membership organizations handle this work within their membership departments and do not pay any outside companies for it. If this is your reality, then skip over this line in the budgeting process; it only applies to the fees paid to an outsider for handling this function.

Periodicals pay different postage rates depending on the type of permit they obtain from the USPS, and the price often is lower for members than for nonmembers. (Chapter 9 includes details.) This sample budget estimates postage at $.51 per member copy and $.63 per nonmember copy.

If your organization is planning to distribute copies in retail stores (a subject also covered in Chapter 9), then you would pay shipping fees for those bulk shipments. Your printer can often help you estimate these shipping fees. The sample worksheet below shows none.

Printers also charge a fee for putting postage or shipping labels onto the copies and delivering them into the distribution service. This fee is usually a fixed amount for each issue. The sample shows $180 per issue.

Ad sales commissions. Nonprofits commonly pay advertising salespeople some combination of a salary and a commission based on sales. The salary appears in the first section of the budgeting worksheet because it is a fixed expense. But commissions vary depending on the level of sales. (Chapter 4 contains more information about compensating salespeople.) The sample budget shows a 19% commission rate.

CROSS-REFERENCE

Several chapters describe different aspects of the variable costs of publishing, which are captured in this part of the budget. Chapters 5 and 6 cover the costs of acquiring or developing content, including articles, artwork, and graphics. Chapters 7 and 8 describe the costs associated with producing publications, either in print or online. Chapter 9 covers distribution costs of printed publications, and Chapter 10 covers advertising sales costs, including commissions.

Nonprofit Publishing Budget Worksheet, continued

VARIABLE EXPENSES		January	February	March
Content-Related Costs				
Freelance writing	Cost per edit page $100	$ 6,400	$ 1,200	$ 6,200
Photos, illustrations	Cost per edit page $75	$ 4,800	$ 900	$ 4,650
Design, art direction	Cost per edit page $55	$ 3,520	$ 660	$ 3,410
Copyediting, proofing	Cost per edit page $40	$ 2,560	$ 480	$ 2,480
Subtotal of content costs		$ 17,280	$ 3,240	$ 16,740
Print Manufacturing				
Pre-press charges	Cost per issue page $150	$ 10,200	–	$ 10,200
Printing costs	Cost per copy $1.03	$ 19,941	–	$ 19,941
Website Production Costs				
	Cost per year $7,500	$ 625	$ 625	$ 625
Subtotal of manufacturing costs		$ 30,766	$ 625	$ 30,766
Distribution				
Circulation fulfillment	Cost per member copy $0.07	$ 1,050	–	$ 1,050
Postage: Member copies	Cost per copy $0.51	$ 9,874	–	$ 9,874
Postage: All other copies	Cost per copy $0.63	$ 1,638	–	$ 1,638
Total postage costs		$ 11,512	–	$ 11,512
Bulk distribution costs	Cost per copy	–	–	–
Printer Distribution Fees	Cost per issue $180	$ 180	–	$ 180
Subtotal of Distribution		$ 12,742	–	$ 12,742
Ad Sales Commission	Percent of sales 19%	$ 16,074	$ 608	$ 19,409
Subtotal of variable Publishing Costs		$ 76,861	$ 4,473	$ 79,656
TOTAL PUBLISHING COSTS		$109,328	$ 36,940	$ 112,123

Revenue

Publications generally have three kinds of revenue: dues or subscriptions, donations, and advertising. Many organizations attribute some portion of a member's dues to the publications they receive as a benefit of membership. (This issue is addressed in Chapter 9.) Donations coming in through a publication are rarely counted as publishing income. But advertising revenue is always associated with the publishing project, for the tax reasons discussed earlier in the chapter.

The sample budgeting worksheet below shows ad revenues, plus dues income of $.60 per member copy.

Advertising revenue. Typically, there is a different price for different types of ads, and you must budget for each one separately: classified ad pages, small business or professional ads, ads from members who might get a discounted price, ads from outside companies, and ads that your organization runs to promote its own programs, which are often run for free or for a nominal charge to some other department. (All of these options are covered in detail in Chapter 10.)

Some nonprofits do not allow outsiders to advertise on their websites or in their email newsletters, but many do. The worksheet enclosed here has room for calculating those revenues; skip this section if your organization does not allow online ads. The sample shows $1,400 in total online ad revenues per month.

Donations. Organizations generally account for donations separately from their publishing activities, since donations can come from a number of sources outside of the publications. However, the worksheet provides a space to include donations that could be traced directly back to a magazine or website. The sample budget shows no donations income in the publishing department.

Memberships. As with donations, many organizations record membership dues income separately from publishing activities. However, some organizations do allocate a portion of dues to publications.

A recent survey found associations attribute an average of $15 per year out of dues to "pay" for a subscription, but the same survey found that 68% of the responding organizations do not actually include that money in their publishing budget. In other words, the member thinks he or she is paying about $15 per year for a publication, but the revenue is not actually going into the magazine's budget. If your organization decided to allocate some dues income to the publishing department, you would enter that figure in this section of the worksheet.

If your organization sells paid subscriptions, then you will need to expand this spreadsheet to accommodate those revenues. The sample budget shown below does not include paid subscriptions.

Nonprofit Publishing Budget Worksheet, continued

REVENUE				
		January	February	March
Classified ad revenue	Revenue per page $900	$ 1,800	–	$ 2,250
Small business display ads	Revenue per page $2,500	$ 5,000	–	$ 5,000
Outside display ads	Revenue per page $8,000	$72,000	–	$ 88,000
Internal ads	Revenue per page $1,000	$ 3,000	–	$ 2,500
Subtotal of print advertising revenue		$81,800	–	$ 97,750
Website ad revenue	Revenue per unit $400	$ 2,800	$ 3,200	$ 4,400
Advertising revenue, total		$84,600	$ 3,200	$102,150
Donations from print	Amount per issue $3,500	$ 3,500	–	$ 3,500
Donations from online	Amount per month $2,000	$ 2,000	$ 2,000	$ 2,000
Memberships	Amount per member copy $0.60	$ 9,000	–	$ 9,000
Reader revenue, total		$14,500	$ 2,000	$ 14,500
TOTAL PUBLISHING REVENUE		$99,100	$ 5,200	$116,650

CROSS-REFERENCE

Later chapters of the book offer guidance to help you with decisions that affect other areas that will have an impact on budgeting concerns. For example, there is a discussion about setting advertising prices in Chapter 10, and a discussion about subscription and membership income in Chapter 9.

Net Publishing Income

Finally, the budgeting worksheet shows how to calculate net publishing income. Do not be alarmed if your results are negative. According to one benchmark survey, more than 65% of nonprofits do not earn any net income from their publications. (See "Lessons Learned From a Publishing Survey," below.)

If you get a disappointing outcome when you get to the Net Income line in your worksheet, you can go back and change some of the assumptions made in the earlier section on publishing assumptions—for example, publish fewer copies per year or fewer pages in each issue.

And remember to include any nonfinancial outcomes that you can attribute to your publications, as discussed earlier in this chapter. The sample worksheet below includes correspondence between members and editors, volunteer service hours, and conference attendance.

CROSS-REFERENCE

The last piece of the budget is a tally of the others. This is the proverbial bottom line that shows how all of your other decisions will add up—either producing net income from publishing or generating net expenses. Chapter 11 includes some survey information from nonprofit publishers that shows which ones are generally profitable, and which ones are not. The budget worksheet also encourages you to add in some nonfinancial gains from publishing, such as gains in your communications with members or the hours donated by volunteers, and you will find those items discussed in Chapters 1 and 11.

Nonprofit Publishing Budget Worksheet, continued

NET PUBLISHING INCOME (Revenues Minus Expenses)			
	January	February	March
	$ (10,228)	$ (31,740)	$ 4,527
Nonfinancial gains			
Letters and emails to editors	300	75	400
Volunteer service hours	3,000	2,500	3,200
Conference attendance			4,600

Lessons Learned From a Publishing Survey

A recent survey of membership societies and other associations found widely different practices among small, medium, and large organizations. Small ones typically hire only one editor, while bigger ones average 20 people in the publishing department.

 A majority of organizations of all sizes outsource at least some of their publishing functions. All of the smallest organizations and nearly half of the medium-sized ones reported spending more on publications than they earn from them. Only the largest organizations were publishing profitably.

Publishing Benchmarks	Smallest	Medium	Largest
Annual revenues of the organization	$100,000 or less	Up to $4.9 million	$5 million or more
Number of publishing employees	1	5	20
12 issues/year or more	17%	51%	83%
Median pages per issue	28	70	97
Median copies distributed per issue	6,250	32,660	93,750
Percent reporting any publishing net income	0%	49%	100%
Total annual publishing revenue	$13,660	$894,245	$9,281,950
Total annual publishing costs	$133,974	$866,255	$6,935,966
Net publishing (loss) or profit	($120,314)	$27,990	$2,345,984
Outsourced functions:			
Editorial	50%	22%	33%
Production	75%	35%	50%
Design	83%	50%	17%
Circulation	25%	23%	33%
Ad sales	25%	55%	50%
Nothing	0%	6%	0%

Source: Society of National Association Publications, 2005.

Finding and Hiring Help

Once you've clarified your publication's focus, the next step is to decide what people you need to get it produced. Some of the contributors will likely be part of your nonprofit's regular staff. Some may be existing staff who don't work full time on your publication but can be tapped to handle certain tasks. And some will likely be freelancers, consultants, or independent contractors outside the organization.

This chapter describes how to corral the human resources you will need to publish successfully, whether it's hiring publishing employees, recruiting talented freelancers, or coaxing current coworkers into expanding their duties and knowledge.

Even if you are not in a position at your nonprofit to hire additional people, this chapter will be useful in explaining what functions your organization should be looking to fill and where it can look to find the best help.

Common Tasks and Staffing

If you look at the masthead listing those who work at most publications and websites, you'll likely see that there are at most a handful of names of people involved in producing it. At the vast majority of nonprofits, these people are jacks-of-all-trades, individuals who take on all the roles needed to pull the issue or edition or current incarnation of the website together. But whatever their titles or duties, at most publications, some people focus on the editorial process of producing each issue or edition, and some focus on the business process of financially supporting the publication.

While there are a number of jobs to fill in producing a publication, the reality is that many nonprofits scrape by with barebones operations, often with one or two people in charge of everything. Another common arrangement is for one person to act as editor and handle all editorial side functions, and another as business manager and handle all business side functions. This tiny crew will outsource work to freelancers or perhaps pull in another staff person during the end of the production to pitch in—to proofread, for example.

With larger nonprofits and publications that have wider circulations, there are more people involved and a greater division of labor. At the very largest national nonprofits with publications resembling slick, commercial magazines, you may find staff positions comparable to consumer publications of similar size and circulation.

Most small to medium-sized nonprofits have staff somewhere in between those two extremes. A standard arrangement on the editorial side is to have a head editor; one other editor who doubles as a staff writer, photographer, and copy editor; and a hybrid designer-production manager. A typical structure on the business side is to have the organization's chief financial staffer double as publisher and, if the publication accepts advertising, an ad manager or ad rep to handle transactions.

Editorial Functions

There are a number of editorial functions commonly required by most publications—and your organization will need to fill them, too. Depending on the size and scope of your publishing activities, you may need from as few as a couple people working part time to a dozen full-time staffers. As you read through this chapter, consider where your project fits on the spectrum and whether you know of any ideal candidates to fill the various roles.

Editing. Editors generally generate and develop story ideas, solicit and assign work from staff and freelance writers, write articles, and shape the words that appear on the pages or website. Editors also work on their own or with designers to determine how the publication looks, how it's arranged and organized, and whether its appearance gives readers the right impressions about the content. And an editor usually serves as the main point of contact for members of your editorial advisory board. (See "Establishing an Editorial Advisory Board," below, for details on this.)

Managing the workflow. With so many different people and tasks involved in producing a publication, someone needs to keep track of who's doing what and when it needs to get done. The project or workflow manager, dubbed the managing editor at some publications, generally checks in with editors and other contributors to make sure everyone sticks to the schedule. This person often also tracks editorial expenses to make sure the costs of producing each new issue or posting are within budget. In low-budget operations, this may not be a full-time job for one person; the work will simply be folded into the duties of a staffer who does other things. An office manager or general work coordinator, equipped with the right spreadsheets and calendar, may be able to handle this function.

Proofreading. Publications are produced by humans, and humans make mistakes. Publications need proofreaders or copy editors with sharp eyes to look over nearly-final versions for misspellings, bad punctuation, poor grammar, typos, captions that don't match their photos, and all sorts of other errors and inconsistencies. These people also make sure the words written conform to the style rules of your publication to keep it consistent over time. People with a love and command of language who pay much attention to detail are good choices for this role.

CAUTION

Recognize the value of a second pair of eyes. Regardless of how small the staff is at your publication or how diligently they work, it is critical to have at least two pair of eyes review material before it is published. Errors have a remarkable way of cloaking themselves in invisibility, no matter how eagle-eyed the reader.

Web editing. Many organizations hire a person, either on staff or as a freelancer, who can specialize in converting printed articles to a Web-friendly format using stylistic norms that are becoming common online. The Web editor might also be responsible for producing original articles and site features. For example, this person might have the task of adding links to an article that was originally published in your newsletter and making sure the accompanying photographs are properly fed to your site. And in addition, he or she might develop an online reader poll to gather feedback on the story.

Designing. Designers establish and oversee the overall visual appearance of a publication. In print publications, they typeset the copy and lay out pages, arranging the text with images to invite in readers and help tell the story. Designers also work with editors to figure out the best images to complement a story, then search for and commission the appropriate artwork. And an organization that publishes many richly illustrated publications may hire a dedicated art director who can concentrate on supervising the contributing illustrators and photographers hired to provide artwork. If your nonprofit's publication is ambitious enough to warrant a number of designers, usually the top person will act as art director while the other designers on staff carry out the director's vision. For smaller nonprofits or those with limited budgets, the roles are usually rolled into one.

Publishers often hire a professional designer to develop the fundamental style for a magazine or website on a one-time basis. The design's underlying structure is called a "grid" in publishing parlance. (See Chapter 6 for more detail on this.) Here, it's important to note that with a design grid in hand, staffers or freelancers who do not have previous design experience can maintain a site or produce magazine issues that look as though a professional produced them. They only need to be trained in how to use the grid.

Production. Once the words and pictures or graphics for the publication are established, that work must be translated into the finished product, whether it's a newsletter, magazine, or website.

At a print publication, this involves sending the completed electronic files to the printer, communicating with the printer about materials such as ink and paper, and troubleshooting all sorts of problems that arise while producing the physical product. Find a detail-oriented person with the natural ability to inspire cooperation as well as technical expertise, because your production staff will be charged with keeping everyone else—from the editors to the printing company—on schedule and people skills are a real necessity.

If your organization publishes substantial numbers of newsletter or magazine issues throughout the year, you may need to have a full-time person acting in this role. If not, you may be able to fill gaps in your publication's knowledge with consultants or a designer who also understands production issues. (See "Freelance Production Help," below, for more details on filling this position.)

For online publications, the equivalent role is someone who is responsible for converting the files into other formats that can be uploaded to the right servers; fixing software glitches; testing the website before it goes live to see that all the links are working and everything looks right; and tweaking parts that didn't appear correctly, such as a special font or a photo with an unusual size. This person may need to have a computer programming background and some specialized technical training in Web systems.

Business Functions

In addition to the common creative and technical functions required to produce content, there are a number of activities typically required on the business side of most publications.

Publisher or business manager. At a commercial publishing company, the publisher's job is generating revenue—and hopefully, profits. The publisher is usually closely linked to advertising sales, but this person may also oversee all marketing, subscription sales, and budgeting activities. And typically, the person who has the title of publisher is also the top salesperson or business development manager.

At nonprofit organizations that do not sell ads or subscriptions, there is rarely a person on staff who holds the publisher's title. Instead, nonprofits commonly use the business manager's title to designate the senior person on the business side of the publishing activities: the person focused on staying within budgets, negotiating vendor contracts, and generating revenue.

If a publication does sell ads, the publisher or business manager, not the editor, is responsible for overseeing advertising sales activities because there are some ethical issues about having editors manage the sales force. (See Chapter 10 for a complete explanation.)

Sales and advertising. If your publication accepts and sells advertising, someone will need to create media kits, sell ads, and handle customer service for advertisers. Organizations often end up with a sales team that is a combination of staff employees and outside contractors. If there are several people at your nonprofit working on ad sales, then there will be a sales manager who avoids conflicts among them by making sure that every salesperson has a unique list of clients to manage. (See "Freelance Salespeople," below, for details on hiring outsiders.)

Distribution and fulfillment. Every issue of your publication must be delivered to your readers—through the mail, a website, email, or newsstands, or at drop-off locations and news boxes. Someone will need to be responsible for managing and perhaps expanding the channels through which your publication is distributed. And if you sell subscriptions, someone should be responsible for signing up new readers and renewing existing ones. And, ultimately, there needs to be a person who will make sure that readers are actually receiving your publication and investigate and fix the problem if they are not.

Establishing an Editorial Advisory Board

While they are not on staff at your nonprofit and do not usually work directly on its publications, an editorial advisory board is a group of people—usually stakeholders of the organization's editorial mission—who meet regularly with staff to advise on the editorial direction of the publication. They can include readers or members, experts in the subject area, experts in publishing, or members of the nonprofit's board.

Any publication should consider forming an editorial advisory board to help support its publishing activities. Advisory boards can be extremely useful for generating or spotting story ideas, helping staff stay on top of trends or news about the publication's editorial focus, occasionally writing articles or helping identify and connect staff to writers for articles, critiquing the publication, and serving as guest editors.

> **TIP**
>
> **Editorial boards can be sounding boards, too.** Editorial advisory boards can be invaluable for acting as a general sounding board for quandaries or controversies, such as whether to accept a questionable advertiser or article submission. A board can also work as a buffer between readers and publication staff, or between the nonprofit's wider staff and publication staff. One editor who worked for a professional publication that often got into trouble for printing material that the nonprofit staff thought reflected badly on the profession remembers how two prominent editorial advisory board members would often smooth things over. "They would say, 'I'll take care of it,' and the problem would go away," said the editor. If you are lucky enough to find members with this kind of pull and who are in your camp, you will have more independence to work on your publication.

Ideally, editorial advisory boards are composed of people who have expertise and interest in your area of editorial focus and who are also enthusiastic about sharing or explaining that information through your publishing activities. When searching for editorial board members, look for people who are passionate about reading and about the format of your publication. Ask potential board members what publications they read and what websites they visit. Notice if they carry publications around with them or refer to any particular sources when discussing current events.

If you are publishing a newsletter or magazine, look for advisory board members who are familiar with many different types of print publications. Your staff will benefit from that type of sophistication and exposure to different styles. Board candidates might be the staff at other publications, faculty members of local schools' journalism or communications programs, members or leaders of magazine or writers' professional associations, or members of media advocacy organizations.

If you are publishing online, look for advisory board members who are savvy Internet users and frequently click through online publications. They will know what innovative design or technical approaches websites are using and can pass those insights on to you.

For all types of publications, aim to assemble an editorial advisory board that represents a good cross-section of your publication's constituencies. This may include the organization's management, leadership, members, readers, experts or practitioners in your field, and other publishing professionals.

You can break down areas of expertise even further and find individuals for those slots. For example, an editorial advisory board for an environmental publication might include one person who specializes in air pollution, another in water pollution, another in developmental sprawl, and so on. Editorial advisory boards that include prominent or famous people can help raise the profile of your publication. But make sure that everyone involved has the necessary time and energy to make a meaningful contribution to your project. Otherwise your advisory board will be little more than a list of names or may become more hindrance than help.

There's no "right" number of members for an advisory board; that depends on your publication and its needs. Boards typically convene at least once or twice a year but can meet quarterly or even more frequently. Make sure, however, that one of your meetings falls in late autumn or early winter so that you can incorporate any ideas or suggestions into the planning process for the coming year's editorial lineup. Most editorial advisory boards function informally, but depending on how involved your members are, your board might benefit from a chair or designated leader to help manage, communicate with, and organize the group.

The editorial board can be useful for many functions. But it's important to set expectations and boundaries so that members do not end up missing meetings, micromanaging your publication, or demanding to review it before it goes to press. If you intend to rely on the advisory board to help generate stories or spot trends, ask board members to email those ideas regularly or to present them at each meeting. If members are expected to write articles, let them know how many and work with them to deliver the goods.

It's also a good idea to draw up a set of guidelines, such as those offered below, to distribute to members. This can help head off misunderstandings of many kinds.

The guidelines can explain the board's composition. It's a good idea to specify the length of terms and rules for renewing membership to have the opportunity to cycle out members who may not be contributing, and to constantly inject new energy and ideas into your publication.

Guidelines can also set out meeting obligations and duties—stressing members' advisory nature and spelling out their obligations and providing at least some details of how they can meet those obligations.

CD-ROM

The Editorial Advisory Board Guidelines shown below are also included on the CD-ROM in this book. You can tailor them to your needs and give them to all who become board members.

Sample Editorial Advisory Board Guidelines

Welcome to the editorial advisory board of [name of publication]. Thank you for contributing your time, energy, and talent.

Composition of the Board

The editorial advisory board consists of [X] members who serve staggered terms of [X] years each. New members are nominated by current members and staff and need to be approved by the executive director of the organization. Any member may be removed by a majority vote of the board or the nonprofit's board of directors if he or she does not fulfill board responsibilities.

The editor of the publication and the organization's executive director will serve as ex officio members of the editorial advisory board.

Members shall elect a chairperson to work with the publication's staff and a secretary to record the board's decisions and output. Each of these positions shall be one-year terms.

Editorial Board Meetings

The editorial advisory board meets [X] times per year, with at least one regularly scheduled meeting falling prior to the setting of the publication's annual editorial calendar. Board members are expected to attend all meetings.

Board Member Duties

The role of the editorial advisory board is to provide informal advice on the content and direction of [publication name] so that it can best fulfill its editorial mission. Members are expected to suggest ideas for possible stories on trends in the field or on sources and events that could be useful in developing content. Members are also expected to provide feedback and criticism to staff about the development of content, and on already-published content when consulted.

Members should come to each meeting with several story ideas or subject areas they feel should be covered in the publication.

Outside of board meetings, board members are expected to:

- regularly read the publication or visit its website to stay familiar with its content
- be available to staff to answer questions, review manuscripts from time to time, and give general advice, and
- contribute content by writing articles or identifying and approaching writers.

The editorial advisory board also generally represents and promotes [publication name] to the readership and wider public.

The editorial advisory board does not control or review the contents of [publication name] before publication, nor does it have the authority to remove or add content.

[If applicable to your publication.] The editorial advisory board members may also be called on from time to time to apply the advertising policies of [publication name] if staff is unable to resolve an issue on its own. [Or you may call on the editorial advisory board to develop, enact, and update advertising guidelines for your publication.]

Determining Staffing Needs

Deciding on the kind and amount of help you'll need to work on your publication and then finding appropriately skilled people to take on the work is often a challenge. The most important considerations are how frequently you publish, the size and complexity of your publication, and the size of your budget.

For guidance, look to comparable organizations and comparable publications—or those that you'd like to emulate. When evaluating how your publication compares to others, take a number of factors into account, including:

- **the nonprofit's size and income.** As a general rule, the larger and more high-visibility your nonprofit, the higher the standards and expectations both readers and management will have for its publications. Larger nonprofits tend to have more money to devote to publishing ventures and to run more-sophisticated programs or services that will generate more possibilities for content. Consequently, readers, donors, and others may expect a glossy or thick publication with substantive articles or a website that is updated frequently and has more bells and whistles than they would expect from a small nonprofit with meager funds.

- **the frequency of the publication.** Publications that are issued fairly frequently—bimonthly, monthly, or weekly—require more people to put together than those issued quarterly or semi-annually. They simply need more articles, more fresh ideas, more editing, more artwork, more design work. As you go up the scale in frequency, the publishing cycle also shortens and the schedules of multiple issues overlap. Staff at a quarterly publication, for example, may work on one issue at a time, completing one issue before beginning work on the next one. But those at a monthly publication do not have the luxury of doing that and must start work on the next month or even the month after that before ending the cycle for the current month. That requires juggling more tasks and schedules—and usually having several people to help do it successfully.

- **the size or scope of the publication.** A 40-page publication with five pages of advertising takes more work than a 16-page publication with no advertising. Similarly, a publication website with five different pages and additional links on each page is going to take more work than a website that only contains links off the home page. Unfortunately, it's not possible to use a straight proportional formula to calculate how much time and work is required per page. For example, it wouldn't be accurate to say that a 40-page publication requires double the time and work of a 20-pager. Rather, the number of additional departments, stories, and components in those 20 additional pages is a better determinant of how much more work is needed. If those 20 pages contained two long feature stories, they would require less work than if they contained two departments, a feature story, an interview, and a photo essay.

- **the subject matter.** If your publication regularly covers complex subjects, such as scholarly or scientific topics, or if it publishes peer-reviewed papers, you may need more help or hire experts to solicit, evaluate, and edit manuscripts.

- **the circulation and scope of distribution and coverage.** A publication that covers local issues in one city and is circulated to 500 people is going to have different staffing requirements from one with a national circulation of 50,000. Readers will expect news from all over the country in a national publication, which may require you to hire freelance correspondents—something the local publication can do without. Handling delivery of 50,000 issues of a publication versus 500 will also require more people and perhaps more vendors.

What to Do When Short-Handed

It is common for nonprofit publications to be short-staffed. Often, this is because funding is tight across the board and the budget for publishing activities suffers—sometimes disproportionately. Another reason, however, is that people with little or no publishing expertise often fail to understand the level of resources and staffing needed to produce a quality publication.

If you find yourself short on help, you may be able to make do with current staff members by expanding their duties, scaling back on the size and scope of your publication, or supplementing what you have with help from outside the organization. Another option is to lobby for more staff. This section discusses both options in more detail—and gives practical pointers for putting them in place.

Getting Help From Existing Staff

Some staff members may be interested in taking on more duties. For example, there may be an editor who is willing to learn more about website software and maintenance who can eventually double as the publication's website manager. You may have a receptionist at your nonprofit who pays great attention to detail and has chunks of free time between fielding phone calls. This person, if given some training, might become an excellent proofreader for your publication. Or he or she might have an outgoing personality and phone manner that is just right for selling advertising.

> **TIP**
>
> **You won't know unless you ask.** If you need help with a defined task, you might consider advertising within your nonprofit organization by posting an informal "help wanted" sign on the lunchroom bulletin board or sending out a group email. Many people have hidden talents and passions such as drawing or writing that could be put to use for your publication. A quick email could flush out the aspiring novelist who'd make a perfect proofreader.

You can also supplement current staff with part-timers, volunteers, interns, consultants, and freelancers or contractors. Perhaps you publish a bimonthly and want to beef up the content by adding one additional feature story per issue. That might translate into five additional pages, which will in turn mean, perhaps, 40 extra hours of writing, editing, designing, and copy editing. A part-time or freelance editor may be the perfect solution. It's hard to know exactly how long a project will take, but you can try to get a sense of the answer by consciously tracking how long it takes you to do something similar. The next time you produce a feature story, for example, ask everyone who worked on it—which may include a writer, editor, copy editor, and designer—to note how much time they spend on it.

Finding Training to Bolster Staff Expertise

If you will be asking more varied work of your publication's staff members, help them develop the skills and knowledge to do their jobs by sending them to training or continuing education courses.

There are many places to look for classes that will help bone up skills needed for publishing.

Local universities or colleges often offer extension courses in a variety of disciplines. Look for publishing courses taught by the journalism or communications departments. Universities with graduate departments in journalism often have special programs for working journalists and editors.

Community colleges and adult schools affiliated with your local high school or your city often offer all kinds of continuing education courses. They are good places to look for general classes on editing and copy editing.

Professional associations, such as the Society of Professional Journalists, the National Association of Hispanic Journalists, and the Society of Environmental Journalists, often offer workshops or seminars at annual conferences to develop their members' skills.

Most printers offer onsite production training once or twice a year, and some paper mills also offer these programs. The more you know about production technologies, the more efficient your publishing operations will be.

Finally, media training organizations often offer a variety of courses your staff can attend—from copy editing, to reporting, to designing websites.

Perhaps you publish a quarterly publication that trots along comfortably for the earlier and middle stages of your production cycle but is always scrambling for people to proofread and manage the production process at the very end. Consider contracting with a copy editor or a production manager to come in four times a year and help.

Or maybe you would like to carry some advertising but just can't afford to keep a salesperson on the payroll. There are independent advertising sales firms you can hire to sell ads for your publication. (See "Freelance Salespeople" for more on this.)

You can always try volunteers and interns for simpler functions, such as responding to missed issue requests or compiling the Letters to the Editor section. These workers are often eager to learn about the inner workings of a publication or nonprofit organization and can often provide valuable services in return. In exchange for free or inexpensive labor, however, be prepared to invest more time in training or supervising.

Lobbying for More Help

If your publication has enough work to merit taking on additional in-house staff members, you may need to lobby management to hire them. Of course, this is much easier said than done. You must do some homework so you can justify the cost.

First, figure out who or what group of people at your nonprofit can make the decision to grant more resources and learn the best time to approach them. Usually, it's optimum to lobby for more funds when the organization is assembling its annual budget for the next fiscal year. At most nonprofits, the budget and any changes need to be approved by the board of directors, usually at a major meeting. So broach the topic of increasing the publication's staffing budget when you know money discussions are being considered, but well in advance of when a final decision will be needed.

Be sensitive as well to the overall financial standing of the organization. If money is tight and there's been talk of layoffs, your chances of being able to add new positions will probably be nil.

After you have decided who to approach and when to do it, prepare your argument. If you have already completed an analysis of your publication compared to publications at similarly sized nonprofits, this is the place to use those findings. (See Chapter 11 for more information about using your budget, industry performance benchmarks, surveys, and other data to justify adding staff or increasing expenses.) If you know of other nonprofit publications that are superior in quality to yours, show copies of them to the people you need to convince to demonstrate that it is worthwhile to devote more resources to your own publication. Explain what benefits the strong example likely produces: more donors, more members, or more subscribers. Display the results visually by creating a chart that shows the factors you analyzed for each publication—including number of staff members, number of pages, frequency, and size of the operating budget.

Beware, however, that it may not be enough to simply point out disparities in staffing between your publication and another one. Decision makers at your organization simply may not aspire to match other nonprofit publications. It's better to make the case by demonstrating how increased resources for the publication would help achieve your group's particular goals.

It's also key to track and highlight any tangible benefits that past investments in the publication have yielded for the organization. (See Chapter 11 for ideas on how to measure the publication's influence.) For example, if your group's main reason for publishing is to change public policy, point out how the increase in payment rates for freelance writers last year resulted in better-reported stories, which in turn led several lawmakers to subscribe to your publication.

Finally, enlist cheerleaders. If certain members of your board or staff are particularly strong supporters of your vision for the publication, ask for their help in convincing decision makers. Always save laudatory letters to the editor and relevant feedback from readers.

You may not get exactly what you want in additional staffing or resources, but you will increase the likelihood of getting some additional needed help if you do your homework. And the chances that you'll get anything at all are zero if you do not ask.

Hiring New Staff

The reality for most nonprofit publications is that they never will be as robustly staffed as needed. That's why it's so important to find and hire the best people you can afford. To do that, you'll need to figure out where publishing professionals look for work. For most nonprofit publications, it's also crucial to develop a strong pool of professional freelance writers, artists, and editors.

Details about hiring freelancers to fill particular positions are covered in the next section of this chapter. This section addresses hiring full-time or part-time staff for your publication positions.

First, write a job description. Job descriptions set and clarify everyone's expectations. Both the employer and employee have a written document to refer to when questions or ambiguous situations arise. They are also often useful legally if anything goes awry in the work relationship. A job description should include these basics: the job title, duties, and responsibilities, and how the position fits into the overall organization. It should also include a description of any special tools, equipment, skills, or knowledge needed to do the job.

RESOURCE

For detailed information on how to phrase job descriptions and what to include in them, see *Job Description Handbook*, by Margie Mader-Clark (Nolo).

You can also get a rough idea about job descriptions used in publishing from the magazine *Folio*, at www.foliomag.com. It conducts annual salary surveys that include details about the duties associated with each job title for editorial, production, sales, and distribution jobs.

Finding the Best Prospects

Once you've completed the job description, post it—along with other relevant information such as optimal hire date and contact information for your nonprofit—where qualified people are likely to find it.

In addition to the general online job posting outlets including Monster, Career Builder, The Vault, and Craigslist, send your job description and other particulars of hiring to:

- journalism or media careers online bulletin boards and websites

- the websites and alumni email distribution lists of graduate schools of journalism, undergraduate journalism programs, and art schools

- associations for Hispanic, Asian, African American, gay and lesbian, and Native American journalists and publishing professionals; this is also a way to diversify your applicant pool

- associations for journalists, such as the Society of Professional Journalists and American Association of Magazine Editors, and for designers, such as the Communication Arts Network or the American Institute of Graphic Arts, a group for graphic artists

- associations for publishers, such as the Society of National Association Publishers, at www.snaponline.org

- the websites or email networks of groups supporting media, such as the media activism organization Media Alliance, at www.media-aliance.org, or the media reform group Free Press, at www.freepress.net

- websites and job listings for nonprofit jobs, such as Idealist.org, Nonprofit Times, Opportunity Knocks, and the career page of the *Chronicle of Philanthropy*, and

- newspapers and other specialized publications; for example, if your publication is located in a job market in which potential applicants are likely to check the newspaper classifieds for jobs, by all means post your listing there. If your publication concerns a very specialized field in which many applicants read a certain publication, consider advertising the position there as well.

You can also proactively network to locate good candidates. Join the local chapter of a few journalism associations and attend their mixers to meet other people who work on publications. You might bump into an editor who is looking to change jobs or knows someone else who needs a position.

Websites Most Likely to Lead to Good Candidates

The job market has traditionally been difficult for writers, editors, and designers, as there always seem to be many more people looking than there are positions to fill. Competition is fierce, and the few available jobs get distributed far and wide through numerous websites and job banks.

Here is a list of some of the most well-known websites that you can contact with information on particular positions.

To find writers and editors

- **Journalism Jobs, at www.journalismjobs.com** A well-organized and extensive national database of media jobs. Candidates can search by industry, position, location, or keyword.

- **Craigslist, at www.craigslist.org** One of the most popular ways to advertise jobs. Post your position under the "writing/editing" and "nonprofit sector" categories.

- **The National Diversity Newspaper Jobs Bank, at www.newsjobs.com** Devoted to diversifying the news and media industry.

- **The Journalist's Toolbox, at www.journaliststoolbox.com/newswriting/jobs. html** The job bank of the American Press Institute.

- **The Magazine Job Board,** sponsored by *Folio and Circulation Management*, at www.magjobsonline.com.

- **The University of California at Berkeley's J-Jobs, at http://journalism.berkeley. edu/jobs** Linked to UC Berkeley's graduate school of journalism, J-Jobs is free for posters and draws employers and job seekers from across the country.

- **The Detroit Free Press Jobs Page, at www.freep.com/legacy/jobspage** This website acts as a big portal to many other job websites.

- **Editor & Publisher's Online Classifieds, at www.editorandpublisher.com/ eandp/classifieds/index.js** The online classifieds section of the oldest journal covering the newspaper industry.

- **Journalism Next, at www.journalismnext.com** A website geared to helping journalists of color find jobs and helping employers find diverse candidates, the site allows job seekers to post resumes and receive automatic notification and delivery of matching jobs.

- **National Writer's Union** has a job posting feature at its site at www.nwu.org.

To find designers and graphic artists

- **Creative Hot List, at www.creativehotlist.com** One of the leading websites where designers go to post their portfolios and look for work.
- **AIGA, at www.aigadesignjobs.org** The AIGA is a professional association for designers. It costs $95 to post a job for AIGA members, and $195 if you're not a member. Jobs stay posted for 90 days.
- **American Showcase, at www.americanshowcase.com** American Showcase is a directory of individual designers, artists, and photographers. It's a good starting place because all categories of graphics freelancers are listed there.
- **The Graphic Artists Guild** has a job listing feature at www.gag.org. This union represents freelance photographers as well as professional illustrators. Its job posting rates are reasonable, only $45 for four weeks, and a list of available jobs is emailed to members each week.
- **National Press Photographers Association, at www.nppa.org,** also has a job bank.
- **The Professional Photographers Association, at www.ppa.org,** also allows publishers to post jobs at its site.

TIP

When seeking applicants with specialized knowledge. If your publication specializes in a particular topic, such as the environment, health care, or education, seek out professional associations formed about the subject. Search the Internet for societies and associations of media professionals specializing in your topic. There is, for example, a Society of Environmental Journalists and an Education Writers Association. Many of these groups help their members find work, so they are great places to spread the word about an opening with your publication.

Tips for Sifting Out Good Prospects

When it comes to deciding which person to hire among a number of possible candidates, it's worth thinking through and being clear about the skills, experience, and qualities needed for your particular position, as well as what your publication has to offer and what tradeoffs you may have to make in your final decision. A person who has more experience, for example, will probably demand higher pay. But if you need only part-time help, you might be able to afford the hire.

In addition to keeping in mind all the traditional goals of finding a reliable, hardworking person, consider the following qualities.

Enthusiasm for the mission. Be attuned to whether a candidate seems to share your enthusiasm for the mission of your organization and its publication—and whether he or she can articulate why.

Relevant experience. On the editorial side, it's best to stick to candidates who have experience writing, editing, and designing for periodicals, as opposed to those who have worked in marketing, advertising, copywriting, or other industries, since the focus in those fields is very different—journalism, instead of sales. The same is true for the business side. Crafting renewal solicitations for a publication is different from crafting credit card offers or invitations to wine clubs. With advertising sales, it often pays to find salespeople who are already familiar with the advertisers they will be working with for your publication.

Availability. If you are hiring a part-time copy editor or designer, find out whether the person's work requirements and schedule will fit into your publishing schedule—including the probable lulls and crunch times. It's common around the end of a production cycle, when the files are due to the printer or website manager, for staff to work long hours to make deadlines.

General compatibility. While it may be difficult to discern in a meeting or two, be attuned to whether a candidate has the right mindset for your nonprofit organization and for the available position. Many nonprofit groups have more casual, collaborative work environments and attract staff people with eclectic backgrounds. Consider whether a candidate who comes from a more corporate environment will fit in and feel comfortable without a clear-cut corporate hierarchy—or be frustrated by a more consensus-based decision-making style.

Matching Experience and Job Needs

In today's job market, it is common to be flooded with eager applicants, many of whom seem frustratingly unqualified for the job you need to fill.

For example, say you are an editor for a small nonprofit magazine who needs to hire a new designer. You compose a job description, post it in the right places—and a flood of applications rolls in.

As you begin to review the candidates, you notice that some people appear to be very talented designers, but their portfolios do not show any magazine experience. Instead, they consist mainly of corporate catalogues and brochures. How should you evaluate these candidates?

As a rule, choose candidates who have the most experience matching the type of work you want done. Designing a periodical requires a different set of skills and knowledge from designing a one-off piece or even a publication for a big corporate brand. As just one example, the designer must know how to develop and maintain a consistent visual identity for the publication, but at the same time innovate within those constraints, month after month. Understanding how readers read or relate to publications is another skill that candidates without editorial design experience may lack.

Given the choice between two seemingly equally talented candidates—one with publication experience and one without—go for the one with the relevant expertise. If no candidates have experience matching your needs, go for the one that comes closest.

CAUTION

Don't overlook the obvious. No matter how charmed you may be by a particular candidate, pay attention to the attributes he or she shows and how they will help or hurt in the job you're looking to fill. Don't hire a copy editor whose cover letter and resume is riddled with typos. Don't hire a designer whose resume is arranged in a way that's hard to read. Don't hire a website coordinator who does not seem familiar with essential website management terms and software.

Questions to Ask Job Candidates

Here are some sample interview questions to help you vet applicants and jumpstart your thinking about what you should be asking.

TIP

Additional ways to gather information. To help check out candidates' track records in advance, ask them to bring samples of their work to the interview or send them to you in advance. When interviewing writers and editors, ask candidates to bring clips of articles they have written or copies of publications they've edited. Ask designers to bring their portfolios.

If you are hiring editors or copy editors, you could ask them to take an editing test as part of the interviewing process. A general editing test usually consists of a poorly-organized news story that the candidate is asked to improve, and a copy editing test consists of a story with typos and grammatical errors that the candidate is asked to correct.

CD-ROM

These interview questions are also available on the CD-ROM included with this book, so that you can tailor them for your own use, print them out, and compare the answers you ask all potential candidates once the interviews are over.

Interview Questions for Job Candidates

General Nonprofit Experience [For candidates for all positions]

• Why are you interested in working for our nonprofit?

• Have you had previous exposure or dealings with this nonprofit?

• How does what you are seeking in a career fit with our mission as a nonprofit?

• Do you have experience working at nonprofits? If not, how do you think you would need to adjust to one?

For Editor and Writer Positions

• What other publications have you written for or edited?

• Do you have any particular expertise in our nonprofit's subject area?

• What's your understanding of our editorial mission, and how do you envision carrying that out?

• [If the publication has already been launched] How would you improve the content of our publication or website?

• [If the publication has already been launched] What do you feel are our publication or website's strongest and weakest areas?

• How would you balance the desires of the larger organization for self-promotion with the desires of readers for more objective content?

• What's your understanding of our readership or audience—and how would you increase it?

• What kind of editorial personality or tone should we be projecting?

• Describe your experience working with freelance writers and artists and managing the production of a publication or website.

For Designer Positions

• What other publications have you designed?

• What's your understanding of our editorial mission, and how do you plan on carrying that out?

• What's your approach to design and communicating with readers?

• [If the publication has already been launched] What do you feel are our strongest and weakest areas of visual presentation?

• What kind of visual image should we be projecting?

For Business and Advertising Sales Positions

• What publications or websites have you worked with previously?

• What kinds of companies were advertising there?

• How much do you know about companies that we are targeting for our publication? [Show the candidate a list of your publication or website's prospects.]

• What additional types of companies might be good targets?

• What experience do you have growing and managing nonprofit publications or websites?

RESOURCE

For detailed information on legal constraints on interview questions and hiring, and complete information on other employee concerns such as wages, benefits, and workplace safety, see *The Employer's Legal Handbook*, by Fred Steingold (Nolo).

Don't Need to Know, Don't Ask

Stay away from questions during job interviews related to topics that are legally dicey. Straying into these sensitive areas could form the basis of a discrimination lawsuit.

In general, the law prohibits an interviewer from asking questions or making remarks related to:

- race
- color
- gender
- age
- religious beliefs
- national origin, or
- disability.

There are laws in some states and locales that also prohibit you from inquiring into a number of other areas—and it is safest to avoid them, including:

- marital or family status
- pregnancy
- sexual orientation, and
- genetic testing results.

There are, however, ways to gather information from a candidate that is related to his or her ability to do the job. Say, for example, you are hiring an editor for a publication geared to a 20-something readership and you want the person to understand and be able to connect to that age demographic. Instead of asking the candidate's age, which would be an illegal question, ask how well the person understands the readership and plans to develop relevant content.

Deciding How Much to Pay

For nonprofits, the fact most likely to limit you from being able to hire the person you want is the lack of money. Nonprofits are usually not able to match what a person might earn at a commercial enterprise. The staff at consumer magazines tend to make more than those who work at comparably sized nonprofit publications. And, not surprisingly, the staff at smaller publications with lower circulations generally bring home smaller paychecks than their counterparts at larger publications that have wider circulations.

But an increasing number of workers value things about a workplace other than earnings. And there are advantages to working at nonprofits that should be highlighted in your negotiations with or pursuit of a person you'd like to hire. If you are flexible with work hours, let people work from home, offer paid sabbaticals or more vacation in lieu of more pay, offer generous health benefits or nonstandard benefits, or are even willing to let staff bring their pets to work, these pluses may be able to outweigh the minus of a lower salary. Many experienced, talented workers look for jobs that allow them to be home when their children are home or help them achieve a better life-work balance by not requiring that they work excessive hours.

Finally, at most nonprofits, employees work together for a cause in which they are interested. Publishing professionals at more-advanced stages of their careers with more-stable bank accounts may actually be more than happy to accept lower salaries in exchange for contributing to an organization that they feel is making a difference.

There's no perfect database of salaries tailored to nonprofit publishing positions. Rather, you need to arrive at appropriate salary ranges by using various sources. For example, you might find out what editors at a similarly sized for-profit organization earn and what the general salary scale is for a nonprofit of your size and extrapolate from there.

RESOURCE

An excellent resource for salaries is *Folio* **magazine's handy online compensation calculator at www.readexsurvey.com/foliocalc/ salary.asp.** It shows compensation for different levels of employees at business and consumer magazines broken out by geography, total sales volume, level of responsibility, and years of experience.

Very generally, people working on the editorial side of nonprofit publications tend to make somewhere in the high-$20Ks to mid-$50Ks. Individuals with more experience or higher up the masthead make the upper end of the range.

On the production end of things, *Folio's* recent salary survey found that staff production managers with three years of experience command an average salary of $45K to $50K in an organization with revenues of less than $1 million. Salaries go up from there, depending on how much work the manager must oversee and how many employees they will supervise. There is no formal training for this job, and most people fall into it after working as graphic artists or salespeople at printing or paper companies.

For in-house sales staff, you can easily find out what other advertising salespeople typically earn at comparable publications. *Folio's* most recent figures show that for a publication with less than $1 million in annual advertising revenue, the top sales executive who sets policy, manages other people, and has five or more years of experience should earn at least $91,536.

A salesperson for the same organization who calls on advertisers and sells ads but has no management responsibilities should earn $36,000 with five years of experience and nearly $53,000 with ten years on a similar job. By the time you add up salaries, plus marketing and overhead expenses, your in-house sales team will probably cost between 20% to 30% of the revenue they generate.

RESOURCE
There are a number of additional resources to consult for salaries:

- Idealist.org, a networking and job website for the activist and nonprofit communities, maintains a handy page of links to nonprofit salary surveys at www.idealist.org/career/salarysurvey.html.
- *Nonprofit Times*, a publication for nonprofit managers, also conducts salary surveys that you can find on its website at www.nptimes.com.
- The Vault, an online job resource center, publishes salary information for publishing positions that are self reported by individuals at www. vault.com.

Hiring Freelancers

There are often advantages to hiring freelance workers or consultants to work on your publication. You can hire such workers as needed, paying them only for the work that must be done. Working with freelancers often allows you to bring in expertise in a wide range of topic areas, something that would be impractical to develop and maintain among in-house staff. And when acquiring artwork for your publication, fusing a number of different freelance photographers, illustrators, and other artists allows you to choose among a variety of visual styles that could never be found in just one person's work.

So short of adding more staff positions and rallying a whole army of volunteers and interns, the most common way to expand your publication's capacity is to work with freelance writers and artists, editors, production managers, designers, photographers, illustrators, salespeople, marketing consultants, distribution consultants, and anyone else you think you might need.

RESOURCE
For detailed information on hiring and working with freelancers, including the most recent IRS rules, see *Working With Independent Contractors*, by Stephen Fishman (Nolo).

Employees and Independent Contractors: More Than Just Semantics

The law identifies workers as either employees or independent contractors. Freelancers and consultants are usually considered independent contractors from a legal standpoint. The distinction is important because the two groups of workers are subject to the controls of differing state laws and IRS reporting requirements.

The main difference between the classifications is that employers can control the way in which employees work, but also have certain responsibilities and obligations to them, such as paying unemployment or workers compensation or withholding federal and state taxes for them.

Independent contractors, on the other hand, are their own bosses and the hiring firm is their client. Employers cannot control the way in which independent contractors work—meaning they cannot specify when, where, and how the job gets done as long as it gets done. But they also do not have to offer independent contractors any benefits or do the paperwork and pay the taxes that come with hiring employees.

When working with independent contractors, be careful not to treat them as employees by controlling when, where, and how the project gets done. And if you have workers who are employees, don't pretend that they are independent contractors. Either behavior could subject you to complicated legal liabilities and potential fines.

Freelance Writers and Artists

Don't hesitate to approach writers and artists about working for your nonprofit publication. Freelancers are always looking for work, and you'd be surprised how often those in the mainstream—even those who are well known—are willing to work on the cheap for a small nonprofit publication, perhaps because they believe in your mission.

Finding Freelance Writers

Most editors who have worked in the publishing business for a while amass Rolodexes full of writers they trust who produce the kind of writing they want. You can do the same. Collect the names and writing samples of journalists whose work you admire, and build a database of writers you like. It doesn't matter if they are writing for the nonprofit, trade, or consumer press; keep the names of writers who seem like good candidates for producing an article for your publication.

Local daily papers are another good place to look for freelance writers. Reporters at newspapers are often assigned to cover a particular beat—and many of them become experts on a subject area or event. Such seasoned reporters may be willing to freelance to try their hand at magazine writing. Or if it's a subject they know a lot about, they may just appreciate having more space to tell the longer version of the story that won't fit in the number of inches they're allotted at the newspaper.

Writers and journalists who have a book to promote can also be excellent potential contributors to your website or publication. Depending on who holds the copyright to their work and how it's held, they may allow you to run a short book excerpt free with the proper attribution or for a very small fee. And in some cases, authors are also happy to write a new piece in exchange for the opportunity to promote their book to your readers.

CROSS-REFERENCE

Publishers are often able to secure copyrighted articles, artwork, and photographs in print publications and on websites simply by asking for permission from the person who owns copyright to the work or by paying a modest fee for the work. See Chapter 6, "Getting Permission," for a discussion of this. The CD-ROM included with this book also contains the forms required to secure such permissions.

> **CAUTION**
>
> **When recycling bears a bad name.** Some freelance writers are willing to work for a low rate because they feel they can squeeze more income out of a story they've already written by doing a bit more research or refocusing the angle to adapt it for your publication. In such cases, be careful that the work is indeed different from what's been published elsewhere.

Helping Writers Find You

Editors at nonprofit publications can do a couple of things to get their publication's name out to the freelance writing community and increase their chances of receiving quality queries. The first is to formulate a set of writer's guidelines for potential contributors. The second is to get listed in some of the directories that freelance writers commonly consult to find work. Both options are discussed in detail below.

And sometimes, as described below, editors don't need to look for writers. Once a publication is up and running, much content gets developed through query letters that freelance writers send to publication editors. Writers use queries to pitch editors a story idea in hopes of convincing the editor to commission them to write the story.

> **TIP**
>
> **Getting the right help through reverse queries.** Sometimes talented writers could do a fine job on a story but just don't have the specialized knowledge or access to sources necessary to pitch it in the first place. If you haven't been able to find a writer through your usual networks for a story and you don't want to wait around for a writer to pitch you, try putting out a reverse query. Reverse queries are exactly what they sound like: story pitches that are generated by editors and targeted at the freelance writing community.
>
> To get this ball in motion, compile a list of fairly developed ideas for stories you'd like to publish, and ask your networks to distribute them freely. Forward them to media email lists, professional associations, previous

freelancers, and other editors. Ask those who receive your pitch to pass it on to writers they think would be interested. Reverse queries are also useful in giving freelancers a better idea of the types of pitches you are seeking and in attracting qualified writers with whom you don't already have a relationship.

Using writers' guidelines. Writers' guidelines should provide basic information about your publication, such as how frequently it's published, how widely it's distributed, who its readers are, and the average length of time between when the publication receives a draft of an article and when it will likely appear in print. They should also clearly explain the publication's editorial mission and what kinds of stories, topics, formats, and structures fit best in the publication.

Be sure to specify how a writer can submit a request to write for your publication—for example, whether email is acceptable, or only regular postal mail—and whether you accept unsolicited manuscripts. To help you better assess potential writers, request that all query letters include a brief resume summarizing the writer's background and two or three clips of previously published stories.

Writers' guidelines not only are a handy and succinct way of responding to random inquiries about writing for your publication, but also can serve as an inspiring document that introduces your publication's editorial mission and affirmatively describes the type of content it wants to publish.

Once you've developed writer's guidelines, make them easily available to potential contributors. Post them on your website with a prominent link. If you publish a print product, add a regular section to each issue describing how to contribute and referring readers to the link.

For direction when writing guidelines for your publication, check out other writers' guidelines to see the various ways publications describe themselves. This can help you develop a way to communicate your own unique set of requirements.

Below is a sample, a part of the guideline for *Glimpse Quarterly,* a magazine that promotes cross-cultural understanding among young adults through coverage of international news, travel, and culture. You might use them as a model when crafting your own writers' guidelines.

Submission Guidelines

Eligibility

While the bulk of Glimpse content is written by study abroad students, anyone who is living in another country for a month or longer is eligible to contribute. We are less inclined to accept stories from "on-the-move" travelers; we are primarily interested in the experiences of those volunteering, working, and/or studying in a single place for an extended period of time.

You do not have to consider yourself a "writer" to contribute to Glimpse. The Glimpse editorial staff undergoes a personal, intensive revision process with each and every contributor, teaching those with all levels of writing experience the basic tenets of compelling creative nonfiction. While not all submissions are ultimately accepted, all contributors are given a chance to work collaboratively with an editorial staff member to revise or refocus their submissions.

Compensation

Contributors write for us on a volunteer basis. If you require pay for your work, please do not submit. By contributing to Glimpse, you support our mission to promote cross-cultural understanding; you also receive comprehensive editorial guidance and international exposure for your work. We syndicate a portion of our published pieces to other newspapers and magazines. In the event of syndication, a contributor may opt to either receive a percentage of the syndication fee or donate it to our developing Glimpse Fellows Program.

Platform

If you are studying in a country that will be spotlighted in an upcoming print issue and would like to write a piece that relates to the Spotlight theme, you may submit directly to *Glimpse Quarterly*. Otherwise, your piece will be considered for online publication. All articles published online are eligible to be included in a future issue of *Glimpse Quarterly*.

Content

Feature Articles

Glimpse articles are NOT essays; they are stories rooted in your personal experience. We want you to think small. Focus on a single experience or cluster of experiences that share a common theme. Keep your story rooted in tangible detail. What is around you? What do the streets, buildings, landscapes look like? What conversations have you had with people? Follow the golden rule of creative writing: Show, don't tell. Instead of telling us that Iran is a country caught in transition, show us how this transition is evident in your daily experiences and interactions.

As your piece begins to take shape, you'll eventually need to step back from the detail in order to incorporate a reflective element. Examine your details: look for patterns of similarity, difference. What do they mean within the context of your developing cultural understanding? Be careful here: We don't want any sweeping cultural generalizations. When reflecting on your experiences, make sure we know where you're coming from. How has your own cultural lens influenced your perception of the scene at hand? What's your bias? (Everyone has one!) Why are you biased in this way? Such elements should be implicit in your article.

If your article is accepted for publication, you will be asked to provide accompanying photos. If you don't have images that specifically illustrate events described in your piece, send us the most

Submission Guidelines, continued

relevant photos you have. We prefer to feature at least three and up to ten images for each article. If you would like to submit additional photos for our database, please read the "Photographic Database" section below.

Word Length and Format

Feature articles should be between 800 and 2,000 words. Include your name, phone number, and email address in the top left corner of the submission. Conclude your submission with a 2-4 sentence bio telling us a bit about yourself.

Submission Process

Step One:
Register as a Glimpse Contributor in our Contributor Database. We use our database as a means of keeping track of all interested contributors and occasionally for soliciting content for our print issues.

Step Two:
Send submissions by email to editor@glimpsefoundation.org. Paste submissions into the body of the email AND attach them as Word documents. Use SUBMISSION as the subject of your email.

We prefer to receive submissions via email. If you do not have email access, you may send submissions via postal mail to:
Glimpse Magazine
The Glimpse Foundation
17 Gordon Ave, Suite 201
Providence, RI 02905

Postal submissions MUST include a self-addressed stamped envelope or else Glimpse will be unable to notify you about the status of your article.

Copyright

All contributors must be prepared to transfer copyright interests for their submission to Glimpse in the event that their pieces are accepted. Exceptions are sometimes made for experienced free-lance writers who have previously been published and compensated for their writing.

Editing Process

Contributors must respect the right of Glimpse editors to edit submissions as they deem necessary. Our editors will undergo a comprehensive, collaborative revision process with each accepted contributor and will not make any structural/content-related changes without notifying the author. Don't be surprised if Glimpse editors request a revision from you of your first draft—this is a routine part of the process.

Contributors will be asked to provide photographs if their submission is accepted. We prefer to receive photos as scanned attachments; however, if such resources are unavailable, all photos and scannable work can be sent to us via postal mail. We will provide more-detailed information upon acceptance.

Listing in *Writer's Market*. If you pay for freelance articles, another way to get your publication's name out into the freelance community is to promote yourself as a venue for freelance work.

Many freelancers use a primary reference called *Writer's Market* that publishes critical information about publications that commission freelance content. The listing for each publication includes the most pertinent information for freelance writers—including the general pay scale, to whom query letters should be pitched, contact information, and basic information on readership and distribution.

To get listed in *Writer's Market*, request a questionnaire by sending an email request to wmupdates@fwpubs.com or using the "Contact Us" feature on the website at www.writersmarket.com.

Using the job listing opportunities at associations. As mentioned earlier, many writers belong to professional associations that allow publishers to recruit them through their websites. These free listings can lead to long-term relationships with professional writers who have an interest in your mission or subject area.

Finding Freelance Artists

In the context of producing publications, "artists" are photographers, illustrators, font creators, sometimes designers, and anyone who contributes visual materials, as opposed to text, to your publication or website.

Hiring freelancers to produce art images for publications is usually the purview of the art director or whoever is handling the design. Just as you would do to find good writers, you should regularly troll publications and collect the names of artists you might like to hire or whose work you admire.

TIP

Consider saving money by using stock images. The least expensive way to add photographs and illustrations to your magazine or website is to use stock images. For a fraction of what you'd pay someone to create a new image, you can select something an illustrator or photographer already has on hand. Chapter 6 explains more about using stock images. If you do choose to hire someone for a fresh, custom-made drawing or photo, expect to pay about as much for the artwork as you paid the author to write the article. And allow the same amount of time for the creative process.

Most photographers and illustrators who are interested in contributing to publications and who are serious about keeping a roof over their heads create their own websites and post their portfolios online. You can usually locate more information about a particular artist by typing his or her name into any major search engine. Many freelancers also offer "stock" images on their websites that are available at discounted prices.

If you don't have a particular person in mind, you can browse online and in printed catalogues, frequently called "source books." Sections of these catalogues also list representatives for artists who might be able to help direct you to the kind of art or artist you need.

Organize samples of artists' work into categories that will be useful to you when you are generating ideas for specific artwork. You can, for example, keep a separate binder for photographers and one for illustrators. For illustrators, you can categorize artists' styles—such as realistic, fantastical, whimsical, cartoonish—and subject matter specialization: people, objects, concepts and ideas, plants, animals. Some photographers excel at setting up and photographing shots in controlled studio settings; others are great at capturing subjects in any setting.

As with freelance writers, don't be hesitant about approaching professional photographers and illustrators, even well-known ones, to do work for your publication.

If you hire someone to create a custom illustration or photograph to accompany an article, be prepared to give that person a great deal of creative freedom. For example, after showing the artist the kind of art your publication or website normally uses, and giving him or her the article to read, don't spend too much energy specifying exactly what image you want. Instead, step back and let the artist surprise you with something fresh. That way, you will usually wind up with the best work, and your publication will benefit.

Good Sources for Finding Illustrators and Photographers

The vast majority of freelance artists market themselves through numerous portfolio websites and catalogues. Below is a list of some of the most well-known places to search for a freelance illustrator or photographer.

- **The Black Book, at www.blackbook.com** A resource for the creative community. Includes a creative industry directory and portfolios online, and also publishes multiple catalogues of photography, illustration, and mixed media. You can sign up on the website to receive a complimentary copy of its publications.

- **Workbook, at www.workbook.com** Also a national resource for the graphic arts community. It also posts portfolios and keeps an extensive database of contact information.

- **Alternative Pick, at www.altpick.com** Another website that presents artists' work to those who buy art.

- **Directory of Illustration, at www.directoryofillustration.com** The Graphic Artists Guild publishes the *Directory of Illustration* and sponsors the website, where you can see thousands of illustrators' portfolios. The source book is issued every November. Go to the group's website to see whether you qualify for a free copy.

- **American Society of Media Photographers, at www.asmp.org** Offers an extensive online directory of photographers who have experience photographing for publications. You can search by state, metro area, subject specialty, or name of a photographer.

Art schools are another good possibility for finding affordable photographers and illustrators. Students or recent graduates are eager to get published and sell their work. Sign up for and attend open house showcases for the photography and illustration departments of art schools in your area. Call and make connections with instructors who may be able to direct you to their most talented students. The flip side is that art students with little experience may work slowly or may need much more attention and guidance to get the result you want.

Helping Artists Find You

Many freelance illustrators and photographers drum up jobs by regularly sending out postcards of their work to people who buy artwork and by paying to be listed in the source books discussed. They will sometimes also email or cold call designers or art directors. But if your publication is not well known or on the radar screens of the art community, you probably won't be approached.

You can start networking, however, to get your publication's name out. Some simple things you can do are to ask artists who interest you to add your publication to their mailing lists and to contact the local chapters of illustrator or photographer associations to ask if they keep a database of art buyers that they share with their members and ask to be included.

As with freelance writers, you can use guidelines to solicit contributions from artists. It's harder to use submissions for illustrations, as they are often conceptual and need to be custom-created to perfectly match the message and tone of the article. But if your publication regularly uses a certain style or format of illustration in a particular section or department, such as a black-and-white line drawing of a neighborhood skyline for a community newsletter, you could certainly try setting parameters in guidelines and entertain submissions.

It's easier to solicit photo contributions. But try to be as specific as possible about what you are and are not interested in, to avoid receiving photos of someone's vacation. Again, *Glimpse Quarterly's* contributor guidelines, reproduced in part below, include a section on how to submit photos.

Photo Submission Guidelines

The following submission guidelines for photos are fairly specific, but they all exist for a reason, so PLEASE do your best to adhere to them. Contributors who follow all instructions get major brownie points.

Photo Formats

If scanning print images or slides, photos MUST be scanned at 300 dpi or higher, with dimensions of at least 7x10 inches. You can adjust dpi and photo size before you scan. If submitting digital photos, send the largest/highest-resolution file size you have available.

If mailing, either prints or slides are acceptable.

Sending Photos

You may send photos to us via email or snail mail. If emailing:

- Send to photos@glimpsefoundation.org. Send *one photo per email* with the caption written in the body of the email. See below for captioning guidelines.

- Save each file as **Firstname_Lastname##**. For example, Joe Smith would save his first photo as **Joe_Smith01** and his second photo as **Joe_Smith02**. Etc.

- Match the subject line of each email to the name of the file contained therein.

If mailing, send to:

The Glimpse Foundation
ATT Editor
17 Gordon Ave, Suite 201
Providence, RI 02905

Include a self-addressed envelope for return of your photos. If you do not enclose an envelope, your photos will not be returned. Include captions in a separate typed document; be sure that it's clear which captions corresponds to which photo. See below for captioning guidelines.

Making Assignments

Once you have a story or artwork you want to commission, whether it was generated internally or you were approached by a freelancer with the idea, the next step is to make the assignment.

Get in touch with the freelancer and discuss and develop the assignment in more detail. Go over the basics, such as the freelancer's availability, your publication's timeline, what your publication is about, and who your readers are.

Checklist of Topics to Cover Before Making an Assignment

Discussing details of work and your expectations with freelancers in advance will save you many headaches down the line. Before finalizing an assignment, make sure that you have covered the following topics:

- **Focus and angle of the article or art.** Will it be a news feature, op-ed, essay, book review, or Q&A? Will it be a studio portrait or an environmental portrait? Will it be a watercolor illustration or a cartoon or a line drawing?

- **The publication's editorial mission.** Discuss what you're all about, who your readers are, your circulation, your publication's tone and style.

- **The publication's editorial process.** Which and how many editors will the manuscript pass through? Will the person need to deal with a fact checker? Does artwork need to be approved by the top editor?

- **Timelines and deadlines.** Include dates for first drafts, revisions, and final drafts.

- **Number of revisions.** Some publishers set a final number of revisions the freelancer is expected to accommodate.

- **Compensation, terms, and schedule of payment.** Are expenses included? Will the freelancer be paid upon publication, or will half be paid upon final submission and the rest after publication?

- **Use of the work.** This is more important for artists than writers, but still good to cover with both. Will the image be used on the cover or on the inside? Will the article be used as the cover story, or as one story in a department?

- **Rights to the work.** (See "What to Include in a Freelance Contract," below, for more on this.)

- **Kill fees.** Explain what happens if your publication decides not to use the material but the work was partly performed. Does your publication pay a percentage of the originally agreed amount, also called a "kill" fee? Is the writer or artist free to take back his or her work and shop it around to other publications?

- **Method of delivery.** Should the writer email the story or send a disc? Should the photographer post photos online or overnight a disc?

This also gives you the opportunity to firmly establish what you are looking to publish and for the freelancer to clarify what he or she will deliver. For example, you may think a particular freelance writer is qualified to do a story on a particular topic but want him or her to take a different angle or perspective or write a shorter or longer piece than proposed. Discuss this to be sure the writer is willing and able to produce the story you need.

When hiring freelance artists or photographers, thoroughly discuss the story they will be illustrating. (See "Checklist of Topics to Cover Before Making an Assignment," below, for guidance.) In addition to relating the subject matter or key players in the story, hone in on the point or message you want to convey with the written words. Sometimes this will require you to oversimplify the story's meaning, but, it will help the artist zero in on creating a striking image. Also explain the mood or tone you are hoping to establish in the story to help the photographer or illustrator pick the right color palette, style, or even medium to use.

This is also the time to establish any other significant items such as deadlines, the number of revisions the writer or artist is expected to accommodate, the publication's editorial process, the payment process and schedule, what happens if the publication decides not to use the material, and so on.

Paying Freelance Writers and Artists

When determining what to pay freelancers for their work, it's crucial to have a general idea of the market standard.

Some freelancers are willing to work for a nonprofit for less than they would a for-profit group, because you are making less money from their work. And with all freelancers, it's usually possible to negotiate lower rates —especially if you are a regular client and send a lot of work their way.

Rates for writers. The industry norm for writers is to get paid by the word, usually the number of words they are assigned to write, not the number of words the article eventually gets whittled down to when it's finally printed. The glossiest consumer publications with heavy national advertisers generally pay the most per word ($1.50 and up), and tiny publications with little or no advertising pay the least (from almost nothing up to 75 cents). Most writers do not consider a publication to be a truly viable or "serious" venue for freelance work unless it pays $1 per word. As a nonprofit publication, you will probably be able to afford only rates at the lower end of the pay scale.

It is sometimes a good idea to set flat fees for pieces, rather than agree to pay by the word. It's easier on your editors and on your accounting department if your publication has a rule of paying a fixed amount for features, for shorter news pieces, or for contributions to a certain department. If you are commissioning an expert to write a series of articles of varying lengths, for example, it would be more straightforward just to pay for the package.

TIP

Checking the *Guide* for guidance. See the "Rates and Practices" section of the *Freelance Writer's Guide* (National Writers Union) to get a firm idea of appropriate freelance rates to set.

Rates for artists. It is more common for artists to set their own rates for the work they produce. When setting their rates, many of them will be most concerned with how your publication will use the work and how much money you are going to make from using it.

They will likely charge more for a photograph or illustration to be used on the cover of a publication than for a small image on the inside, for example. And as your circulation and amount of advertising goes up, so will the artist's rates. Freelance artists who are not widely known will generally work for less than the established ones. But if the market is down and there's not much work to go around, most artists will work for less than what they might command when business is good.

RESOURCE

The best source for current rates and hiring practices for photographers and illustrators is the book *Graphic Artists Market* (National Writers' Guide).

Tips for Keeping Costs Down

Photographers can get quite expensive, so try the following tips to save some money.

- Tell the photographer what you want and ask what would be the least expensive way to get it. Perhaps he or she already has an image in their files that would suffice.
- Use stock images.
- Encourage people on your publication staff to learn to take good photographs. Usually many people take better photos by simply taking two giant steps forward to tighten up the frame on a subject.
- Limit the scope of rights that you buy so that you're not paying for more than you'll be using.

Photographers usually charge a set amount for the usage you want—such as a cover or inside shot of a full page—or charge you a day rate to shoot an event. Photographers may have different rates for shooting in a studio or on location, so be sure to ask. A photographer might charge you from several hundred up to thousands of dollars for a cover, depending on how much work is involved or whether assistants are needed to help to set up a shot. Day rates typically start around $600 to $800 and up. If the shoot will be quick or won't take a whole day, ask if the photographer is willing to work at an hourly rate or charge for only a half day. (See Chapter 6, "Obtaining Artwork," for ideas for accessing photographers' stock archives for inexpensive art possibilities.)

Illustrators tend to charge a little bit less than photographers, because they have fewer expenses. They often work out of their homes and don't have to hire assistants. For illustrators, what's important is the use and the level of detail required. Will it be full color or black and white? Is it a drawing with shading and perspective, or a simple line drawing? Experienced illustrators can charge $800 to $1,000 and up for a detailed cover illustration. Student illustrators might be able to produce something for a few hundred dollars.

Freelance Production Help

Production people who are able to understand and coordinate the process of getting your publication's digital files properly translated into what the printing press cranks out are valuable, potentially saving you time and lots of money. As mentioned earlier, there's no formal training for this kind of position; much of their expertise is learned on the job.

If you do not have the resources to hire someone, consider leaning on a freelance graphic designer or production consultant in the beginning. Production consultants and designers can get your systems up and running so that you barely need their help later on. These consultants are generally more expensive by the hour than for full-time staff; either will probably run $75 per hour or more. Find one with suitable skills willing to coordinate with your printer or website vendor to ensure that every detail comes out perfectly.

Expect to work at least six months with a consultant developing the tools and connections in your system. And be sure to ask him or her to build something that handles every task you need—from word processing to Web publishing and archiving.

As with other types of freelancers you might hire, find someone who has a track record handling the same work for comparable organizations. Check references, both with publisher clients and with printers. In fact, it makes great sense to ask printers and other publishers to help you locate an appropriate consultant. You can also find them listed in industry directories and through publishing associations.

Some publishers hire a freelance graphic designer to create a master design grid or template for a newsletter, magazine, or website. (See Chapter 6 for details about grids.) Some graphic designers have knowledge about production issues as well as design challenges. They know how to communicate with printers, supervise their work, and negotiate printing contracts. But this is not true of all designers. Many of them want to stick to design, quitting at the page layout stage. Even such designers can usually help you find someone else—an independent prepress service, another freelancer, or even the printer—to complete the production tasks.

Outside prepress vendors are available to help convert your page layouts into printable digital files. Many printers also offer this service. Specialists like these, at either your printer or a separate company, are likely to keep up with changing technology better than your nonprofit staff can, and they may have much more experienced staff than you can hire on your own. So hiring a freelancer for this task may be preferable over hiring someone in house to do it.

RESOURCE

Find production consultants through *Folio* magazine at www. foliomag.com and the graphic arts magazine *How*, online at www.howdesign. com. Consultants advertise in both publications.

Freelance Salespeople

Nonprofits often end up with a sales team that is a combination of staff employees and outside contractors. It's quite common to have an inside sales manager and an outside sales force. The inside manager, who may also sell ads, is responsible for keeping track of which salesperson is assigned to which advertising account to avoid overlap.

EXAMPLE: *Kentucky Living* has 2.5 salaried sales employees, two commission-only contract salespeople to handle certain accounts, and an independent sales firm that sells ads to companies located outside of Kentucky. On average, the entire *Kentucky Living* team can sell about 45 ad pages per person per year. This is a reasonable level of productivity to expect for a well-established publication that already has relationships with a few hundred advertisers.

RESOURCE

A good resource for finding independent advertising sales firms is the National Association of Publisher's Representatives (NAPR), a professional association of sales firms. Its website has a database of firms by location and valuable tips on hiring and managing ad salespeople at www. naprassoc.com.

When looking for freelance salespeople to work for your nonprofit, keep in mind that familiarity with your publication's world of advertisers is a plus.

Give each salesperson or firm a well-defined and unique area—by geography or product type, for instance—so no two people ever accidentally call on the same advertiser.

And create a compensation program that rewards the kind of sales you want to achieve. For example, if you want new accounts, give a bonus for them. If you want existing advertisers to buy bigger ads or more of them, give a bonus for upgrades. If you want a whole new category of ads, give a prize for the first salesperson to break into that category.

Publishers generally pay outside sales firms or freelancers about 20% of the advertising income each person generates. If your publication doesn't have much ad potential or is just getting started, you may need to pay more than 20% to make the assignment worthwhile. There are other costs your outside salespeople will expect you to cover—including media kits and other promotion materials, travel expenses, and sometimes a guaranteed minimum monthly draw against future commissions.

Adding everything together, an outside sales team will probably cost between 25% and 30% of sales revenue. Keep in mind, however, that an experienced, professional sales representative who has well-established relationships can often generate more advertising revenue, more quickly, than someone from your own staff who must build each new advertiser relationship from scratch.

What to Include in a Freelance Contract

Once you and a freelancer agree on an assignment and its terms, it's wise to make that agreement official by signing a contract. The contract documents your agreement and protects your publication in case the freelancer does not live up to his or her obligations. It also provides the freelancer with protection if you do not live up to your end of the bargain.

Your contract with a freelancer should cover the following basic areas.

- **Services to be performed.** It's not necessary to go into extreme detail, but do make clear what the work commissioned and subject matter is and what the final product should be. For example, you might write that the freelancer will "report and write a 3,000-word feature article about the effects of pesticides on migrant farm workers" or that an illustrator will "produce an 8.5" x 11" watercolor depiction of a Siamese cat."

- **Payment.** Specify what you will pay the freelancer for the work: a flat amount or an hourly, daily, weekly, or monthly rate. If there is a maximum limit you will pay the person for the work, write that in. Also spell out here whether you will pay a kill fee, or percentage of the fee if the work is not published. Kill fees are usually 20% to 50% of the original fee, depending on how much work was done.

- **Terms of payment.** Specify how and when you'll pay the freelancer. Most publications pay within a certain number of days after publication, but you may choose some other arrangement. You can also specify here the terms under which a kill fee will be paid— including what percentage you will pay if the writer has already done a first draft or an illustrator has done the first round of sketches.

- **Expenses.** If the assignment will require the freelancer to incur expenses, such as travel fees or renting special equipment, specify whether he or she should bill for them separately. It's wise to set an upper limit for expenses, and you might require that expenses over a certain amount first meet approval by the publication. You should also require freelancers to submit receipts as proof of the expense.

- **Materials.** Specify that freelancers are required to provide their own materials.

- **Rights and use.** People who create particular work retain the copyright to it unless they give it up. When you publish a freelancer, you buy certain rights to use their work. In your contract, specify what rights you are purchasing to the work under the contract. Most publishers buy first and one-time North American serial rights. This means your publication will be the first in North America to publish the work, and that the freelancer can't run off to a different publication or a competitor and sell them the same work. These rights are in effect before the publication date and for a set length of time after—usually 60 to 90 days. If your publication wants to post the material on your website, you should also specify that you are buying that right.

- **Releases.** In the case of photographing subjects who must give permission for their pictures to be taken and their likenesses to be used, the contract should specify whose responsibility it is to secure the release: the freelancer or someone on staff at the publication.

- **Modifying or terminating the agreement.** Your needs may change. Perhaps there's a breaking news development that indicates that the short 300-word story you assigned should be expanded into a 5,000-word feature story. Detail how either your publication or the freelancer could modify the agreement.

There are also other clauses that are wise to include as part of the contract to ensure that the freelancer can never be interpreted to be an employee of your publication, because employees have certain legal rights. These clauses make clear that freelancers are responsible for paying all their own state and federal taxes and that the publication is not buying workers, compensation insurance nor paying unemployment or fringe benefits for freelancers.

The Struggle Over Copyrights

With the increasing uses of the Internet, online versions of publications, and other forms of media, many publishers have been demanding more and more rights to freelance work.

Understandably, the freelance writing and graphic arts community has loudly protested these developments and freelance professionals try to negotiate hard against all-encompassing contracts. As the National Writers Union explains in its *Freelance Writers' Guide,* "Of late, a less draconian but still highly objectionable kind of contract has become common, one in which the magazine requests exclusive one-time publication rights and nonexclusive (and ongoing) secondary rights in other categories." The NWU urges writers to demand additional compensation for any type of republication.

Graphic artists have the same concern about specifying exactly what rights a publisher buys. An artist may retain ownership of his or her work and may also limit your rights to a certain time period, geographic location, or medium. These details should be clearly described in your contract. Everything not specified in the contract is usually available for an additional fee, but you have to ask about it.

Your publication will have to determine what position on rights is best to take. First publishing rights and the right to post the story on your publication's website seem to be a pretty standard arrangement these days. But it's worth asking for more if you need it: Many freelancers will be more flexible with a nonprofit publication than they would be with a commercial one.

RESOURCE

The National Association of Publisher's Representatives offers information about how to find advertising sales representatives at its website, at www.naprassoc.com.

For general information on drafting a freelance contract, including sample language to use, see *Consultant & Independent Contractor Agreements*, by Stephen Fishman (Nolo).

Managing Freelance Arrangements

Developing successful working relationships with freelancers doesn't end when you sign a contract—or even after the work is finished.

Stay in touch with freelancers, especially as deadlines approach, to evaluate the progress of the work and determine if the freelancer is having any difficulties or encountering obstacles that might prevent or delay completing the assignment.

Call up writers once they've had a chance to do some reporting and ask how the story is developing. Has its direction changed? Has the writer discovered a slightly different angle that should be pursued? Is the writer having trouble securing interviews? Perhaps the editor can help or suggest additional sources to contact.

When working with photographers, check in before the shoot to ask whether your art direction is clear, find out whether there are any questions, and remind them of certain elements or needs you may have. For example, if you may be using one of the shots as a cover image and your covers require a vertical versus horizontal shot, be sure to tell the photographer to take plenty of vertical shots. Sometimes editors or designers accompany photographers during a photo shoot to make sure the needed image is captured.

Illustrators will typically submit two to three conceptual sketches for your approval before they begin working on the final piece. Take this opportunity to fully discuss and give guidance to the illustrator because once you approve a sketch, the illustrator is free to proceed to final art based on that sketch. Changes are much easier to make to sketches than to final art, and possibly less expensive, too.

Designers can also show you a "sketch" or rough approach before proceeding to a finished grid or website template design. And you should ask them for this interim step to prevent unhappy surprises down the road. For example, someone who is designing a template can usually show you the fonts they want to use and the color palette before proceeding to the finished design.

Once an assignment is over, if you liked what the freelancer produced, it's also wise to cultivate the relationship. Call that freelancer occasionally, just to chat. Or take him or her out for lunch or coffee, keeping the lines of communication open. ●

Creating Compelling Content

Hashing out editorial missions, budgets, and personnel decisions is a necessary part of sustaining a healthy nonprofit publication. But none of those activities will be as important and meaningful as the words within it. That's what your readers consume and what they will use to judge your publication. Depending on the strength and presentation of the content, readers could decide that your publication provides indispensable information and merits an hour of their precious reading time and $5 from their wallets each month. Or they could decide that it is worthy only of the recycling bin or the delete button.

This chapter covers the entire procedure of gathering, selecting, shaping, packaging, and presenting content for your nonprofit publication. It explains how to come up with ideas, decide what's newsworthy, transform an idea into an article that will attract your readers, and write headlines that will make readers itch to read on. And the tips in this chapter will also help you get the best work from freelancers and others who might contribute articles to your website or magazine.

Developing Story Ideas

Coming up with ideas about what to publish is not a science. Inspiration can come from many different sources.

The first logical step is to encourage everyone involved to be well informed about relevant news and trends on your topic—and make the effort yourself, too. Read daily papers, community newsletters, consumer magazines, industry and trade publications, online blogs, and any related technical publications. There are many ways—some more systematic and logical and others more random and subjective—to generate a rich and successful mix of material for your publication. Readers crave news, information, and entertainment; it's providing those things on your targeted topic that will prompt them to pick up and spend time with your publication.

Refer to the editorial mission that you developed earlier or inherited from others (see Chapter 1). It should spell out who your readers are and what you strive to do for them. You can learn to understand your readership's wants and needs even more thoroughly through various kinds of surveys and reports. (These are discussed in Chapter 11.)

To a degree, certain subjects and how you will cover them will naturally flow from your editorial mission and the specific type of nonprofit your publication covers. But a publication with truly great editorial content transcends this level of coverage to produce material that might be unexpected or even surprising to its readers, that challenges them in ways in which they didn't know they'd appreciate being challenged, and tells them things that help them in their jobs—or that they couldn't easily find elsewhere. In the best publications, all of this is wrapped up in a package that's accessible and engaging, both to read and to see.

One prerequisite for most editorial content is that it is should be news to readers. That is, the information should be about events, people, phenomena, and activities that they don't already know or have never been presented to them in quite the same way.

EXAMPLE: You publish an electronic newsletter for a nonprofit concerned with environmental issues. A writer proposes a story on global warming, a topic you've covered before. However, it could still merit publication if the writer has an exclusive interview with a noted scientist on the subject who has never before granted an interview.

Information that is newsworthy tends to meet certain criteria. Most often, it is timely and significant, directly affects readers, involves prominent people, includes struggle and conflict, or is quirky and strange. For some readers and publications, the more quickly a story is told after the events happen, the more likely it is to be newsworthy. And events that affect large percentages of populations or groups are often newsworthy. Think Social Security reform or a change to some other major government program.

Things that prominent people say or do can be newsworthy. Events surrounding topics that your readers care about or that affect their daily lives, or those of their family, friends, or loved ones, are newsworthy. Stories that fulfill more than one of these requirements quickly climb the scale of newsworthiness.

Where to Look for Story Ideas

It can be hard coming up with issue after issue of story ideas, especially good ideas. Sometimes you are low on inspiration. Sometimes it's refreshing just to seek some diversity outside your own mode of thinking and conception of the subject matter. At these times, it might be helpful to consult others.

Here is a list of some options to try.

- Hold a meeting to share and bounce stories off a group of people at your nonprofit and massage ideas to make them most compelling for readers. By brainstorming and inviting skeptical, critical questioning at story meetings, you can refine and elevate average, humdrum ideas into thoughtful, unexpected, and salient stories.
- Ask your editorial advisory board members for story ideas and trends they are observing. (See Chapter 4 for more on editorial boards.)
- Conduct a focus group of readers about what they'd like to read about but never see in the publication or website.
- Establish working friendships with other editors through journalism associations and ask them if they'd help you refine story ideas or let you bounce ideas off them.
- Convene your best freelance writers, or take them out to lunch one on one, and solicit their ideas. In particular, ask them whether they've had ideas for stories they'd like to write for your publication but did not pitch because they did not think your publication would accept them.
- Attend conferences, seminars, and meetings in your publication's field of interest. You will meet new sources and learn new ideas.

TIP

Keep the reader firmly in mind. Always consider story ideas from your readers' perspectives. Ask honestly whether they would be interested in an idea or whether it's simply something that personally interests you or someone on your staff.

Choosing the Right Treatment

Pick any publication off the news rack, flip it open, and you'll see a wide variety of forms in which to present content. Or click through some different online publications and you'll see the various components used to create their Web pages.

If you're researching magazines, notice that in the front section of most of them, you'll find shorter, briefer, newsier stories. Some are no more than blurbs of 35 to 50 words. In recurring departments, you might find columns or essays. In the middle, you'll typically find the long features, the cover stories, and narrative articles. You might see a photo essay or charts, graphs, or lists instead of typeset text. These might be the body of the story or could be sidebars to the main story. Many magazines end with a first-person essay or a slightly more light-hearted, humorous piece.

Newsletters usually consist of many shorter stories, but they often include departments with a recurring columnist or a section of longer features as well.

Online publication articles are shorter still. Many Internet articles max out at 400 to 500 words. There are exceptions, of course, but since it is physically difficult to read on a computer screen and different content is always just a click away, Internet publishers keep stories short to accommodate readers' short attention spans.

Described below are some common formats with some advice about when they work best.

News stories or news briefs read like articles that appear in newspapers. They state the news in the first paragraph and get to the point quickly.

Story length is flexible—but ranges from 40 words or less for a news snippet to 800 words for a news feature. These articles tend to be shorter and state the topic at hand in the first sentence or paragraph. This format works best for reporting news or other information that will lose its timeliness quickly. Even when news stories lead with a short anecdote, the news usually follows within a couple paragraphs.

Features are generally longer stories ideal for showcasing in-depth reporting on a topic. Depending on the size of your publication, they can range from 2,000 to even 10,000 words. Good features are often propelled by strong narratives, subjects, or protagonists. The relevance of features doesn't expire as quickly as news stories or may never expire. The best ones, however, are topical for some reason or related to something that is currently newsworthy. They may be a detailed examination of a phenomenon or idea that has been around for a long time; it's just that they're covered more in depth or with some unique focus. In features, writers tend to spend a longer time with a source or subject, to take time describing the events or setting the scene for a story they are relaying. Features can be funny, provocative, or disturbing. What they all share is some goal to entertain readers in some small way beyond what a regular news story would deliver.

Essays are analytic compositions on one topic. They work well when the writer wishes to make an argument or persuade the reader to his or her point of view. They are also good for introducing and explaining a concept or idea that may not be widely known or understood, or misunderstood. Think political essays or commentary.

First-person stories can be quite powerful when a writer has first-hand experience with the subject matter. With first-person stories, however, it's usually a good idea to encourage writers to interview others in similar circumstances just to be able to expand and add some variety to their examples beyond their own lives.

Question & Answer formats can be great for presenting a person's thoughts and opinions—particularly a person who is well known, famous, or likely to be of interest to your readers. Since conversations can ramble, Q&As often require intensive editing for the best questions and content. It also helps if your publication can ask tough questions, or if some controversy surrounds the individual. Q&As can be an easy format for someone who does not write well, since such pieces involve conveying another person's thoughts rather than crafting a story, which can be good or bad for your publication.

Tables, charts, maps, diagrams, guides, and lists are helpful when presenting information that is not necessary to process in prose form or that is only relevant for some of your readers, so readers can quickly zero in on the information they need.

EXAMPLE: If you wanted to make your readers aware of all the farmers markets operating in your state, you might break down the markets by county and list them that way, so that readers can immediately spot which markets are closest to where they live. Or you could do a map with blow-up listings. An entry might read "Ogden Valley Farmers Market. Produce, meats, dairy, bakery. Open M, W, Th. 10 a.m.-4 p.m., 3000 Main Street." If you chose to present that information in the body of an article, you would be making the information more difficult to access for your readers.

Imagine if you wrote the following for each of dozens of markets: "The Ogden Valley Farmers Market is popular among surrounding neighborhoods and hosts vendors selling a wide variety of produce, meats, dairy, and bakery items. It is open Mondays, Wednesdays, and Thursdays from 10 a.m. to 4 p.m. The market is located at 3000 Main Street, just blocks from the downtown plaza." This type of entry might be appropriate if you were highlighting various markets, but if the purpose is to convey a lot of information quickly, this would be the wrong approach.

TIP

Match graphic forms to the information. Some information can best be imparted not through words, but through graphics. Something that can be tedious to read can be understood at a glance through a picture. For example, complicated legislative processes can easily be explained through flow charts. A long chronology or history can be grasped through a timeline. The rollercoaster value of a company's stock can be shown on a graph.

There's no end to the forms in which you can present content. The overriding concern should be to make the content the most accessible for your readers. Consider the nature of your nonprofit organization and the best tone and style to reach readers.

If your organization exists for networking or social purposes, the publication might be chatty and informal. If you are a scientific professional association, your readers may expect the content to be presented in a more formal and academic style. If you publish for visual artists, more of your content will probably be presented graphically. If you publish for a group of linguists, more of it will be presented as text.

EXAMPLE: You publish a newsletter for parents raising bilingual children and wanted to inform your readers about all the public and private immersion schools and programs available. You want to provide all sorts of useful info: the name of the school, location, cost, languages offered, entry requirements, date enrollment begins, motto or philosophy, special features, contact info, website address. It might make the most sense to present this large amount of data as a table with well-defined headings that readers could scan and consult, instead of forcing readers to read this information as prose and dig out the information they seek.

On the other hand, if the same publication reports on a recent study showing that high school students in language immersion schools did not appear to score any better on College Board language exams than students who learned through conventional programs—an invented scenario—this should probably be presented as straightforwardly as possible. This would be grave, perhaps disturbing, information for many of your readers and might best be treated as a serious story or with analysis. This doesn't sound like a breezy, "Didja know?" 100-word story. Nor is it necessarily a sprawling, 5,000-word first-person narrative in which the writer follows the blow-by-blow activities of the scientists who conducted the study.

Experiment with forms. And if you see a great presentation in a publication, even one that deals with completely different subject matter from what your publication covers, there's no reason you can't adapt it for your purposes. For example, magazines that focus on the rich and famous, beauty, and fashion often have sections in which they show photos of a few best-dressed or worst-dressed celebrities and invite critics to provide—often hilarious—commentary on their outfits. Perhaps this same format could be used to critique something else: computer gadgets, or books, or day hikes. Be creative, be clever, and have fun. Readers will appreciate your efforts to keep them entertained and surprised—and they'll keep coming back for more.

Combining Form and Substance to Catch Readers' Minds

Some publications have invented incredibly innovative ways to present content.

For example, *Harper's* magazine runs a recurring department called "Annotation" that takes an image of an object—usually a close-up photo —and educates readers through short, factual notes pointing back to features of the object. It once "annotated" an American Automobile Association membership card to illustrate how the AAA uses much of its dues money to lobby for automobile-friendly and transit-unfriendly policies.

The magazine is also famous for its "Harper's Index," a one-page line-by-line listing of little-known facts and numbers that are meticulously researched, presented, and juxtaposed in such a way that the reader can't help but draw certain conclusions about the data.

As another example, *Bay Nature*, a magazine for people who appreciate "exploring, celebrating, and understanding" the San Francisco Bay Area's natural habitat, runs a department called "Naturalist's Notebook," in which the author and illustrator highlights some feature of nature, whether it's the ecosystem of a single beach or the life cycle of a species of native bird, by mimicking what a naturalist might sketch or doodle into his or her notebook. All text on the page is handwritten, not set in type, and illustrated by hand-drawn and watercolor-painted artwork. The text and artwork are not laid out in a traditional grid format but appear in a more freeform arrangement on the page. The page is so unlike the usual fare in print publications that it immediately grabs readers' attention.

Turning Ideas Into Words

At some publications, editorial responsibilities focus more on soliciting and shaping content for print. At others, members of the staff report and write stories that are published. Even if you are not doing as much direct reporting and writing, it is critical to know the basics to communicate with your writers, set standards, give writers ideas when they are stuck, and spot holes or trouble in stories.

If you have little or no experience and would like to learn more, there are many textbooks, most of them aimed at journalists and journalism students that cover the basics thoroughly and carefully. And your local community colleges, adult schools, media associations, or university extension programs may also offer introductory journalism courses that can help you understand the fundamentals.

 RESOURCE
A few good books on news writing basics are noted here.

- *Melvin Mencher's News Reporting and Writing,* by Melvin Mencher (McGraw Hill): This textbook is often used to teach journalism students the fundamentals of the news reporting and writing process. It covers everything from how to quote sources, to writing leads for feature stories, to properly reporting the score of a basketball game.

- *The Associated Press Guide to News Writing,* by Rene J. Cappon (Peterson's Guides): It distills the famous newsgathering coop's straightforward approach to writing the news—including what makes a good news story, how to construct a good lead, how to use quotes and cite sources, and how to keep your writing clear and concise.

- *The Elements of News Writing,* by James W. Kershner (Allyn & Bacon): Also an introduction to news writing, but reads less like a textbook and more "how-to." Kershner spends more time on reviewing the rules of grammar and usage and offers a 15-step guide to writing a news story.

Reporting

Reporting refers to gathering news and collecting the data, quotes, and other information that will be used in assembling or writing a story. The most common methods of reporting include interviewing people; researching and procuring documents, such as press releases, reports, public records, or previously reported news clips; and observing events in person by attending meetings, gatherings, or other functions.

However the news is gathered, it is essential that you make sure it is accurate and fair to maintain your publication's integrity—and avoid legal problems.

Accuracy

One of the tenets of reporting, and perhaps the overriding one, is accuracy. All the writing in your publication must be factually correct. This applies to everything in all stories—from the middle initial of a zoologist you are quoting, to the species name of her pet iguana, to your explanation of her groundbreaking research into a little-studied branch of chimp evolution. Inaccuracy always causes a publication to lose credibility, often prompts angry letters from exasperated readers, and occasionally even acts as a catalyst for lawsuits from subjects who feel they have been wrongly portrayed.

Some publications add a step called "fact checking" to verify the accuracy of their content. Checking reference books and documents gathered by the writers, calling sources, and sometimes even delving into the writer's notes, fact checkers scrutinize each factual statement in the story and determine whether it is true as written and flag or fix problems they find. Even if your publication's staff is not large enough to do comprehensive fact checking, it's possible to do some to institute a measure of quality control. For example, you could make it a practice to check new writers, or particularly controversial stories, or all proper names and information that's easily accessible through a quick Internet search.

One way that writers often get in trouble is through sloppy sourcing. "Sourcing" refers to attributing information in a story. It tells the reader how the writer learned or knows the information. The most common sin occurs when information is attributed incompletely or not at all, misleading readers to believe that the writer talked directly to a source. For example, the writer might include a statement in quotes, followed by "said so-and-so," when the quote actually came from a previously reported news account in a different publication. The writer didn't actually do the work to track down and talk to this source but found it in a news clip search or Internet search and decided to reuse it. Proper attribution for such a quote would read "said so-and-so when interviewed by such-and-such publication in March 20XX."

The same goes for information learned elsewhere that's stated as fact, such as why a company went bankrupt or why scientists think autism is on the rise. Generally, information that you do not independently gather should be attributed. Basic, well-known facts, such as Ronald Reagan winning the presidential election in 1980, do not need to be attributed.

Where it gets tricky is in publishing information that is not widely known and must be learned through intensive research and individual initiative. For example, if you were publishing a story about how the use and disposal of computer and electronics equipment is poisoning the environments of low-income communities and relied heavily on information from a months-long, groundbreaking investigation by reporters at the local newspaper, it would be wrong to use the information without crediting the paper. Often, writers do not intend to "steal" information from other sources; they simply find it difficult to incorporate the attribution without disturbing the flow and pace of the writing. But failing to give proper attributions is plagiarism—and wrong.

Avoid this problem by attributing any publication from which you take information and also making a few phone calls to experts on the topic, even the same sources who were quoted in the story to which you are referring. There is no rule against calling the same sources and collecting quotes of your own to add to your article.

There will be grey areas, and your publication will have to make its own policies as to what attribution it requires. Some publications consider a fact widely known or public knowledge if it was reported in at least three major newspapers. In general, though, the vast majority of the content you publish should be independently reported by the people writing your stories.

For the Record: All About 'Off the Record'

In movies, secretive but knowledgeable sources always want to go "off the record" with reporters.

But do you know what that really means? In journalistic lingo, "off the record" means the information cannot be used in any way and can only be stored in the reporter's head. It cannot even be taken to a different source for confirmation.

When most people ask to go off the record, what they want is to avoid seeing their name appear in print with the information or the quote. Sometimes you can negotiate with the source to describe him or her generally, but not by name, such as "a county official with the health services department" or "a high school history teacher in Pittsburgh."

Be careful about anonymous sources, though. Unless you cannot get the story any other way, steer clear. Remember, anonymous sources never have to publicly stand behind the information they reveal and may harbor hidden agendas by selectively disclosing it to you. The information often can't be verified or fact checked easily, and using too much unsourced material can breed distrust among readers.

Fairness

Most writers are now expected to be fair. This does not mean that they must present all sides of an issue or include dozens of quotes from every person who has something to say on the subject. Rather, they should seek and consider different viewpoints in their reporting and must not ignore information or fail to explore arguments that contradict their assumptions and conclusions.

This is especially true for publications that advocate a viewpoint, as many nonprofit publications do. Advocacy publications start out with a set of assumptions, generally found in the editorial or organizational mission statement, then launch their news reporting from there.

EXAMPLE: An environmental publication may start with a fundamental belief that it is not sustainable or wise for people to live out of balance with the natural environment, to take more from the earth than they give back. If it were running a short news brief updating its readers about a piece of legislation that would tighten auto efficiency standards, it wouldn't be obligated to run long antiregulation quotes from the auto and oil industries, in the name of being fair. It might be useful, however, to note that those industries oppose the bill.

An example of unfairness would be a publication that runs a long examination of the legislation and fails to mention that the auto manufacturing lobby actually supported the bill.

Usually, working in or dealing with viewpoints that don't fit neatly into the expected views on a topic produces a more nuanced and sophisticated story.

Fairness also means that if you are going to attack or criticize a subject, or accuse it of wrongdoing, that you give it a chance to explain its side of the story. Even if your facts are unassailable, readers will wonder what the person or group will have to say for themselves.

Structuring a Story

There is no one right way to write a story. The most provocative feature stories often break many conventions. But as with artists and architects, writers who break the rules most successfully must first master the classic forms used in their art or craft.

The most basic story structure used in most publications is the news story. Articles may be long or short, or start off with an anecdote about a person or a scene-setting paragraph, but almost all share the same structural elements. The vast majority of news stories follows the "inverted pyramid style"—a colorful term that means placing all the most critical information at the beginning of a story and leaving little details that the reader does not necessarily need to know at the end. For example, if somebody died in a car accident, you need to state early that the person died and how, and probably also where, when, and why. You do not need to include up high that the person collected porcelain frogs as a hobby.

News stories typically consist of:

- a lead to begin
- a "nut" paragraph that explains to readers why they should pay attention or care about this story if that was not already made apparent in the lead
- some background information to give the story some context
- explanatory material that supports or further explains the nut paragraph—usually told chronologically or grouped together by theme, and
- to close, a "kicker," often used in magazine features, consisting of a few paragraphs that wrap up the story by looping back to a protagonist or ending on a thought-provoking quote.

A lead is considered one of the most important elements of any story. This is the first sentence that readers will encounter, and it will often determine whether they keep reading or stop. So it's important for writers to craft leads that will pique reader interest.

Leads can be direct or delayed. Direct leads are usually a statement of the news that includes the who, what, where, when, and sometimes why of what happened. They are self-explanatory. Delayed leads are the ones that relay a little story, tell a short anecdote about a situation or person, or set the scene. They must be chosen carefully, for they are meant to set the tone for the story and crystallize the subject of the article.

Anecdotal leads should serve as a mini-story that represents the points you will make in the larger story.

EXAMPLE: The *New York Times Magazine* once ran a story examining how researchers are figuring out the best ways to interrupt people in this technological age without distracting them so much that they lose all productivity. The lead told a quick story about how one of these "interruption" scientists got interested in the subject because when she moved from a quiet, isolated lab position to a professor position, she discovered that she was hardly able to get anything done due to constant disruptions from cell phone calls, email, coworkers, and other distractions.

Nut paragraphs are meant to explain to readers why they should care about the story they are reading. In these paragraphs, writers usually zoom out to show readers the big picture: the magnitude of a problem, how many people a story touches, how much money is being wasted, what it means for the reader's future if the problem or conflict is not resolved. These paragraphs often try to quantify the problem through some use of statistics and may be useful for conveying why your publication is telling a particular story. The trick is to write them in a way that leaves readers wanting to know more, instead of divulging everything at once so that there's no incentive to keep reading.

Background sections catch readers up to speed on a subject, whether it's on the history of a conflict or background information on how airplane wings work, so that they can move forward and understand the rest of the story.

Explanatory material, sometimes added after the background or historical section, usually organizes the rest of the story body chronologically or by grouping similar ideas or material. These paragraphs support and expand on the points the writer made in the nut graph about why the story is important to readers.

A kicker, used to end some stories, ties up loose ends and may forecast what might happen next for the story subjects or issue. Kickers often revisit the person or situation in the lead of the story or pose questions that can't be answered yet but are prompted by the reporting.

There are an endless number of ways that you can tweak and twist this structure, but if you examine all stories closely, you'll see that most of them follow this form, however loosely.

In addition to the news story form, there are other things to know about what makes good writing.

For example, striking the right tone and pace for a story is important. Tone refers to the "voice" or manner of expression communicated through the writing. Pace is the flow of the story—that is, how quickly or slowly it moves from scene to scene or one area of information to another.

EXAMPLE: If you are presenting a 4,000-word profile on your university's latest Nobel Prize winner, it wouldn't sound right to start out with a traditional news lead about why he or she won the award. Readers settling in for a long story need to be drawn in and invited to sit down for tea. Such a profile might begin instead by setting a scene from the person's life that illuminates the road to achieving such an award. In contrast, a short news story announcing the award would get to the point quickly and not delay readers, who are expecting to move from beginning to end without dallying.

RESOURCE
There are a number of good books that include advice on good writing.

- *The Art and Craft of Feature Writing: Based on the Wall Street Journal Guide*, by William E. Blundell (Plume): This great little volume teaches nonfiction feature writers first how to better craft an interesting angle to a story and then go about reporting, organizing, and writing it. Blundell uses excerpts from real news stories to deconstruct the thinking and writing process.
- *Bird by Bird: Some Instructions on Writing and Life*, by Anne Lamott (Anchor): Lamott offers less nitty-gritty writing advice than other books but is so empathetic about the psychological challenges of writing—writer's block, jealousy of others' success, anxiety at being discovered a fraud—that it's still a worthwhile read.
- *Follow the Story: How to Write Successful Nonfiction*, by James B. Stewart (Simon & Schuster): In this book, Pulitzer Prize-winning Stewart teaches nonfiction writers how to use the narrative devices of fiction to improve their writing, with chapters covering topics such as leads, dialogue, description, and humor and pathos. He offers many examples, particularly from his bestselling book on the 1980s junk bond and insider trading scandals.
- *The Journalist's Craft: A Guide to Writing Better Stories*, by Dennis Jackson and John Sweeney (Allworth Press): A collection of essays by writers, editors, and writing coaches, this book focuses on what makes good storytelling, in addition to covering other basic topics such as how to generate good ideas and the mechanics of language.

Lobbying Restrictions May Limit Your Content

IRS rules on tax-exempt organizations also put some restrictions on how much lobbying some of them may conduct, which may also affect the kind of content you can carry in your publications.

But the antilobbying rules are widely misunderstood—and not as restrictive as many people assume. Part of the problem is in confusing "lobbying" with "advocating." Lobbying here means attempting to influence specific legislation by contacting the sponsoring politicians or others directly involved with it, or encouraging members of the public to do so. As explained below, some nonprofits must curtail some of this type of activity or risk losing their tax-exempt status.

By contrast, advocacy work is the lifeblood of many nonprofit organizations—many of which consider it their reason for being to, for example, reduce highway accidents or curb tobacco smoking among teens. Nonprofit associations are freely allowed to communicate with members about legislative issues, to conduct research about policy issues, and to testify before legislators when invited to do so about public policy. That's considered advocacy.

Nonprofits that are not in the 501(c)3 category *can* legally urge readers to vote for or against specific candidates and measures or to contact their legislators. Trade unions, typically 501(c)5 entities, and business trade associations, 501(c)(6), fall into this group, as do all 501(c)4 groups, commonly social welfare organizations.

Even 501(c)3 charities that wish to engage in lobbying may do so legally. However, under IRS rules, that activity may not be a "substantial part" of its activities. The problem with the stricture is that "substantial" in this context remains undefined, causing some groups to shun or curtail all potential lobbying activities rather than be subjected to a vague standard that might set off the IRS sensors.

If your nonprofit contemplates quite a bit of activity that could be dubbed "lobbying," another option is to notify the IRS that you wish to be covered under section 501(h) of the tax code. This election, available since 1976, allows qualified groups to spend up to $1 million on lobbying annually, based on a sliding scale tied to annual exempt expenditures.

You can find more information about how to safely navigate the lobbying laws in these publications:

Lobbying Restrictions May Limit Your Content, continued

- *Worry-Free Lobbying for Nonprofits,* a 12-page brochure that you can download free from the Alliance for Justice at www.afj.org.
- *The Nonprofit Lobbying Guide,* by Bob Smucker, a 158-page book that you can download free from the Center for Lobbying in the Public Interest at www.clpi.org.
- *The Lobbying and Advocacy Handbook for Nonprofit Organizations,* by Marcia Avner (Amherst Wilder Foundation).

Finally, relevant IRS Publications, available at www.irs.gov, include "1828 Tax Guide for Churches and Religious Organizations" and "557 Tax Exempt Status of Your Organization."

Editing

The manuscripts that writers turn in are rarely ever ready to go directly into a publication as written. Even good writers can suffer from being poorly organized in expressing themselves or failing to write concisely when they haven't done enough reporting. They typically need the sharp, red pen of an editor to excise the flab of words, to tease out a clear message from a rambling rough draft, or to ask tough questions and prod them to go reinterview a source.

Depending on your publication and the expertise of those involved, editors will operate in a number of different ways. This section explains what editors can strive to do for their publications to produce the most readable content for their readers.

The editor as stylist. If you've ever looked through one of those Hollywood celebrity tabloids, you know that many beautiful, famous people make amazingly poor fashion choices when they are allowed to dress themselves. That's why they have stylists and publicists who determine for them every aspect of their appearance: their makeup, wardrobe, and hairstyle, and sometimes even the company they keep. These stylists know what image the celebrity needs to project to the public to achieve star status—and they package and present the person accordingly.

Good editors do for their publications what these stylists do for their stars. They shape and promote a strong image and voice for their product. You'll notice that some of the most prominent consumer publications carry a strong brand identity among readers and even the wider public. It's almost as if these publications have a personality that readers recognize and embrace. For example, when you see *Rolling Stone*, you know the magazine will focus on the newest thing in popular music and what's hip and cool. When you see *Sports Illustrated*, you know you'll find coverage of famous athletes and jock culture.

> ## TIP
>
> **Get a publication stylist of your own.** If you're not sure of the right image to project, consult your publication's mission statement (see Chapter 1), or your editorial advisory board (see Chapter 4), or conduct surveys of readers, members, and the organization's staff (see Chapter 11).

Identity is important. It can dictate whether a reader chooses to subscribe to your publication or the one your competitor produces. Both publications might have similar content or run stories about similar topics but present or package them in drastically different ways.

Publications that successfully create an identity and attitude for themselves start by understanding who their target readership is, then carefully selecting and developing their content to engage that core group of people. Do some research to try to know your readers well—their basic demographics, whether they're urban or suburban, why they read your publication—so you will know how to position stories that are provocative to them in some way. (See Chapter 11 for more detail on how to better understand your readers.)

Your gauge of your readers' knowledge of your publication's subject area, the way you address them through content, the assumptions you make about what they think is good, and what makes them mad—all of that adds up to an image and attitude that your publication projects.

Your content could echo what readers have been observing about their lives: "Broke Paying for Gas? A Special Exposé of Which Oil Companies Are Getting Fat Off Your Wallet."

Or your content could pique their curiosity or prurient interests: "You Can't Be Good All the Time: Five Notable Greens and Their Biggest Environmental Sins."

Or your content could fulfill a need readers have: "How to Invest in Responsible Businesses—And Make Buckets of Money, Too."

Or your content could challenge your readers' conventional wisdom or push their buttons: "Why Going to the Gym Is Bad for Your Health."

EXAMPLE: Imagine there are two vegetarian living magazines. The first magazine is published by a vegetarian support network in Nebraska, the Beef State, for its members. Its intent is to help new or beginning vegetarians expand their culinary horizons and introduce them to foods, such as tofu, that they may not understand well or is not readily available in local supermarkets. It assumes the audience doesn't know much about tofu and needs a little education and coaxing to incorporate it into their diets.

The other publication is 12 years old and published for California vegetarians in urban areas including San Francisco, Los Angeles, and San Diego. This magazine's readers are already familiar with tofu and ready to use it in unusual ways, such as baking it or making it into desserts.

Now imagine that both publications ran stories about tofu. The first magazine titles its story "Tasty Tofu" and discusses how tofu is a good source of protein for vegetarians, how it's made, the history of tofu, and the different kinds of tofu, and offers several recipes and where you can buy it. The second magazine runs a story titled "Have Your Tofu—And Eat It, Too" and explains how readers can easily substitute tofu into many dessert recipes to incorporate protein and avoid all the weight gain and guilt that comes with traditional desserts. It then offers five dessert recipes using tofu as a main ingredient.

The second magazine's readership probably wouldn't have much interest in the first magazine's article on tofu. The treatment of the subject matter is too elementary for advanced vegetarians. It's unclear whether the first magazine's readership would like the second magazine's tofu article; it might appeal to them, but then again, making tofu desserts might sound a little too strange. Or they might have trouble finding the type of tofu needed in the areas they live.

The editor as word tinkerer. In addition to shaping ideas and stories, editors also handle the nuts and bolts of fixing, rearranging, and cleaning up copy so that paragraphs read in logical order, sentences flow smoothly, and you don't print "pubic" when you meant "public." There are as many ways to edit as there are editors, but here is an outline of the general process editors follow.

After a story is turned in, most editors start by reading it through once just to understand what the writer presented and get an overall first impression of it. If you are the editor, at this point you should be asking: Did the writer deliver what was assigned? Are there major gaps in the story or questions left unanswered that will confuse readers? Does the story fail to include a required response from somebody? If the answer to some of these questions is "yes," and the piece requires more major chunks of material, return to the writer and ask for the information or suggest a rewrite of certain portions.

Once you are satisfied that the reporting is done and you have all the material you need, the next step is to make sure the story is organized logically, clearly, and artfully for readers.

From this point on, you will probably be moving copy around, and the mechanics of this will differ. Some editors prefer to edit on a hard copy of the story and, if there's time, return a marked-up version to let the writer take a stab at making changes—and help teach the writer how to make the final copy more acceptable. Some editors do this electronically, highlighting copy, inserting comments, and asking questions in different colors or in brackets [] for the writer to fix or answer. And some simply return to the writer a new, edited version of the story to review for accuracy and approval. As an editor, you know you've done a good job when the writer can't quite tell what's been changed—just that it's better—because you have preserved the writer's thoughts and style.

After the story structure is finalized, most editors then take a final pass through it, moving through the story sentence by sentence to tighten language, clarify meaning, and fix grammatical mistakes and misspellings or typos.

Avoiding Legal Hot Water

Consider also whether any parts of the story could be libelous or potentially libelous.

You can find many legal definitions of libel for your particular state in journalism guidebooks or on Internet websites, such as www.medialaw.org, but a general definition of libel is a false statement published about a person that injures his or her reputation. If the person about whom the statement is made is a public figure—that is, a government official, a celebrity, or some other well-known person—then the publisher must have either known the statement was false and published it anyway or recklessly disregarded whether the statement was true or false. Generally, it is easier for a private individual to prove libel; he or she must show only that the publisher did not act "with due care" before publishing the damaging false statement.

If you wrongly print that someone has been convicted of a crime, you could be in trouble. If you wrongly print that someone is bankrupt, you could be in trouble.

So scour your stories, especially controversial ones, for possible libel. To decrease your liability, you might soften how something is phrased or triple check a fact.

Don't forget to check headlines, pull quotes, and photo captions. If you find something that might be potentially libelous, check with someone who can give some good advice, such as a media attorney, a professional journalism association, or a nonprofit such as the Media Law Resource Center, at www.medialaw.org.

RESOURCE

The *Elements of Style,* by William Strunk, Jr. and E.B. White (Allyn & Bacon), is a time-tested little volume for editors. It covers many principles of use and composition, such as omitting extraneous phrases or words—avoiding "most unique" or "Suffice it to say," and using active voice instead of passive, such as "The boulder crushed the hiker" instead of "The hiker got hit by the boulder."

If you have made extensive changes to a written piece since the writer last saw it or might have altered factual information, it is usually a good idea to show a copy to the writer one more time.

The final step before the story is handed off to be designed is proofreading, sometimes called copy editing. This is the stage where you make sure "Social Security" is capitalized, that you mean "consist of" instead of "comprised of," and that there are absolutely no mistakes in your publication. Readers catch errors and will develop a bad impression of your publication as unprofessional, sloppy, and untrustworthy if they find typos in your copy.

RESOURCE

You can find the correct spelling of most words in any good dictionary, but for tougher questions, consult the *Associated Press Stylebook and Briefing on Media Law* (Basic Books). It is widely considered the bible of copy editing and use among professional journalists.

Also keep track of your publication's particular usage quirks to create a "house stylebook." It is important to stay consistent from issue to issue and within each issue. If you combine commonly used words such as "health care" into "healthcare," stick to it and don't present it both ways. The failure to be consistent can make your publication look sloppy and amateurish.

If your publication is small and you do your own copy editing, try to recruit a coworker to check copy as well or consider paying an outside proofreader to give the final stories a look. Having another set of eyes review your publication provides a valuable quality control check. Often, another person can catch mistakes that you've glossed over because you've seen the copy one too many times.

RESOURCE
There are many good sources to consult for help with copy editing.

- *Garner's Modern American Usage*, by Bryan A. Garner (Oxford University Press): This book is "the authority on grammar, usage, and style." It says so right on the cover. Listing words and terms alphabetically, like a dictionary, this reference book explains the word's correct usage and, most important, provides an example sentence or two showing the word in proper context. A word is often listed with other words that are misused in its place.

- *The Chicago Manual of Style*, by the University of Chicago Press staff (University of Chicago Press): This is an essential reference guide for copy editors, covering grammar, punctuation, common misspellings, the proper presentation in print of names and terms, numbers and money, foreign languages, quotes and dialogue—the list goes on. For example, should the name of an opera be in quotes or italicized? (Italicized.)

- *Merriam-Webster's Collegiate Dictionary* (Merriam-Webster): Many people forget how useful the dictionary is for looking up the proper spelling, capitalization, and hyphenation of a word. When in doubt, check here first.

The editor as packager. It's not enough to create good stories and pictures that meet readers' needs and interests. Editors must know how to shape, present, and promote content by using headlines and other devices to grab readers' attention. Think about your audience and what forms of visual and text presentation are most likely to arouse their interest or convince them to look at your publication.

The one problem editors seem to share is that today's readers are increasingly pressed for time and their attention spans are short. The publication must be readable and look and feel friendly and digestible. Editors need to consider a variety of approaches and formats to draw in busy readers. Many readers will shy away from long blocks of text with no pictures or images. Similarly, photos or illustrations that are all essentially the same kind of picture—the same angle, same lighting, same composition, same mood—can quickly fail to hold readers' attention.

As a result, the better publications present content in smaller and quicker portions and break up the monotony of pages in hopes that even if readers do not have time to read an 800-word story, maybe they will look at a picture and read the related 200-word sidebar, a sidelight to the main story. If they like what they read, maybe they'll keep going.

Here's a rundown of some common presentation components and when and how to best use them.

Headlines are the titles that you use for stories. They are also sometimes called "banner" or "display" copy because they often run across the top of a story or page and are the first chance to tell the reader what the story's about. One of the best ways to sell a publication's content is through the skillful use of headlines. Unlike newspaper headlines, which tend to function as the shortest possible summary of a story, periodical publication headlines should convey the topic but pique reader interest by being clever or including a twist. As the examples below illustrate, editors often do this by writing headlines that are double entendres, have multiple layers of meaning, or involve word play.

CAUTION

When cleverness can dilute your search. While clever headlines are great for capturing reader interest, they are terrible for helping online users find what they are searching for on the Internet. A story about new wind energy technology titled "Winds of Change," for example, contains few of the key words Internet search engines would use to locate appropriate content. If you put your print content up on a website or publish online, be sure to rewrite the stories' "tags" to provide more-specific information than just the headline. (See Chapter 8 for more about search engines.)

Some publications, such as magazines, also use **deks**, illustrated below, which are one or two sentences appearing with the headline that summarizes the story's main themes and, especially if you've picked a headline that uses word play, "explains" the headline.

Magazines also use **cover lines**, which are headlines or copy that you use on the front cover to entice readers. They can be the same as the inside headline of the story, but it is often more effective to write a different cover line that is shorter and more dramatic. Be careful you don't frustrate readers by writing cover lines that completely lose their connection to the corresponding story inside. Some editors regrettably treat cover lines as an expanded table of contents instead of writing copy to sell what's inside. Numbers and rankings can work great in cover lines. Readers always want to know the "10 Best [fill in the blank]," the "Five Worst [fill in the blank]," the "Complete Guide to [whatever]." Don't promise what you don't deliver, though.

Here are some examples of headlines and deks that illustrate the principles described above.

For a profile of a young working student who has no health insurance. Young adults constitute one of the largest groups of uninsured in California and the United States.

Cover line: Putting a Face to the Uninsured

Headline: Access Denied

Dek: Chris Taylor is 25, is working, and hasn't seen a doctor in six years. Join the club.

For a feature about the difficulties of balancing life and work for parents who home school their children.

Cover line: Get a Life! How Homeschooling Sucks Your Time

Headline: Extra Homework

Dek: Now that Sandra Becker's full-time job is to home school her three children and still be a mother and wife, she rarely leaves the house. Surely this isn't what they meant by stay-at-home mom?

For a package of mini-profiles on prominent environmentalists and their biggest earth-unfriendly sins.

Cover line: 10 Famous Greens Confess Their Worst Environmental Sins

Headline: Caught Green-handed!

Dek: Even the best of environmentalists have wasteful habits and secrets. How do you stack up?

As you can see, the cover lines, headlines, and deks are written to stir up reader curiosity and emotions. They sometimes ask probing questions of the reader. They don't tell everything about the story, just enough to get readers asking, "Hmm, wonder what that's about?" or "Gee, I need to know about that."

Writing arresting banner copy can take a group brainstorming effort, so enlist all the help you can get. You might try gathering staff in a heads and deks meeting and have a big word play session. Ideally, you should distribute final drafts of the stories and require that staff read them before convening, so that everybody fully understands the angle and tone of the article and can offer fitting suggestions. Generating banner copy together can be fun and rewarding, but be careful not to get mired in group indecision and writing bland headlines "by committee."

In publications with a table of contents, **TOC lines** are the short summaries that appear next to the article listings on that page. For readers who instinctively turn to the table of contents to browse a publication, TOC lines are critical. For example, a story about 10 famous environmental activists and their biggest transgressions could read: "It's hard for even the best of us to be green all of the time. We teased the worst earth-unfriendly habits out of 10 notable environmentalists."

TIP

Appealing to your readers. The biggest problem that most editors and publication staff have in writing this kind of copy is remembering to pitch content from the reader's perspective. Often your audience wants to read things that they think will make them more beautiful, smarter, richer, funnier, or happier. That often involves tapping into your readers' emotions, their hopes, fears, joys, worries, or anger.

Sidebars contain content that is tangential but related to the main story and often appear as a box or inset. They are great for highlighting content that deserves some special attention. They are also useful for sectioning off content that needs to be told but doesn't seem to fit in anywhere or would interrupt the flow of the main story.

EXAMPLE: If you are running a story about the county fair, you could run sidebars about the quirkiest contests, such as who can eat the most Spam or who grew the biggest tomato.

Lists are a kind of sidebar and can summarize or build on the story's main points in a concise and memorable way. Some classic ones are lists of "Dos and Don'ts", or "In and Out." But you can run lists of nearly anything. Run a list of what the reader can do to help fix the problem, if it's a story meant to inspire activism, or list the top 10 culprits, if it's a story about major corporations that incorporate offshore to avoid paying taxes.

Resource boxes often appear at the end of a story and point readers to where to find more information on a topic. They can contain website addresses, books and other publications on the topic, or lists of organizations.

EXAMPLE: If you ran a story about the rise of asthma among children in low-income communities, you could list websites where readers can learn more or track asthma statistics, associations and support groups to join, or local medical clinics that offer discounted asthma care.

Pull quotes are snippets from the main story that are provocative or attention-grabbing in some way and pull readers into the story. Good pull quotes will make readers think, "Wait, did someone really say that?" or "What are they talking about here? I have to find out."

EXAMPLE: In a story about one city's effort to encourage residents to take transit by forbidding cars downtown, it would be better to pick a quote such as: "People hated it at first because they've forgotten how to walk. But eventually they come around. Some people love it so much that they've moved downtown," instead of: "It was difficult for people to adjust at first, but we've made progress."

Adding Art to the Package

The best editors think ahead to how art and graphics will complement the words. Since editors are most familiar with the content they've been shaping, many help signal essential information about it to the art director or designer who will later acquire artwork and configure the page. They do so in a succinct "art memo," similar to the sample below. (See Chapter 6 for a complete description of the design process.)

CD-ROM

A template for an art memo, which you can tailor to your needs, is available on the CD-ROM included with this book.

Sample Art Edit Memo

Publication: *Pinnacle*, the alumni magazine of Arch University

Issue: March/April 20XX

Editor: Leslie Lee

Writer: Angela Taylor, [contact info]

Headline: Corporate Branding

Dek: Sports director Eugene Hays can get Arch University's stadium rebuilt practically for free. So why is half the campus calling him a sell out?

Synopsis of story: Arch University is in dire need of seismically retrofitting its sports stadium, Elysian Fields, but hasn't been able to raise the funds. Athletic director Eugene Hayes has caused a huge uproar on campus by persuading a major pharmaceutical company to pay for virtually all of the construction in exchange for the right to rename the facility Narcophlage Arena. The campus is deeply divided, with some thinking that the name is not as important as getting the stadium rebuilt and others thinking that this kind of corporate influence is not worth the money. The board of trustees is set to vote on the proposal in mid April.

Story angle: The article profiles Hayes and spotlights his controversial efforts to rebuild the stadium in exchange for naming rights. Hayes is an unlikely bad guy. Traditionally beloved by the school, Hayes had always been an opponent of corporate sponsorship, protesting advertising in the stadium and on team uniforms. But in this case, he decided there was no other way the stadium would get rebuilt and that the benefits of a strong sports program outweighed the negatives.

Key themes/concepts: Public good versus private gain. Selling out. Corporate influence. Reluctant bad guy.

Main subjects and contact info:

Eugene Hayes, sports director, (XXX) XXX-XXXX

Max Emerson, president of the board of trustees, memerson@arch.edu

Theresa Huang, president of the student body, (XXX) XXX-XXXX

Steven Schlosberg, football team quarterback and captain, (XXX) XXX-XXXX

Marian Walters, CEO of Narcophlage Corporation, m_walters@narcophlage.com

Brent Scott, business school professor, (XXX) XXX-XXXX, bscott@arch.edu

Editor's suggestions and comments: Writer says Hayes is pretty photogenic and expressive.

Writing for the Web

Most organizations post their magazine or newsletter articles on their websites. And some organizations also write Web-only material that appears exclusively on a website, never in print.

In both instances, writers should be encouraged to accommodate the Web writing standards that have begun to surface in recent years. Edit the printed articles so that they're easier to read online, for example. And train your website writers to follow these style standards as much as possible when creating new material for your site. If you do, readers are far more likely to benefit from the content you provide to them and to return for more.

Most writers and editors got their basic training in the world of print. They are habitually writing for that medium rather than the Internet, and you may have to retrain some folks to write in a more Web-friendly style.

Here are a few suggestions about writing and editing habits that are proving effective on websites.

Help readers skim. Newspapers always put the most important information in the first paragraphs of an article and summarize the main points early on so that readers can quickly decide whether or not to keep reading all the way to the end of the article. Online, you can take the practice a step further by putting less-important details on a different page and linking to them rather than adding clutter to the main article. Deeply interested readers can follow the links, while others can skim the story and move on.

Be concise. Because computer screen resolution is not as sharp as print on paper, people tend to read up to 25% more slowly on computer screens than they can read from a printed page. You can speed up the website reading experience for people by removing words that are not essential to your story before you post it online. For example, if the print version of a newsletter article is 500 words long, try editing the Web version down by half, and try keeping most sentences below 20 words.

Break up long paragraphs. Always a turn-off for the eyes, a solid block of text is even harder to read on a screen than on paper. Before posting to a website, cut the length of paragraphs and use lots of subtitles to help readers find their way through the article.

Identify links. Online publications often combine sidebar and graphic elements with links contained within, at the top or bottom of, or at the sides of stories that can immediately jump the viewer to additional, detailed information or related articles on the topic. Besides other articles and graphics, websites often link to photo slideshows, video- or audio-casts, and other useful websites. Make sure to tell readers what they will find behind a link and why they should go there. For example, instead of "Next page," use a link that says "More energy-saving ideas."

Use searchable terms. Search is one of the major distinctions between print and online writing. A reader who opens up your newsletter can scan all the pages to see what it's about. But many people will find themselves reading one of your online articles after using a search engine. And metaphors are confusing to search engines. Google can't tell if your "Cutting Red Tape" article is about sewing or politics. For that reason, many editors rename articles that are moving from print to the Web and add technical markings (called "meta tags") that help search engines find it. (Chapter 8 contains detailed information about working with search engines.)

RESOURCE

You can find additional advice about tailoring writing to website audiences in a number of books and Web resources, including those described here:

- *Hot Text: Web Writing that Works,* by Jonathan Price and Lisa Price (New Riders Press): Not the most groundbreaking book, but one that covers all the bases, including CMS, tagging, and the other searchability issues described in this chapter.

- "The Web Content Style Guide," by Gerry McGovern, is an online source at www.gerrymcgovern.com/guide_write_01.htm: McGovern is a Web content consultant and author of a book by the same name as this article. The book includes a sample style guide for websites. The ten-part article includes highlights and also serves as an example of excellent online writing.

- "Writing for the Web," an online article by Daniel Will-Harris, can be found at www.efuse.com/Design/web_writing_basics.html: eFuse. com is a website about building websites, created by a professional typeface designer who is also a freelance writer. This short article covers both writing style and formatting issues.

- *Writing for the Web,* by Crawford Kilian (Self-Counsel Writing): This 140-page book is especially useful for translating print content to websites by contrasting the reader's response to the different mediums. The author also has a blog about the subject at http://crofsblogs.typepad.com.

Effective Email Campaigns and Newsletters

Writing effective emails is a greater challenge than composing Web pages or print articles because your email messages must compete with so many other items in a reader's mailbox.

Experts offer the following tips.

Remember why you're writing. Email is an action-oriented format, and email campaigns are usually designed to stimulate readers to make a donation, renew a membership, visit a website, or sign up for an event. Consider why you're sending each message and focus 100% of your content on that purpose, no distractions.

Consider the subject line. People scan the subject line to determine whether or not to open a message, and one could argue that there is no more critical part of the message than the subject line. Never use exclamation marks, words, or other symbols in a subject line that might trigger a reader's spam filter, such as "sex" or "free." And always use a few compelling words that convey your purpose and invite a reader into the body of the message, such as "Registration Deadline Approaches" or "Join Us on March 23."

Keep the message focused. Use call-to-action phrases and include steps a reader can take immediately, such as links and phone numbers. Short sentences and paragraphs also help readers stay focused on the purpose of your message and make an email easier to read graphically. (Chapter 6 includes more tips about design formats that work best for emails.)

Designing Print Publications and Websites

A magazine, newsletter, or website with a great design not only grabs and maintains reader interest but, over the long term, helps establish its identity, personality, credibility, and professionalism. Bad design makes readers stop reading or, even worse, repels readers and prevents them from even cracking open your publication or giving it more than a moment's glance when it comes to their inboxes. It can also make you appear amateurish or outdated in the way you handle the subject matter.

By the end of this chapter, however, you'll be well versed with what works in Web and print publication design, the design process, how to collaborate with design professionals, and how to successfully design your publication on what's usually a tight nonprofit budget.

Design Terms Decoded

As in many other fields of work, people who design publications, usually called graphic designers, often throw around a lingo all their own when talking about their work. It will be helpful to become acquainted with some basic terminology so that you can break through this language barrier. You will likely encounter dozens of unfamiliar terms as you continue to work with graphic designers, but the ones below should provide you with a basic working vocabulary.

- **Art** refers to all images other than words, including photographs, illustrations, paintings, icons, and even text that's set in a distinctive way so that it functions as a visual element that breaks up the page.
- **Bleeds** are any ink that's printed off the edge of a page and is cut off when the pages are trimmed after printing. When ink prints off all four sides of the page, it's called a full bleed.
- **Copy or text** are used interchangeably and refer to the written words in publications. You might hear designers say that "the copy is running long and needs to be cut." They simply mean there are too

Design Terms Decoded, continued

many words to fit in the space or to live easily in the design of a print or Web page.

- **Cropping** is when parts of an image, usually a photo, are chopped off. A designer may choose to crop a photo because part of the image is irrelevant or not print-worthy or because he or she wants to focus in on a subject.
- **Folio** refers to the words and numbers, usually at the bottom of the page but sometimes in other unusual locations, that identify the publication title and page numbers.
- **Layout** is how all text and art elements are positioned on the page. When designers gather and arrange copy and art, they are creating layouts or "laying out" the pages.
- **Spread** in a print publication refers to two pages facing each other.

While some of these terms apply to designing both print and Web publications, a number of additional terms are unique to websites.

- **Animation** refers to an image on the screen that changes over time, whether it's a sequence showing waves rolling into shore for an aquatic preservation nonprofit's website or a rolling ticker showing our national deficit.
- **Banners** are visual elements, usually rectangular in shape, that appear in prominent positions along the top, bottom, or right and left sides of the screen. Banners are usually Internet advertisements but can be used for other purposes, too.
- **Home page** is the first page that appears when you go to a particular website. This is the equivalent of a print publication's cover and is the first impression your website will make on readers.
- **Navigation bars** are groupings of graphic or text buttons that visitors to a website can click to link to other pages within the same website. They indicate how the website is organized and help people quickly move from section to section of the website.
- **Rollovers** or **mouseovers** are elements on a screen that change when users move a cursor over a particular section of the screen.

The Function of Design

All by itself, the written word is pretty hard to read. Plain copy on a printed or website page looks like big gray blocks to the scanning eye. Designers arrange text on printed or website pages into columns or boxes and add graphic elements such as bold headlines to help people read it. And it's the visual presentation that will keep readers interested: the photographs, illustrations, drawings—and the composition, balance, and interplay of text and art.

Navigation is another essential function of design for both print and Web publications. Designers help people find the way through a long article by adding headlines, subheads, and page numbers. Otherwise, readers will stumble when the writer shifts gears to a new topic. And many of them will choose to bail when they hit a stumbling point.

Websites present the greatest challenge when it comes to helping readers navigate through text because they lack the physical cues people rely on in printed publications. A reader can see two 8.5-x-11-inch pages of a newsletter article at one time, but only about a computer screen's worth of the same article on a website. The magazine or newsletter designer can include a lot of graphic elements and navigation cues on a two-page article spread that will not be visible on a website.

Another function of design is that it must meet readers' expectations. Websites generally conform to an unwritten standard presentation format these days. The publisher's identity is displayed near the top, navigation elements appear in a column or bar that's easy to find, and pages are generally about the same size, fitting within the common dimensions of computer screens. Newsletters and magazines also have unspoken design standards. Following those norms generally helps to convey a publisher's professionalism to readers—and keeps the content from seeming jumbled and confusing.

These design conventions have also been widely adopted because they work so well at transforming grey blocks of type into a satisfying reading experience. But novice designers often violate the standard practices by adding borders, colors, or bold letters to "liven up" what they think looks dull. They might use three different sizes of text in a headline in the effort to make it look "different." They might plop a photo down in the corner of a page because they feel the page looks plain without it.

Publication design is both more subtle and complicated than that; it is about communicating meaning to the reader. The overarching goals of publication graphic design are to grab readers' attention, pull them into the content, help and encourage them to move through the publication, and make the reading experience enjoyable. Inserting a number of different colors or art elements in a haphazard way is like putting barriers across a hiking trail. Rather than helping readers absorb information, these elements are likely to confuse or annoy them. And when that happens, the reader stops reading.

Good designers manipulate art and text to create something that is more than just the sum of various parts. As one experienced designer puts it: "I try to give the reader something with the art that you can't get with words. That way, the art serves an editorial function and it keeps it from just being decoration." In other words, the visuals should also help tell the story. Art and text work together; take away one element, and the whole package falls short.

Researchers have devoted many studies to scrutinizing how readers read. But the basics are these: Readers rarely consume a magazine or newsletter as they would a novel or other book, by starting at the first page and reading through consecutive pages. Holding the publication in their hands, readers quickly browse through the pages, scanning for something that catches their attention. They might flip from the front or from the back.

Another way readers typically approach a publication is by following the pull of some arresting line or photo on the cover and quickly paging inside for that specific content. (See "Covers and Home Pages," below, for details on cover design.) They might also quickly thumb through the front, looking for the table of contents and then jumping somewhere deeper into the publication. When readers do stop at a page or spread, they scan from top left to top right before working their way down.

The critical information to absorb from all this analysis is that since a print publication is a three-dimensional object that readers skim quickly, the areas of the pages they actually see are the outer upper left and outer upper right of each spread. The areas closer to the center of the page remain hidden from view until the reader stops for some reason.

Internet readers scan more unpredictably, from top left to right, then down or to whatever catches their eye on the screen. Users now automatically seek out buttons or links that help them get exactly where they want to go, as when looking for an address or a staff contact. Some use a search box to quickly locate answers or information.

The point is to understand how readers read—and design publications to take advantage of these patterns and to work with, not against, them.

RESOURCE

There are a number of books that offer good help and advice on editorial design:

- *Editing by Design: For Designers, Art Directors, and Editors—The Classic Guide to Winning Readers*, by Jan V. White (Allworth Press). One of the reference bibles of the principles behind solid editorial design. It covers everything from fonts, to appropriate line spacing, to how to evoke different reactions from readers through page layouts. Includes many visual examples of everything, often drawn in the author's whimsical style.

- *Learning Web Design: A Beginner's Guide to HTML, Graphics, and Beyond*, by Jennifer Niederst (O'Reilly Media). Niederst leads Web design virgins step by step through the entire process, from explaining what the Internet is, to editing Web graphics, to purchasing server space and getting files uploaded. For those who want to delve further, look up another of her books, *Web Design in a Nutshell: A Desktop Quick Reference* (O'Reilly Media).

- *Magazine Design That Works: Secrets for Successful Magazine Design*, by Stacey King (Rockport Publishers). A good overview book with many examples of successful magazine design; not much technical information about creating layouts.

- *The Non-Designer's Design Book*, by Robin Williams (Peachpit Press). A practical, nuts-and-bolts guide to good editorial and graphic design for people with no design background. It covers four basic design principles and helps you recognize why something is badly or well designed. Includes a large section on typography.
- *The Non-Designer's Web Book*, by Robin Williams and John Tollett (Peachpit Press). A just-the-basics book for someone who doesn't know the first thing about designing a website. Even if you'll be outsourcing the job, this primer on the process will help you understand the process and know how to assess a good design.
- *Professional Web Site Design From Start to Finish*, by Anne-Marie Concepcion (How Design Books). While it leaves the details of writing HTML to other volumes, this simply written book delivers all the other important aspects of Web design useful to nonprofit publishers, such as setting site goals, deciding the site architecture, managing the process, trafficking files, subcontracting, and analyzing Web log data.
- *Surprise Me: Editorial Design*, by Horst Moser (Mark Batty Publisher). A comprehensive guide to editorial design featuring many examples.

Your Publication's Design

As discussed below, publication design encompasses both the overall look and feel of the publication and also how individual stories are presented. Both are critical for communicating with readers.

A design template captures all of your individual decisions about type fonts, colors, and page formats into one place so that you don't have to revisit all of those decisions for each new article. (See "Creating a Design Grid," below, for a complete explanation.)

The Overall Look and Feel

The look and feel of your publication—the typefaces, use of color, kinds of photos, and styles of illustration—all combine to give readers their first general impression of it. Just as you will size up someone you're meeting for the first time by observing the person's choice of dress, hair style, body posture, and manner of speaking, so will readers decide whether your publication interests them.

The overall look and feel of your publication is expressed through everything from the logo on the cover or home page to the type you use to how you differentiate various sections of your publications yet tie them together so that it's apparent they're all part of the whole.

Establishing Personality

First, consider the publication's editorial mission and how you want to translate that to your publication's visual personality. (See Chapter 1 for details on establishing a mission.)

To understand a publication's personality, go to the news stand and browse a while, or go online and click through several websites. (The Internet Public Library's Reading Room, at www.ipl.org, is a good launch point for browsing online.) Does that computer gaming magazine project the same image as that women's fitness magazine? What assumptions do you think the editors of that hot rod magazine are making about their readers versus the editors of that alternative medicine publication? What impression do you get from that website for lovers of the Old West compared to one for lovers of Goth culture? By the way they look and feel, publications convey a personality.

TIP

So you want to redesign. Redesigns of publications are different than new designs. Readers are familiar with the old design and therefore have certain expectations of how they'll experience the publication. Redesigns must strike a balance between updating and freshening the publication's look while maintaining some continuity with what came before. Redesigns involve thinking about what you want to keep and what to discard. The best redesigns present themselves as reincarnations of the old publications instead of completely new publications.

Taking the Personality Test

Every publication should have a distinct personality that it cultivates and strives to project to readers. Unlike a publication for the general public, such as a daily newspaper, nonprofits often cater to a specific, like-minded readership with certain characteristics and sensibilities that they expect to see reflected by the group's publication.

Most legal journals, for example, strive to project a serious and authoritative image to readers. These readers may rely on the journal to provide information that could very well be the last word—the law—on a subject. It may be printed on heavy stock paper, use traditional fonts, and adopt a more linear layout to appear more stately, conservative, and lasting. It would not likely use a rainbow of colors or whimsical illustrations or fonts in its design.

National Geographic, an iconic publication, does a good job of projecting through its design an earnest, scholarly, intellectually curious personality that's in keeping with the Society's mission of "increasing and diffusing geographic knowledge." It is known for its photography of people and cultures and wonderfully detailed maps and information graphics. The fonts are traditional. The layouts tend to be more understated and elegant, relying on the spectacular photography to draw the reader.

A popular newsletter called *Bottom Line* projects its image as a trusted friend who has life figured out and can provide all kinds of inside advice on money, family, and health for busy readers. Instead of using photos that readers may not identify with, it uses a few illustrations and sometimes cartoons to add visual interest. The layout is straightforward and organized. Stories state what they have to offer in clear headlines and are easy to read in short bites, with few or no jumps within a story.

The online magazine *Slate* provides analysis and commentary on politics, news, and cultures. It projects a sophisticated, worldly, savvy image by using muted, understated colors; simple fonts; and one dominant graphic for each page, and staying relatively clean and free of clutter, with more white space than many online publications allow.

Compare that to the gossip news blog "Drudge Report," which is a big, haphazard mishmash of links and photos. By treating almost all content the same, it feeds the sense that there are connections among everything and many bits of information to be gleaned in the news "haystack."

Choosing Typefaces and Fonts

Once the visual personality is established, most publication designers turn to finding a title logo and inside display and text typefaces to reflect it.

The style of type you choose sets a powerful tone for the entire publication. Serif type—the styles with the little jags and embellishments on the tips of letters—are typically more traditional, more suitable for publications catering to a scholarly or professional audience. Sans serif type is generally considered to look more modern and may be a good choice for publications dealing, for example, with counterculture topics, technology, or high design. However, as the number of typefaces grows, these distinctions are less relevant. Today, you can find post-modern serif type that's anything but conservative.

Typefaces are the names given to sets, or families, of fonts. A publication can use just two typefaces, but within each are many different fonts. For example, within one typeface can be different fonts for bold, italic, thick, thin, or condensed versions.

Look at a number of publications that use different typefaces. You'll quickly see that different ones can set totally different moods and conjure up different connotations for the reader.

The logo font, the one used for the title of your publication, must be able to stand by itself, because readers are not only reading the title but also seeing the logo as an art element—much as the Coca-Cola logo reads "Coca-Cola," but has evolved to the point where it mainly serves as a symbol for the entire brand. People no longer need to read the actual words or letters to recognize what it is.

Fonts used for the main text of the publication should be easy to read. They may be the same as the logo font, but need not be. Many publications stick with classic, tried-and-true fonts such as Times New Roman, Bookman, and Franklin Gothic because they have established histories of being easy to read.

Depending on how large your publication is, you might use additional fonts for advertising or other sections. Every publication is different, but the general rule is to use no more than two or three typefaces, encompassing six or seven fonts, throughout the publication. Too many and it will have a disturbingly disjointed feeling.

RESOURCE

If you love to play with words, chances are you'll think fonts are fun, too. To get a better idea of how they set a style and tone, experiment with them on your computer by typing in a sentence and setting it in many different fonts and sizes. Below are also some websites of type developers and publishers to help you explore the universe of type:

- www.emigre.com
- www.houseind.com/house.php
- www.shiftype.com
- www.t26.com/fonts.php, and
- www.typography.com.

Selecting Colors

In fashioning a design for your publication or website, you will also need to decide on a color palette: the group of colors that also helps set the tone for the publication and maintain visual consistency. Some publications use many colors effectively, some use varying tones of one color. And, depending on your publishing budget, some may use only one color: black.

Some print publications use spot color, which is when the press lays down premixed ink in a specific color and you pay for each color you use. This method works well if you are using at most a couple of colors. Other print publications use the more expensive process color, which is when the press lays down little dots of blue, magenta, yellow, and black ink to recreate the entire spectrum of color. This method is used by publications that publish full-color photographs and need the entire range of color. (See Chapter 7 for a complete discussion of using and choosing color in print publications.)

Online publications, because they are viewed on computer monitors, use yet a different way to represent color, called RGB. In this method, pixels of red, green, and blue are combined to display color. When designing for anything seen on a monitor, you must stick to the 216 colors in the Web-safe color palette.

Colors can help convey the personality of your publication. Look at a color wheel to become familiar with the basic colors: the primary colors are blue, red, and yellow; the secondary colors that result from mixing the primaries are purple, orange, and green. In addition, adding various amounts of white and black can change the shade of each of the colors.

Vibrant primary or secondary colors can appear youthful and exuberant, but intense: Think of a rainbow or children's toys. Colors that stick to various shades of one main color are understated and can appear elegant and soothing, but more formal: Think of a flower arrangement in differing shades of red. Colors that appear opposite each other on the color wheel, such as blue and orange or red and green, stand out sharply next to one another and are bold, calling for attention. You'll notice that sports teams often use these pairings of color. Colors that appear next to one another on the color wheel convey a harmonious feeling when used together. Strategic use of white, black, grey, and brown with the basic colors can produce even more effects.

> **CAUTION**
>
> **When money may be an object.** Beware that in print publications using spot color, adding colors costs money, so your palette may constricted by how much you can afford to spend on that front. If you find you need more than two or three colors, consider switching to process color. (See Chapter 7 for details on this.)

Some color combinations evoke a certain time period, which can both help or hurt your publication. If your publication's subject matter concerns a fixed era, such as a newsletter devoted to living the tenets of the Arts and Crafts movement today, using the mellow colors associated with that time can help you more quickly strike the right mood and tone with readers. On the other hand, if your publication is about cutting-edge technology but uses color pairings from the 1990s, readers may well get the impression that your content is stuck there, too. For example, aqua and salmon often remind people of the 1930s Art Deco era and can connote a retro feeling. Black, white, red, and yellow were popular combinations during the early 1970s and can conjure up a mod mood.

And finally, some color combinations evoke a certain setting by echoing the colors found there. For example, using only colors that appear in nature, such as muted shades of green, brown, and blue, can call to mind an earthy feeling and may be appropriate for a publication that focuses on the environment.

Individual Page Layouts

The individual layout component of design is geared toward getting readers interested in particular articles. A headline and how it looks, the accompanying photos or illustration, the placement of copy and art, and the amount of blank space on the page are all intended to draw the reader into reading further.

And while the purpose of establishing an overall design is usually to create a consistent visual framework for readers that reflects the publication's identity, the purpose of designing its individual pages is often to surprise them.

The main goals in designing individual page layouts are to grab readers' attention, quickly give them a sense of what the content is about, convince them to continue reading, and then help them read and maintain interest through the rest of the content. You can do this by creatively but thoughtfully arranging the art in layouts.

"Art" in this context includes photographs, illustrations, charts, drawings, diagrams, and some of the text that appears in a page layout. Typically, dramatic, large photos or illustrations are used as opening art for articles. Once you move into the inside of the story, the artwork becomes more concerned with factual representation about what's happening in the story, whether it's showing photos of people quoted or places events took place or a bar graph to impart statistical information.

Think about how readers read, as described earlier in this chapter, when using art and designing page layouts. There are no hard-and-fast rules, but there are some general principles to follow.

First, put your best art where readers are most likely to see it: in the outer left and outer right sections. Concentrate your most attention-grabbing material in these spaces. Don't hide good photos near the center of the page or force readers to scroll down to find them; place them higher and toward the outside edges. Same goes for headlines, illustrations, and other eye-catching art elements. If all readers see is columns of gray text when they glance at your publication, nothing will make them stop and read.

Conversely, put your weak but necessary art near the spine or down toward the bottom, where it can do its job but doesn't take up valuable real estate that could be used to draw readers. Don't put art in places that will force the reader's eye to jump too far to get to the next line of the story. This is not only tiring, but confusing—and will often cause readers to stop reading.

Also, use a good piece of art as large as you can—and don't try to stretch a bad piece of art into something it can't be. For example, if you have a high-quality photo that captures the subject or point of the article perfectly, don't waste the image as a small photo placed in the middle of the story. Use it large and place it at the beginning of the story. If you have a poor-quality snapshot of your subject, but that's the only photo you have to work with, don't try to enlarge it beyond its technical parameters because you feel the beginning of the story needs a large photo. The snapshot will only turn out grainy and of poor quality. Best to run photos at a size that will retain their clarity and work on other ways to grab readers' attention, such as using a catchy or cleverly set headline.

Finally, have a good reason for using a particular piece of art. The best photos or illustrations sum up the point or message of a story at one glance—and it may take some thought and effort to find or conceive of one that does the job. Images that don't elicit the right mood or conclusion from readers work at cross purposes to getting readers interested and invested in reading the story.

"The most common mistake people make when doing editorial illustration is they show pictures of the nouns," says one publication designer. "They'll run pictures of the things or objects that are mentioned in the story or generally associated with the story subject. For example, in a story about medicine, they'll show a picture of a stethoscope or x-ray, even if the story is, say, about a movement among doctors to pay more attention to the mental health of a patient as part of giving medical treatment. A story is conveyed in the verbs."

Dos and Don'ts for Page Layouts

While there are no hard-and-fast rules for layouts, below are some general guidelines for what to follow and what to avoid.

DO . . .

- Be consistent within the publication and throughout various productions of it.
- Have a reason for what you are doing.
- Think about the readers and how a particular look and feel will resonate with them.
- Spend your money wisely on a few pieces of good art, rather than several pieces of bad art.
- Take the time to write descriptive photo captions that add something extra.
- Leave ample white space to give readers' eyes a rest.

DON'T . . .

- Make every page look too different.
- Use a bad piece of art just to have a piece of art.
- Make the reader struggle to find the next line of the story.
- Pack everything in too tightly.

Email Campaigns and Newsletters

Even though email is easy to send, designing email campaigns correctly can be more difficult that designing for print. That's because a reader's email program can modify how the message appears to the reader before it's opened. And people are using email programs that don't interpret design formatting correctly. For example, some programs do not automatically wrap long lines of text to fit inside a small message window, which forces readers to use a horizontal scroll bar to read long sentences. Most people are willing to scroll down a page, but not through a single sentence.

These simple formatting rules will help ensure that readers see your emails the way you intended them to be seen.

- **Keep it short.** Use fewer than 70 characters in a single line, so that people don't have to scroll through long lines. There should be no more than 25 lines of text in a single message, and only two or three sentences in each paragraph.

- **Plain text.** Older email programs can misread HTML coding, which means that your links might not work, formatted text doesn't read properly, and images don't translate. And sometimes readers set their email programs to read only plain text, even though their email program is capable of reading HTML, to eliminate spam and viruses. For that reason, plain text is always the best option for emails.

- **No images.** Readers can also program their email software to suppress images, and many people take this step. Don't put critical information into an image file, such as a chart or logo, without also including a plain text version of it, because a reader's email program might strip out the graphic.

RESOURCE

Constant Contact is an email broadcasting and formatting service that provides tips for writing and formatting emails in a Learning Center at the website www.constantcontact.com/learning-center. Chapter 9 covers other vendors like this one, and you can check with any email management service for up-to-date tips about formats that are working effectively in their client's email campaigns.

Covers and Home Pages

Covers on newsletters and magazines and home pages of websites are easily the most important page of the entire publication.

If whatever image and text you put on your cover doesn't compel viewers to pick up the publication and open it, all that wonderful content and innovative page design on the inside won't matter a whit, because they'll never see it.

Magazines

Take a look at the covers of different magazines and concentrate on the ones that capture your attention visually.

Of course, no formula exists for how to structure the perfect cover, but there are general principles to keep in mind. One striking image that provides a strong focal point, whether it's a photo or illustration, is usually preferable to a collage of many images. A strong or dramatic color works well, but fads and fashion also factor in the mix. For example, yellow was recently considered the cover color du jour; covers that featured yellow prominently supposedly flew off the newsstands. The blue-green color of teal was trendy in the late 80s and used widely but may appear dated now—at least until it comes back in vogue.

Most people are drawn to faces of other people they find intriguing or photos of landscapes or objects that appear "exotic" in some way. People respond to covers depicting things they desire—whether it's sex, a fancy sports car, or a living room filled with beautiful, expensive furniture. People are also enticed by covers that stand out in the crowd of competing covers. And humor sometimes works well but can be a gamble if your joke falls flat. For some publications, such as an association of independent funeral homes, humor may never be a good fit.

Once you've got people looking at your cover, the cover lines—the words summarizing the main stories inside—had better do a good job of luring them to open the publication. The cover image will hopefully have prompted them to pick up your publication, but cover lines can provide additional editorial ammunition to deliver a one-two punch that convinces them to start paging through or looking for an article that piqued their curiosity. (See Chapter 5 for a discussion of writing effective cover lines.)

Cover lines advertise and promote the inside content to readers in such a way that they feel they're missing out on something important if they don't find out what the story's about. Cliffhanger cover lines are good—luring readers inside to find out what happens. Cover lines that purport to reveal "The 10 Best (or Worst)" of something or "The Complete Guide to" anything usually get attention. Cover lines that claim to share a secret are also popular with many readers.

> **TIP**
> **Don't skimp on cover art.** If you have a limited art budget, spend the majority of it on the cover image. And when you commission a photograph or illustration from an artist, give exact specifications about what you'll need. Cover art usually needs to be a vertical photo or illustration. You must leave room for the logo, cover lines, and perhaps also the address label and bar code if those ultimately appear on your cover.

Newsletters

Because newsletter front pages typically do not contain one dominant image, they are not as dependent on featuring a striking, high-quality piece of artwork or photo—though of course, all publications benefit from good graphics.

For newsletters, a large, eye-catching title logo or masthead; a clean and organized layout; one good piece of art; and headlines that promise the reader valuable information are often enough. Depending on the size of your newsletter, a quickly digestible table of contents somewhere on page one also helps bring people inside. If your headlines are all different sizes, the columns don't align with one another, and your title logo is in tiny 8-point type, you're telling the reader your content isn't worth reading.

RESOURCE

There are a number of good books you can turn to for more guidance in designing newsletters.

- *Design It Yourself Newsletters: A Step-By-Step Guide*, by Chuck Green (Rockport Publishers): The author uses simple explanations of the newsletter design process and offers more than a dozen templates of different design styles so that readers don't have to start from scratch.

- *Newsletter Design: A Step-by-Step Guide to Creative Publications*, by Edward Hamilton (Wiley): Walks readers through every step of the process in designing a newsletter. Offers standard styles and lots of tips, but some complain that the examples look dated since it was first published in 1995.

- *Producing a First-Class Newsletter: A Guide to Planning, Writing, Editing, Designing, Photography, Production, and Printing*, by Barbara A. Fanson (Self-Counsel Press): Fanson takes readers through every stage of the process in creating a newsletter, from how to pick the right title to writing catchy headlines to designing on a grid.

- *Publication Design Workbook: A Real-World Guide to Designing Magazines, Newspapers, and Newsletters*, Timothy Samara (Rockport Publishers): The strong suit of this book is the wealth of real-world examples it provides, but it doesn't stand out as the best introductory book. It is best paired with another book that covers the basics.

Website Home Pages

Home pages are somewhat different from magazine covers or newsletter page ones, because viewers of home pages generally seek them out by clicking on your link or typing in the URL of your website.

There are many different opinions about what makes a good home page, but the best designers start out by clearly understanding the website's purpose. The home page acts as an entryway to all other parts of your site, so it should quickly deliver what users want. Ask yourself why users go to your site. Is it to chat in online forums with other readers? To find articles from past issues that caught their attention and forward them by email to friends and family? What does your publication hope to achieve through the home page? To reinforce your publication and nonprofit's image? To increase subscriptions? The answers to those questions will likely influence how much real estate you devote on your home page to each function, where that will be, and how much emphasis to give to it.

Most of the best website home pages just show some common sense. Your publication's name and logo should be a decent size and in a logical location. Don't make home pages wider than the standard 800 x 600 pixel window size, or readers will be irritated at having to scroll horizontally to read content off the screen. Or worse, they won't be able to find navigation bars or the scroll bar.

Put all your best content, important links, and images in the "upper" area of the home page that users will land on without having to scroll farther down the screen: Again, typically an 800 x 600 pixel area.

Keep the fonts, sizes, and colors to a minimum. But pick type that contrasts well with the background to make reading easy for users— particularly important with online publications since eyes can quickly tire while reading computer screens.

Avoid putting navigation buttons or any other important content in any area within or above any rectangular "banner" shape near the top of your screen. Users apparently have been trained by the Web to assume those are ads and ignore them. Size your images appropriately so that it doesn't take more than five to 10 seconds to load your home page. Make people wait longer and they will go someplace else.

RESOURCE

Here are some books to consult for further homepage and website design.

- *Homepage Usability: 50 Websites Deconstructed,* by Jakob Nielsen and Marie Tahir (New Riders Publishing): Nielsen and Tahir, website experts, review their 113 guidelines, grouped by topic area, for the most usable websites and the reasons behind those rules. They then critique 50 of the most prominent company websites.

- *Webworks: eZines: Explore On-Line Magazine Design,* by Martha Gill (Rockport Publishers): A book that covers just the niche of online magazines, Gill discusses every aspect of starting, designing, and growing an electronic magazine. She collects advice and tips from e-zine staff and analyzes about 50 of the best ones.

A Design Template or Grid

Once you or your designer has settled on the publication's type fonts, colors, headline styles, and so forth—you never have to make those decisions again. Instead, you can capture all those choices in a single design document that will serve every time you create a new article or update a website. In the design world, this is often called a "grid" or "master grid."

A master grid acts as a skeleton around which all subsequent layouts of the print publication or website will be constructed. Design software programs always include a feature that allows you to save page designs as a template or master grid file. If you opened up one of those files, you would see skinny vertical and horizontal lines marking where margins begin and end, where the folio should be placed, and the columns where text should be placed. The grid is invaluable for giving you an automatic, consistent framework for aligning the layout and guaranteeing the accurate placement of elements for every article or Web page that you create.

If you had no grid, you'd waste a lot of time designing each page from scratch. And you would surely make mistakes. Perhaps you would set the folio on one page a quarter-inch to the left of where it appeared on the previous page. Maybe the colored bar you developed to run across the tops of all inside pages would be placed an eighth of an inch higher on several pages. To some eyes, these mistakes might not be as glaring as a major typo in a headline. But most readers will subconsciously find them disconcerting because they break the consistency and rhythm of the publication.

Grids can be simple or complex. Simple ones might only include the lines showing margins and the folio. More-complex ones might show where headlines go, where the text starts, where the department name goes, and where the lines of text in each column are placed. If your publication accepts advertising, make sure that you develop a grid that includes your ad sizes.

Once the master grid is set, you or the publication's designer will create templates off that grid for the different kinds of page layouts that your publication typically uses. You might have one template for features and another for departments. You might have two templates for different kinds of features—perhaps one that is based off two columns versus three columns. Within the departments, you might have three templates: one for news shorts, one for columnists, and one for the announcements page.

Within each template, you can create what are called style sheets that automatically format certain parts of the layout at the click of a button. For example, if a certain department always features no indents in the first paragraph, with the rest indented, you can create a style sheet to achieve that effect and then just click to apply. This saves you time from having to manually format everything. It's common to have style sheets for headlines, bylines, first paragraphs, biography lines, and so on.

The key is for the layouts to have enough differentiation to suit the different kinds of content you'll be presenting, but also to have enough common elements to make the publication look cohesive.

You can also buy a design template and customize it. These templates typically run with QuarkXpress or Adobe InDesign and offer a very low cost way to get a professionally designed product. A newsletter template generally costs as little as $99, and you can buy one specifically for printed or emailed newsletters. Prices for website design templates range from under $100 to more than $2,500.

Email design templates are available free from many sources, including many email broadcasting services. (See Chapter 9 for specifics). But be careful to choose a template that conforms to the design guidelines discussed earlier in this chapter.

RESOURCE

Web design templates can be found free at a site called Open Source Web Design, www.oswd.org. Google, America Online, Yahoo, and other website hosting services also offer some free website design templates that you can customize with your own logo and artwork.

Magazine design grids are usually too complicated to buy in off-the-shelf formats. But you can hire a freelance magazine designer to create your templates for a very reasonable fee. A simple 16-page or 32-page design will cost between $5,000 and $7,500; the price goes up along with the complexity of the publication. If you are also launching a companion website, the designer should be able to give you a separate but compatible grid for each. The price may seem like a steep one at first, but considering that a single template can last for many years, it's usually a worthwhile investment.

Creating a Design Grid

Those starting up a new nonprofit publication sometimes must create their own design from scratch. However, it is usually most efficient to hire someone to establish the overarching parameters of your look and feel. That designer can create a master grid that specifies important features such as a title logo, specific text and display fonts, styles of images to use, and the color palette.

Many publishers hire a seasoned designer to create the original grid and then ask their own employees or a less-expensive freelance production artist to arrange the contents of each issue or website update onto that grid. (See "Getting Help From a Designer," below, for more about getting this first design grid or updating an existing one with professional help.)

If the design template has already been completed and you're not contemplating a redesign, the bulk of the design work entails laying out each page according to the existing template. This job includes locating and procuring artwork for articles and arranging the size, location, orientation, and fitting of every text and art element on a page.

At nonprofits with small staffs, these roles are usually all rolled into one. As the publications grow in size, the design work may be divided among an art director who also does some layout of pages—perhaps the cover or most prominent features—a designer who lays out the bulk of the publication, and a production manager who shepherds the publication to the printer and onto the website.

Going It Alone

If you will be designing your publication yourself, bone up on everything you can about editorial design. (The books and other resources listed in Chapter 12 should help.)

If you can, take an introductory course to graphic or publication design at your local community college, adult school, or university extension class.

And if you have no idea where to start, it is perfectly acceptable to pick a simple design from a publication to copy or use as a foundation to build your publication's look.

You will need a computer that is powerful enough to run software applications for design, and one with a monitor large enough so that you can view whole pages or spreads on one screen. You can run all the major design programs on both Macs or PCs. You'll need software to lay out pages, and also software to manipulate photos and artwork. As noted before, these software programs include features that help you create a design grid.

Getting Help From a Designer

Graphic design, particularly for publications, is a talent and skill that requires practice and training that you may not be able or willing to take on. Unless your publication is quite small and is produced infrequently, such as an eight-page quarterly newsletter, you will probably be better off hiring an experienced professional to design your publication. (See Chapter 4 for specific advice about finding freelance designers.)

Depending on available funds, there are various ways to approach outsourcing your publication's design. For most, the best approach is to hire a freelance designer to create the overall design and also do the page layouts for each issue. You'll usually get the most fitting and most consistent results this way.

If you can't afford to hire an experienced designer for each issue, however, you can shell out more money for someone who is more experienced to establish the overall look and feel of the publication and create the master grid and templates, then pay someone less experienced to do the work of filling out the templates for each issue—or learn to do that yourself.

Whichever route you take, it's a good idea for the designer to create a style manual that documents the publication's style and gives sample pages of how various types of pages and content are treated. This gives the editors and other people who may be working on design a point of reference for how layouts should look. And if you change designers, the new person will have a guide to consult and follow.

Popular Design Software

Most graphic designers use QuarkXPress or Adobe's InDesign. Those two programs have captured almost the entire graphic design market and are in a constant battle for users.

Both programs have more than enough capability to create the types of layouts and files that you will be using for your publication. Which you use is simply a matter of preference and familiarity.

Both Quark and InDesign cost about $800. Quark offers nonprofit pricing for its software licenses. Check out the pricing section of its website, www.quark.com.

Many designers find InDesign to be a good deal because it is often packaged by Adobe as part of its "suite" of creative software that also includes Adobe Illustrator and Photoshop. The retail price of the suite is about $1,200—a good value since Illustrator by itself will cost you about $600 and Photoshop about $700. One of the reasons more people have been using InDesign is because it's bundled with other software they need.

Creating a Map

During the content editing process, you might have a very rough idea of how long articles will be based on the word count, but you never really know how much space they will take once you add in artwork and headlines. Once you have your content, you need to block out where everything goes; how many pages or space it will occupy; and, if your publications carries advertising, where the advertising figures in.

Before ads are incorporated into the print or website page designs, someone in the advertising department usually must make sure the advertisers submitted the right artwork for every ad and that ad placements match advertising agreements. (Chapter 10 covers advertising sales relationships.) In small nonprofits with bare-bones publishing staffs, you may be the one responsible for overseeing all of these details.

To make everything fit right, many publications make a map showing exactly what will appear on every page based on instructions from editors and ad salespeople. Maps also help editors check the flow and pacing of articles. The map is represented as pages laid out in two-page spreads side by side. Some publications make the map life-sized and tack it up to a large wall for everyone involved to consult during the final stages, while some shrink it to fit on several sheets of paper that can be copied and distributed.

Obtaining Artwork

Recognizing that readers need some visual stimulus other than pages and pages of text, most publications acquire art images for each issue. Researching, discovering, and purchasing artwork can be tremendous fun but can also be overwhelming and time-consuming because of the sheer abundance of images available.

In reality, most publications are bound by two major limiting factors. The first is money. Some publishers budget $1,000 or more for artwork to accompany a single article. Others have only $50 or less for art. Luckily, there are lots of low-cost ways to add art, and using stock is the most common one.

Additional limitations are that some images will not be appropriate for the personality of your publication. And some topics might be harder to illustrate than others. For example, stock images of premature babies might be appropriate for medical school textbooks, but not for a sensitive magazine targeting their parents. Instead, commissioning a skillful photographer may be the best way to go.

There are endless artistic styles in photography and illustration—from abstract to realistic, from cartoonish to expressionist, from journalistic to surrealist. And some artists mix styles that don't fit easily into any category. Once the identity of the publication has been established, you'll find that some kinds of artwork will simply look out of place and distract from its tone and personality instead of strengthening it.

Stock Photos and Illustrations

When money is tight, many nonprofits turn to stock images to help illustrate their publications. Stock images are large collections of photos and illustrations—libraries, if you will—that companies maintain, selling the public the right to use the images. You can also usually obtain stock images directly from some photographers and illustrators. Check their websites. Stock images cover a huge gamut of subjects and most today are searchable by keyword on the websites of these companies. (A number of them are listed below.)

Some of the images are generic and meant to stand in conceptually for the subject they represent. For example, you may be publishing a piece on excessive executive compensation in your industry and need photos of men and women in suits to represent these executives. You can go to a stock photo website, type in "business people" and "suits," then browse through the offerings of photos of business types in suits. Some may not be appropriate, if, say the subjects are smiling or have the wrong facial expressions for the tone of your content. But others may work because they set the mood or convey the point you are trying to achieve.

Not all stock images are generic. Some are specific to an event, date, or subject. If your publication is running a story exploring current immigration reform, for example, the big stock photo companies have in their libraries pictures from past and recent massive marches and demonstrations in support of immigrants that took place across the country.

RESOURCE

As you search for photos, you will undoubtedly gather and bookmark a number of fitting sources. The collections of university libraries are often good resources; search online for specifics.

The list below includes some of the best-known stock photo collections. Almost all have a search function to look for an image by keyword. Some sell on an image-by-image basis, others on a subscription basis. Some of the websites are actually run by the same company; the different sites are organized to showcase different styles of photography, including:

- www.ablestock.com
- www.about.reuters.com/pictures/index.aspx
- www.apimages.com
- www.comstock.com
- www.corbis.com
- www.gettyimages.com
- www.jupiterimages.com
- www.magnumphotos.com
- www.memory.loc.gov/ammem/index.html
- www.pacaoffice.org
- www.photonica.com
- www.photos.com, and
- www.sxc.hu.

The big drawback of stock images is that they won't be unique to your publication. Anyone can get access to them for a price. And using too many stock images can give your publication the feel of an annual report or brochure, robbing it of an authenticity you may need. If you're trying to shed new light on an old subject, it will probably help to use fresh illustrations and photographs.

Another drawback to stock photos and illustrations may be that they are not tailor-made for your particular purpose. If you are running a profile or story that focuses on a person who is not famous enough to be in a stock photo collection, for example, you're out of luck. Used judiciously, however, stock images can be a great way to affordably supplement your choices of artwork.

Rights-Managed or Royalty-Free: How to Tell the Difference

Stock images are divided into two categories: rights-managed and royalty-free.

Rights-managed means that the companies are selling a limited use of the image. A rights-managed image can generally be used only once, and the price is determined by the type of organization that wants to use it, such as whether you are an advertising company or an editorial publication; your publication's circulation; at what size and where in the publication you plan to use the image; and in what geographic area your publication is distributed. The creator of the image collects fees based on each use of the image. Rights-managed images tend to be more unusual or difficult to achieve, perhaps with more exotic backgrounds or dramatic lighting.

Royalty-free images can be used more freely but tend to be more generic. Once you buy a royalty-free image, you in effect own it and can use it unlimited times and in unlimited ways. These images can be bought individually, on discs of similar images, or even on a subscription basis, in which you can download a number of images for a set price. The prices of royalty-free images are based on the file size of the image, which determines the quality of the resolution and how large or small you can reproduce it.

Royalty-free images are much cheaper than rights-managed images. For example, a rights-managed photo of a simple crocodile head used in the inside of a publication at up to a half page could cost more than $350. A similar royalty-free shot of a crocodile costs only about $100—and there are no restrictions on how large it can be or where in the publication it can be shown.

While royalty-free images seem like a great deal, be aware that using them has drawbacks, too. As the American Society of Media Photographers points out on its website, royalty-free images circulate much more extensively and widely precisely because they are cheaper, so there's a greater chance that readers may have already seen those images—or, worse, that a competitor or someone else in your field has used it. Don't forget that it's not just other publishers that are using stock images; other organizations may be using these images for various other purposes, too.

Original Photography

There are many affordable ways to add original photography to your publications and websites when you can't find suitable stock photographs. As a general rule, original photography works better for stories about specific people, especially stories that have a central character or characters, a protagonist. For example, if you're hoping to show the beneficiaries of your organization's legal services program, you will want actual photos of the people involved.

On the other hand, a photo often doesn't work well when you are trying to editorialize or state a strong opinion about a subject or when you are trying to describe abstract concepts; in other words, when there's nothing tangible to photograph. For example, a profile on the most important expert in your publication's field would merit a portrait photograph of the expert, but a story about how few new students are going into your field and whether that translates into few advances in knowledge over the next generation would be better suited to an illustration.

Nonprofits with limited budgets often depend on amateur photography to illustrate their publications. A person on staff, perhaps the editor or the writer of the story, will serve double duty as the photographer. This can work if the appointed photographer happens to be talented or if the purpose of the photo is pretty straightforward. For example, you may need only a headshot of a relatively minor figure in a story to identify who is speaking—and most Sunday afternoon photographers can deliver a suitable image of that.

💡 **TIP**

Staff photographers may improve through classes. The least expensive way to get custom photographs of your staff and volunteers on the job is to send a few folks to photography classes and supply them with decent digital cameras. Once they learn the basics of composition and lighting, you can get an endless supply of quality images that genuinely reflect your organization's style and personality.

Often, you can ask the subjects of a story to send in photos of themselves that may work for you to reprint in your publication. Many professionals already have their own headshots and portrait photographs on hand. But try not to rely on this strategy too much, since the quality of snapshots varies widely—and photographs provided by subjects are often either too stiff and formal or too casual and personal to be appropriate for a publication.

If you have the funds available, the preferable choice is to hire a photographer to create an image that conveys the exact message you want to send. (See Chapter 4 for more on finding and hiring photographers.)

There are two basic categories of photography: studio and news or location shots. Studio photographers generally take pictures indoors in an environment where every aspect of the shot—including the lighting, props, subject, and composition—is controlled. News photographers make use of the available light and environment and react more to the situation and circumstances at hand.

Original photographs taken by a professional will cost more than those taken by your staff or purchased from stock libraries. Photographers' prices can vary widely, but most base their fees on the circulation size of the publication. They either charge a creative fee plus expenses, or they charge a day rate. If the photographer must scout locations or shoot a complicated shot that requires the help of an assistant, expect to pay more. For a 300,000 circulation national publication, the going rate for an opening photograph hovers around $800 plus expenses; a smaller shot can be $400 to $500, and a cover shot can run $1,000 to $1,200 and up.

TIP

Use your nonprofit status as a bargaining chip. As a nonprofit publication, you can sometimes bargain for a better rate by pointing out that you are not a profit-making enterprise and appealing to the photographer's desire to support the public good.

Getting Permission

You can include plenty of excellent articles, artwork, and photographs in your print publications and on your website if you take the step of asking for permission from the person who owns copyright to the work. And this is a savvy way to add top-quality content for a modest expense.

Many copyright holders will allow you to use their work free if they support your cause or value the exposure that you give them. Some will charge a fee, but even so, the fee is likely to be a fraction what it would have cost you to acquire the same quality of work from someone else. And if you are careful to respect the owner's rights by requesting permission, this person could become a steady contributor to your publications.

Here are some tips from the book *Getting Permission: How to License & Clear Copyrighted Materials Online & Off,* by Richard Stim (Nolo):

- Allow plenty of time to get permission, because the process can take a month or more.
- Be specific about your needs, including both print and website uses.
- Always include the copyright owner's name and contact information. Usually, the artist or photographer will specify exactly how to credit them.

CD-ROM

The following forms for obtaining permission, from *Getting Permission: How to License & Clear Copyrighted Materials Online & Off,* by Richard Stim (Nolo) are included on the CD that accompanies this book:

- Artwork Permission Agreement
- Photo Permission Agreement, and
- Photo Permission Worksheet.

Commissioned Illustrations

As mentioned, a story that centers on a concept or something else that is intangible is hard to photograph and may be better served by an illustration that visually crystallizes the ideas expressed. An illustration of a main character can also work well to make an editorial point about the person.

Although you may be able to find a competent photographer on staff at your nonprofit, it's not likely that anyone on staff will be able to draw a professional illustration. You'll probably need to hire an illustrator to achieve the effect you want.

The cost of illustrations varies widely. It depends on how complex and detailed the illustration is and how it will be used. The price also depends on the artist's reputation and level of experience. You can usually get the lowest prices from people who are working to establish themselves in the business. Illustrations will run about the same as photography—in the range of $1,000 and up for a cover and $800 and upwards for an inside opener. But illustrations can be a little less expensive because illustrators, who tend to work out of their homes, don't need to travel, invest less in equipment, and generally have lower overhead costs than photographers.

> **CAUTION**
>
> **Know what you're getting for your money.** When you commission a photograph or illustration, you are usually buying first and one-time publishing rights. This means that the artists retain the copyright to their work but promise not to sell it to another entity for a set period of time so that your publication gets to use it first, usually for one time. You can negotiate different arrangements, but expect to pay more if your publication wants to own the copyright, because the artist will no longer be able to generate any additional income from the image.

RESOURCE

Freelance photographers and illustrators advertise and promote themselves by paying to be listed in various directories and by mailing art directors postcards showcasing their current work and styles. Over time, your publication will grow familiar with freelancers whose work is most appropriate for your house style. Art departments will sometimes compile a style guide of different photographers and illustrators and their artistic ranges to better inform and organize the artwork options available to them. (See Chapter 4 for detailed information on finding and hiring photographers and illustrators.)

As with photographers, you can check with individual illustrators to see if they have stock images available. You'll pay significantly less for a stock image than an original one. And a stock image that you get directly from an artist may be of a higher quality than the ones he or she has submitted to the stock libraries.

You can help artists better determine what kind of image you are seeking if you tell them which of their portfolio images drew you to them in the first place. Most illustrators will give you several sketches to consider and then go to final art only on the sketch that you pick.

CAUTION

Resist the temptation to tamper. Once an artist has delivered a final image to use on a publication, courtesy and custom dictate that you do not make any changes to the image on your own. Instead, send it back to the artist if changes become necessary. Normally, an artist will not add extra charges for making small changes, such as resizing an image or repositioning it, so you should give them the opportunity to handle all corrections.

The Importance of Putting It in Writing

When you commission artwork, always discuss the story with the artist, along with some specifics on the kind of image you seek. If you have seen work by the artist that captured a particular style you want, be explicit and refer to that image. Be sure to forward a copy of the article or at least a synopsis with key themes and concepts highlighted. Once you've talked, it helps to memorialize what you've agreed to by sending an art direction memo, as shown in the sample below.

Sample Art Direction Memo
For a photographer
Publication: *Pinnacle*, the alumni magazine of Arch University
Issue date: March/April 20XX
Placement: Cover and interior
Due date: January 18
Dimensions: 8" x 10.5"
Usage: One-time usage, plus image of cover on website
Subject: Eugene Hayes, sports director of Arch University
Contact: Eugene Hayes, (XXX) XXX-XXXX or the sports department admin assistant, Heather Hawkins, XXX) XXX-XXXX
Art direction: "Corporate Branding" is the title (Don't tell him this). Hot red or orange seamless background. Shoot for proud expressions or gestures. A solemn expression would be the fallback. Facial expression will be the only difference between cover and interior shot. The synopsis and story are attached.

Sample Art Direction Memo
For an illustrator
Publication: *Pinnacle*, the alumni magazine of Arch University
Issue date: March/April 20XX
Placement: Cover and interior
Due date: January 18
Dimensions: 8.5" x 11"
Usage: One-time usage, plus image of cover on website
Subject: Eugene Hayes, sports director of Arch University
Art direction: "Corporate Branding" is the title. The synopsis, story, and several photographs of Hayes are attached. Need full-color realistic cartoon of Hayes in some kind of corporate "uniform." The cover and interior drawing will be the same.

CD-ROM

Templates for both of these memos that you can adapt and use for your own assignments are included with the CD-ROM in this book.

Tips for Saving Money on Design

As you can imagine, costs for incorporating art in your design can quickly add up to become unaffordable. This section offers some tips and innovative ideas for stretching and supplementing your publication's art budget.

Set Priorities

Decide what elements are worth investing more money to secure—and which ones you can skimp on if need be. It's usually a good idea to spend more money on the cover image and on opening art for important feature stories. Don't spend a lot of money on small images, which are less likely to be seen by readers.

Negotiate Prices

Prices are always negotiable. And you can often get a bargain rate by capitalizing on the fact that you are a nonprofit publication.

Groups as large as the Associated Press Photo Archive and as small as individual artists charge reduced rates for nonprofit groups. And sources that don't already have set, lower rates are often happy to create them. Often, the reason they don't already have them is because they've never been asked, so be sure to speak up and inquire about a nonprofit discount. Many artists also do not mind letting nonprofit organizations use their work for nominal fees or even free as long as it's for a noncommercial purpose. It gives them exposure in venues where they might not normally showcase.

EXAMPLE: Describing its nonprofit publication, one editor recently hired a very affordable photographer through a listing she posted on Craigslist. org. As mentioned, an inside full-page photo can cost upwards of $800, but this photographer agreed to make no distinctions in price structure for inside shots or cover shots or the size of the shot the publication wanted to use. She just charged a flat fee of $300 for all the photos she shot and gave the publication the copyrights, too.

Try these additional price-cutting strategies:

• If you are located near a school or university, hire talented students to illustrate and photograph what you need.

• Tell freelancers that your publication cannot pay much, but make up for it by giving them more leeway and artistic license than they might normally enjoy.

• Bartering may also be an option; perhaps you can trade artwork for advertising space in your publication.

• If your publication holds any caché, artists might lower their prices just to get published in your pages.

• Search for unpublished work already sitting in artists' portfolios. They may be happy to let you publish their work for a token fee, or even free.

• Look for free art. With the Internet, it's easier than ever to search for free images. For example, there are free stock photo websites. Just be sure to check out that the website is reputable and the images are truly free, or you could run into copyright and licensing issues.

Turn to Unexpected Sources

Some museums and galleries will sell usage of high-quality images in their collections for surprisingly affordable fees. Government agencies and other public data depositories also often let people use their images free or for a nominal fee. The U.S. Geological Survey Library, for example, maintains the world's largest collection of earth science information and houses all sorts of maps and other current and historical images of biology, geology, hydrology, ecosystems, and national parks at www.usgs.gov/pubprod/multimedia.html. Amazingly, most of these images are copyright-free, meaning you can download and use them free, without securing any permission first.

Thinking along those same lines, consider using other copyright-free artwork in your publication. Copyright-free art is artwork for which the copyright has expired or perhaps never existed because it was not properly noticed. When a work's copyright has expired, it enters the public domain, meaning that anyone can use it whenever and in whichever way he or she pleases. Figuring out what exactly has passed into the public domain can be complicated, however, so you may need to do a bit of homework before securing such work.

RESOURCE
There are a number of resources available to guide you in the intricacies of public domain work.

- The Copyright Information Center at Cornell University has put together a handy reference chart, at www.copyright.cornell.edu/ training/Hirtle_Public_Domain.htm, to help you figure out what work is in the public domain.
- Check out the website at www.creativecommons.org to find images and other material in the public domain or with flexible copyrights, meaning their copyrights will be enforced only in certain situations.
- And consult the book *The Public Domain: How to Find Copyright-Free Writings, Music, Art & More*, by Stephen Fishman (Nolo), for a complete explanation of finding and securing public domain work.

Public domain artwork can be used to great effect. One designer collects old *Fortune* and other magazines, scans in interesting images, and reuses them in his publication's designs when appropriate. The vintage magazines are an amazing source of free, retro-style artwork that you might use, too. For example, an article about the increase in high-powered businesswomen who are choosing to become stay-at-home moms could reuse an illustration of a happy, nuclear family with mom in apron from one of these vintage magazines as a powerful graphic for a seeming return to traditional family structures.

Necessity Is the Mother of All Invention

David Loeb and Dan Rademacher, editors at *Bay Nature* magazine, are great examples of people who think creatively about purchasing artwork on a tight budget. Always on the lookout for good nature photography but unable to hire professionals for every shot, they have collected contact information for a large group of amateur and not-quite-professional photographers.

When they know what photos they are seeking, they broadcast email a "photo call" to their photographer list to see if anyone on it has a fitting image already tucked away in their portfolios.

Loeb and Rademacher have also made connections with nearby University of California at Santa Cruz's science and naturalist illustration program and often acquire excellent but still affordable artwork from artists who have passed through the program. In this way, they save their precious art budget for truly outstanding artwork that they'd be hard pressed to get some other way.

"Some photographers are sticklers for getting a certain rate, and it's expensive," said Loeb. "Sometimes they'll say, 'You're nonprofit, we'll do a little lower.' But it's still expensive. We'll use them only if we absolutely have to, if something is absolutely stunning."

Use Typography as Art

You might be able to achieve impressive effects by using free or available typography as artwork. This works best when the visual effect you want to make with the type has some deeper connection or relationship to the meaning of the words being used.

EXAMPLE: One publication running a story about its state hospital trade association's extensive lobbying activities was at a total loss for artwork. There was no money for an illustration and nothing to photograph, since the association did not even occupy its own building, just a space in a high-rise office tower. In a pinch, the editor gave the article "Hospital Heavy" as a headline, and the designer blew up the head into type so large that it swallowed up the entire bottom half of a spread, appearing to squeeze the rest of the spread's copy, thus acting as the heavy.

Conducting Quality Control

It's essential for every publication to establish and conduct a final proofing process before designed pages are sent off to the printer or uploaded onto Web servers.

New errors can be introduced as each piece moves through the final production process. It also helps everyone who worked on an issue or Web feature to see and correct any miscommunications that might have happened. For example, if an advertiser was promised a certain position, the ad sales staff can double check those promises. Taking this quality control step seriously and vigorously checking final layouts will save you much money, headache, and embarrassment down the road.

This type of final proofing is not the same kind of copyediting that articles go through before being sent to the designer. Even content that's completely free of typos and other errors can develop problems once it is type set and laid out as pages. For example, a page designer might accidentally cut off a paragraph at the end of an article, or an outside Web designer might pair the wrong graph with the text that describes it. For no reason, the design software might break a line too early in the middle of a paragraph or further hyphenate a word that already contains a hyphen. Many of these errors must be caught and fixed manually.

The only way to eliminate errors completely is to involve several people in the process and to give everyone a final look before the work goes to press or online.

Creating a Dummy

After all the pages have been designed and lined up in the HTML editor or page layout program, experienced production managers create a dummy issue that everyone checks one last time.

The dummy might be printed on paper for a newsletter or magazine or posted to a protected area of the website for Web updates. For print publications, make your dummy look as close as possible to the finished product. Print double-sided, or use tape or a glue stick to arrange the pages so that page two is the back side of the cover or front page, that pages two and three appear as a spread next to one another, that page four is the back of page three, and so forth.

This way, you can flip through the dummy as it will ultimately be seen. For those who are lucky enough to have photocopier machines with advanced capabilities, check to see if your copier will create "booklets." With this function, the copier can arrange your publication's pages in sets of four as the printer ultimately will, plus bind and staple the pages together to produce an exact replica of the issue.

Circulate the dummy issue among the people who will be proofing. This includes editors, designers, copy editors, and anyone else willing to participate—particularly those who haven't worked on the issue and whose eyes aren't jaded. For publications that carry advertising, it's a good idea for sales staff to take another pass to make sure ad placements and content are correct.

Pay special attention to page numbers, line breaks, captions, article jumps and continuations, the endings of stories, and all links. Have everyone make all changes to the same dummy so that multiple copies aren't floating around and fixes get missed. It helps to create a checklist of everyone who must see the dummy, either on paper or by email, and ask people to notify others when they are done and ready to pass the dummy onto the next person. Give people a set amount of time to review the dummy so that it does not languish. The dummy eventually goes to the designer or Web production person who can enter in all final changes.

Larger organizations often allow as much as a week for viewing the dummy and fixing mistakes. It pays to catch all of your own mistakes before the printer or Web producer ever sees them, because once one of these vendors has converted your work to its system, your mistakes become more expensive to correct. Checking your dummy against the vender's proofs also helps to quickly identify any errors the vendor might have created. When you can prove who made the error, it's easier to get the vendor to pay for fixing it.

Checking Blue Lines or Printer's Proofs

Once you've sent off your final files to the printer or Web person, they will usually produce yet another proof called a blue line for you to review. This is the final, final version that will get physically printed or posted for the world to see. You want to make sure that they have not introduced any errors while converting your documents into their systems. (Printer proofs are covered in Chapter 7, and Web proofs are covered in Chapter 8.)

Blue line is a term held over from the days when a printer produced proofs from film that were printed in blue, like the blueprint for a house. Printer's proofs are not just blue anymore, but the industry still refers to them that way.

When checking blue lines, make sure that all final changes you made to that dummy have been incorporated into the blue line. Your designer will also want to check whether the color balance looks right in photos and throughout, and whether any special "effects" that the designer used, such as a slight shadowing around a headline or a foreground and background color, are properly reproduced.

TIP

Be sure to make a backup. Make backup copies of everything people submit to you, such as articles and photographs. And also back up everything you send to an outside vendor, such as the printer or Web production person.

Creating Archives and Repurposing Content

It may be difficult to imagine today, but you might someday preside over a ten-year anniversary issue of your organization's newsletter or magazine. Or somebody may want to turn your newsletter articles into a book. You just never know when you will need to reproduce material from the current issue or convert it to a different format.

Recycling content can actually become a significant source of extra income for some organizations. In these cases, the same digital files used for the first purpose can be converted to suit the new purpose with minimal additional work. When there is any potential for repurposing, you should include a step in your publishing process for saving copies of the work, labeled and catalogued, so that you can easily retrieve it later. Even if you don't expect to reuse an article or a photograph, it is a good idea to save a copy in your archives—just in case.

Your archiving and repurposing system may be as simple as a plain old storage drive or a box of CDs housing backup copies of all your articles and images in clearly labeled folders.

Sometimes the archiving function is imbedded in other software that you're already using. For example, many page design and HTML editing programs can convert finished pages into the XML formats that are used in Content Management Systems (CMS). A CMS, especially suitable for organizations that publish lots of material, creates searchable digital archives by converting every individual article, photograph, chart, table, video, and sound bite into a format called Extensible Markup Language, or XML.

One technician explained that XML organizes information the way books are organized in a library because each document is labeled, like a library book, with cataloging information—called a markup or "tag"—so that you can easily find it later. (CMS systems are covered in Chapter 8.)

Printing Newsletters and Magazines

Previous chapters focused on creative work—assigning stories to writers and illustrators, editing their work, assembling text and images into an attractive format that's easy to read. The printing step explained here requires a change in focus. While the creative process was driven by your vision and skill, the printing process will mostly be controlled by technology—that is, the equipment that prints your newsletters and magazines.

Decisions about printing should not be made lightly, as both the printing process and the paper it requires are expensive, easily consuming as much as half of a total publishing budget. This chapter explains printing technology and explores how to choose a printer that will meet your needs for the least possible expense.

The first part of the chapter briefly describes the printing process to help you determine what printer would be suitable for the work that you plan to do. The second half explains how to negotiate a good contract and maintain a sound working relationship with the printer you choose.

CAUTION

Sometimes, loyalty doesn't pay. Many nonprofits group all their printing jobs with one company, thinking that will save time and money. But the printer that produces your organization's stationery and business cards is unlikely to have suitable equipment for printing magazines or newsletters. And choosing an ill-equipped printer increases what you pay, adds time to the process—and potentially reduces the quality of your newsletters and magazines.

Finding a Printer

You should be as certain as possible of the physical qualities of the publication you want to print before you can begin interviewing printers or get bids from them. Many of the specific concerns about your publication's look and feel are addressed in earlier chapters, but if you haven't yet decided how many copies to print or what kind of paper to use, this chapter will help inform those decisions.

The main considerations when choosing a printer are color, trim size, issue size, distribution plan, and printing quantity. Each is discussed briefly here, and in more detail later in this chapter.

- **Color** refers to how many colors of ink are printed on the pages. A black-and-white newsletter with your red logo on the cover uses two ink colors: black and red. You would choose a printing company with a two-color press for that job. On the other hand, a full-color magazine uses at least four colors, and you would need to find a printing company with a four-color or six-color press to print it.

- **Trim size** refers to the final shape and dimensions of your publication. Newsletter and magazine papers come in large sheets that are folded and cut—or "trimmed"—to their final shape after they come off the printing presses. Choose a printer that can produce the trim size you want, without wasting paper.

- **Issue size** means how many pages are in each issue of your publication. Many presses can handle a limited number of pages per issue because of their binding equipment. As you increase the number of pages in your publication, you reduce the number of printers that can print it. Look for a printer capable of binding your issues without any difficulty.

- **Print run** means the number of copies of the publication you need. High-speed printers can quickly produce very large numbers of copies, but they're much more expensive to run and therefore only suited to large printing jobs. Choose a printer that normally produces quantities similar to yours.

- **Paper** isn't usually a critical issue in terms of choosing your printer, because most printers can use almost any kind of paper. However, be prepared to discuss your paper choices with printers that you interview, because many of them can help you buy paper.

- **Distribution** means how issues will be delivered to readers. Many nonprofits need the services of a printer that can help with distribution, so it's best to figure out distribution plans before you start looking for your printer. (Chapter 9 covers distribution options in detail.)

Consider Getting Help From a Printing Consultant

Newsletter and magazine printing is a complex technical process. Consider getting an expert to help define what you need, find suitable printer candidates, and evaluate the bids they submit to you. You can find production and printing consultants in *Folio* magazine, at www .foliomag.com, and *How* magazine, at wwwhowdesign.com. Also ask other publishers for leads to qualified consultants. (See Chapter 12 for more about hiring consultants.)

Ask any consultant you are considering hiring to show you comparable printing jobs he or she has managed, and check all references—both with other publisher clients and with printers.

And finally, make sure you understand your consultant's charges. If the consultant customarily adds a mark-up to your printing bill, for example, ask for specifics on what he or she does to control printing costs.

Printer Specialties

Honest printers want you to find a company suited to your publishing needs because they know, perhaps even better than you do, how unfortunate a mismatch can be for everyone involved. Look for a company staffed by people willing to take pains to explain what kind of publications and how many copies it can produce efficiently—and match those capabilities to your needs.

For example, on its website, the Brown Printing Company emphasizes: "Brown's focus is consumer special interest magazines, business-trade publications, catalogs, and inserts with print runs of 30,000 to over 7 million. Our average run is about 140,000." By contrast, the Howard Quinn Printing Company describes itself this way: "We specialize in shorter run lengths, 1,000 to 150,000 copies, so that we can be flexible in scheduling last-minute jobs." A 35,000-copy magazine would look like a small fry to Brown, but a big shot to Howard Quinn. On the other hand, if you need 200,000 copies or more, you should consider only a printer like Brown that is set up to handle those quantities.

> **EXAMPLE:** A small trade union chose Howard Quinn to print 2,200 copies of its two-color, 16-page newsletter because Quinn produces hundreds of newsletters; it's the company's specialty. Added benefits for the trade union are that Quinn is a union shop and located in the same city. The newsletter editor finds it convenient to visit the presses in person when printing is underway.

In the United States, there are about a dozen huge printing companies that specialize in producing large numbers of magazines and catalogs. Each of these top-tier printers owns hundreds of presses in multiple locations around the world and can reliably produce publications as fat as a 400-page bridal magazine or as thin as a 16-page catalog. (See "Magazine Printers," below, for more detail on these companies.)

Next in scale and capabilities are the 40 or 50 commercial printing companies with four or five presses each that print a mix of materials, from annual reports and brochures to small magazines.

And in a third tier, there are hundreds of small printing companies with one press or two that print a vast range of products—from restaurant menus to course catalogs.

Within this mix of commercial printing companies, you will likely find only a handful that focus on producing publications similar to the one you're planning to publish. Ask to see their work, and concentrate your search on printers that spend 30% or more of their time producing magazines or newsletters similar to yours.

> **TIP**
>
> **Seek input on your printing decisions.** This chapter describes various printing technologies so that you can consider what equipment might best suit your publications. But to ensure the best fit, you should also thoroughly discuss printing technology with your designer, and perhaps a production consultant, too.

Newsletter Printers

Newsletter presses are addressed here separately from the ones used mainly for magazines, but some printers take on both types of work.

Newsletters come in various forms and formats. But as discussed here, a newsletter is a publication printed on uncoated 11" x 17" paper that is folded and possibly stapled to form a four-page, eight-page, or 16-page document. Newsletters appear on a wide range of types of paper, including colored stock—and they are generally printed with black ink rather than in color. Some newsletters use one highlight color in addition to black and many include black-and-white photographs and other images such as charts or graphs.

> **SKIP AHEAD**
>
> **If your publication is 32 pages or more . . .** If you are considering a publication larger than about 32 pages per issue, and printing it in full color on glossy white paper, then you should probably think "magazine" rather than "newsletter" when searching for an appropriate printer, and skip to the next section.

There are two choices for printing newsletters: photocopying or offset printing. You can find several of each type of printer in every town. Check the Yellow pages under "Printing." If you want offset printing, look for that word in the ads. Both offset and photocopy printers can work from the final digital files you prepare (see Chapter 2), and both can print on the same kinds of paper, but the quality varies greatly because of the methods used.

Photocopiers use toner powder in cartridges—similar to the laser printers you likely use in your home or office—on both their digital and photocopying machines. Some toners create smudgy graphics and photographs, and some digital printing is expensive in large quantities. If you want bright, clean photographs, or if you need more than about 100 copies of your newsletter, then step up to a commercial offset printer instead of a photocopier.

Offset printers use ink instead of toner, and they can offer many more options in terms of color and format. Ink colors can be custom-mixed to precisely match your logo, for example. (See "Applying Color," below, for more details about colored ink.)

In addition to using better inks and printing technologies, many commercial printers offer services that copy centers rarely provide. For example, some printers can label and mail your newsletters for you. Many of them offer design services, and they can also do some of the technical work required to produce your nonprofit's newsletter. And, if they are already producing a number of newsletters, the in-house designers at most commercial printers may have more expertise about newsletter design than copy center employees, who usually produce mostly fliers and business cards.

Commercial offset printers have cost advantages over copy shops, too, particularly for larger jobs. After the initial set-up costs are covered, an offset printer can run the presses all day, with hardly any extra cost. As a result, it can offer significant price breaks at different quantities. But the last copy from a photocopier costs the same as the first. Consequently, copy shops usually don't offer significant volume discounts.

	Printing Costs for a Two-Color, 16-Page Newsletter	
Here is a comparison of the costs of printing a two-color, 16-page newsletter as quoted by staff at a retail copy center and a commercial printer.		

Number of Copies Printed	Per Copy Cost of Photocopying	Per Copy Cost of Offset Printing
200	$3.81	$3.74
2,000	$3.05	$1.19
5,000	$2.91	$ .73

Magazine Printers

Magazines are generally produced on a different grade of paper from newsletters, and issues typically have more pages. Even the best commercial offset newsletter printer may not be able to handle a 32-page magazine printed in full color for more than 10,000 copies or so.

Consequently, most nonprofits produce magazines at one of the top-tier or middle-tier printing companies using high-speed, computer-controlled presses.

RESOURCE

You can find lists of magazine printers in the "Folio Magazine Super Book" at www.foliomag.com. Printers also often join publishing associations such as the Society of National Association Publications as partner members, and you can find them through the association membership directories. (See Chapter 12 for contact information for publishing associations.)

The top-tier magazine printing companies handle 95% of the magazines and catalogs printed in this country, and the services they offer are very similar. Most of them can handle the whole process for you—from printing your formatted page designs to distributing final copies to your readers' mailboxes or on the newsstands. Many such printers have postal stations right at their printing plants, which work very closely with the United States Postal Service (USPS). For example, printers set up their labeling stations to match the current requirements for periodical postage discounts. (See Chapter 9 for details on postal requirements.)

Some printers will maintain your mailing lists for you, too. And some can bundle the copies you ship to retail stores with copies of other publications, called "pool shipping," which provides substantial savings on distribution costs.

CAUTION

Mistakes that can drive up printing costs. You can unintentionally drive up printing costs dramatically by choosing a format or design for your publication that is expensive for the printer you chose to produce. For example, don't agree to add 40 extra pages to an upcoming special issue unless you know for sure that your printer can bind the fatter magazine. Otherwise, you'll be forced to print the issue at a different plant, with different rules—and probably at a much higher cost.

Avoid these potential mistakes by making sure you or any designer that works on your publication fully understands how the printer will produce your work. If there are any questions, tour the printing plant for a first-hand look.

Magazines can be produced on three different kinds of presses, as described below: sheet-fed offset presses, web offset presses, and rotogravure. Generally speaking, sheet-fed presses are used for quantities of under 10,000 or less; web presses work well for quantities between 15,000 and 750,000, and rotogravure presses are best for very large numbers—even millions of copies.

The terms "offset" and "rotogravure" describe how the ink is applied to the paper, and the terms "sheet-fed" and "web" describe how paper feeds into the presses. In the offset process, lithographic plates are made that transfer ink first to a rubber "blanket" and then to the paper. The process is called offset because the paper does not take the image directly from the plates. Lithographic plates are relatively inexpensive to create, and they hold up well enough to produce up to about a million copies.

The rotogravure process, on the other hand, involves etching images onto copper cylinders, which are both longer lasting and significantly more expensive to produce than lithographic plates. Consequently, the rotogravure process is reserved for high-volume jobs and those that demand museum-quality prints. If you plan to produce fewer than a million copies of a regular magazine, chances are that your publication will be produced on an offset press.

A web is a huge roll of paper that is printed on both sides at once by high-speed presses, typically producing eight, 16, 24, 32, 48, or even 64 pages per side in each pass. One pass of a printing plate on the paper is called an "impression," and the average speed of a web-fed press is 50,000 to 100,000 impressions per hour. This equipment can produce up to 64 pages at one time. A sheet-fed press operates more slowly—the average speed is 10,000 to 15,000 impressions per hour—and can only produce 16 pages at one time. Rotogravure presses produce about 50,000 impressions per hour and are capable of printing up to 96 pages at one time.

RESOURCE

Founded in 2005, the Integrated Media Cooperative was designed to give small to mid-sized publishers the benefits of lower costs on printing, paper, shipping, and general office expenses by consolidating volume purchasing. The group also offers publishers an opportunity to share best practices with each other. You can get more information online at www. imc.coop.

Avoiding Mistakes

All printing presses are controlled by computers that use digital files to manage how ink is laid down on the paper as it moves through the presses. Before the presses start rolling, it's important to make certain the printer's computer system has been set up to print your job correctly. Problems typically stem from both human and technical errors.

Even after carefully proofreading your files (described in Chapter 2), mistakes can slip through. (See Chapter 6, "Conducting Quality Control," for more on this.) Perhaps a photographer submitted the pictures of your convention in a lower resolution than you requested and all the pictures will be muddy if they are not corrected. Or maybe you specified that the cupcake recipe was not supposed to run next to the weight-loss ad in your publication, but it somehow landed there.

Even if your files are completely free of errors, a number of technical problems, such as a formatting error on a disk or a missing line of instructions, can crop up as the printer reads your files into its computer system. And finally, advertisers have been known to submit the wrong ads or to make formatting mistakes in their ads before submitting the files to you.

To catch these potential glitches in advance, the printer will print a proof that shows how its software is reading and organizing all of the files that you submitted. This is called a "composite proof," because every detail is included. The composite proof will look just like the magazine or newsletter—that is, pages will appear in sequence with images and text displayed as planned on every page. If you have included a special photograph and you are worried that the colors require museum-quality matching, you can also ask for a "loose" proof, which checks the color accuracy of one single image or photograph. Expect to pay anywhere from $20 to $45 per page for printed composite or loose proofs from a printer.

For a black-and-white publication, the printer will produce a black-and-white proof so that you can see how the pages are going to look in that format. Color proofing is more complicated because you cannot see exactly how the colors will come off the printing press until it starts producing them. So printers create different kinds of proofs—soft proofs, hard proofs and press proofs—to check color images without actually running the main presses.

Soft proofs are viewed on a computer monitor. But digital images look different on paper than on a computer screen, so you cannot rely on what you see at your standard monitor to predict exactly how the images will appear when printed on paper. For that, you must have either a printed proof as described below or a specially calibrated computer monitor. Most printers can color calibrate your computer monitor to match their proofing equipment so that you can view accurate color proofs on your own screen. This is the most common type of proofing used.

Hard proofs are printed on paper, sometimes with an inkjet or laser color printer. They do not show colors with 100% accuracy because they're not printed on the main presses. Some publishers print their own hard proofs from the soft proof files described above. Printers usually send hard proofs by courier or overnight mail. You will usually have only a day or so to correct any mistakes that you find.

Press proofs are prints made on the printing presses before the full production run begins. The digital prepress process actually does a good job matching colors on the presses, and most publishers will not need to proof the colors in person. But if color is a crucial issue for your organization—say, for example, because you've paid famous wildlife photographers to catch true-to-life images of rare birds—then you should also ask for a "press proof" that will show the colors as the printed pages start to roll off the presses. You will have to visit the presses in person for this kind of proof.

Avoiding Printing Problems: A Checklist

If you follow all of the steps described here, there's a good chance you can eliminate nearly all of the embarrassing or expensive printing mistakes that can arise. (Chapters 6 describes many of these steps in more detail.)

☐ **Make a dummy.** Print a dummy issue from your page design software and thoroughly check for typos, imposition errors (see "Setting Up Pages," below), page layouts, page numbering, and ad positions. Fix all errors until you have a final, perfect proof.

☐ **Check your digital files.** Use your page layout software's preflighting feature to ensure that you have assembled all necessary elements in the correct digital format, including fonts, camera-ready artwork, graphics, and pages.

☐ **Make a backup.** Be sure to make a backup copy of every file before sending it to your printer.

☐ **Check the printer's preflight report.** Fix any formatting errors or missing elements that the printer identifies.

☐ **Double-check the printer's proofs.** Check your corrected in-house dummy against the proofs that the printer supplies. If color reproduction is extraordinarily important, also check color at the press.

☐ **Verify inserts.** Make sure that your printer has received any inserts that you want to include in the issue, and check that the inserts are properly formatted.

☐ **Give distribution instructions.** Provide data files and detailed labeling instructions so that the issues can be prepared for distribution.

☐ **Make postage deposits.** Make sure that postage has been paid so that the USPS will accept your copies into the system without delay.

CD-ROM

The CD-ROM in this book contains a blank copy of this checklist that you can tailor to your needs, print out, and use as a safety check for each of your printing jobs.

A Look at the Mechanics of Printing

When you print a document on a laser printer, you can easily start with page one and continue printing through the whole document in sequence. And you can print as many pages as you like without stopping. But a magazine or newsletter printing press does not work that way. Instead of printing on page-sized pieces of paper, a commercial printer uses large sheets that are cut and folded into pages after printing. Commonly, one sheet of paper can produce four, eight, or 16 pages of a newsletter or magazine.

Every magazine and newsletter is actually a collection of these four-page, eight-page, or 16-page units, called "signatures," which are bound together to make the final issue. And publishers have to design their publications in four-page, eight-page, or 16-page groupings. If you've already got 32 pages in your magazine, for example, you can't add just one more page; you would need to add however many pages were on a whole extra signature. The exact number of pages in each signature depends on the presses and the binding method that you use.

Some of these design considerations are discussed in Chapter 6, but the details described below become important when it comes time to convert your design files into the format that your printer requires. The steps described here take place after the design process is completed, when you are ready to submit your files to your printer. The mechanical details will depend on which equipment your specific printer is using.

Most printers will be willing to explain any questions you have about the process and correctly set up your files to accommodate it. But in case you don't have the information you need, here is a brief summary of how the presses work.

Setting Up Pages

Most commercial printers can produce 16 pages on one huge sheet of paper; some produce four or eight. Each side of the paper is called a form, and the forms are folded together into groups, called "signatures."

As the paper comes out of the printing presses, it travels through equipment that folds it, cuts the oversized sheets into publication-sized pages, trims the edges, and binds the pages together. Say, for example, that you want the pages in your 16-page newsletter to end up in sequence, as shown below.

1	2	3	4	5	6	7	8	9	10	11	12	13	14	15	16

To get this to happen, the printer will have to lay out your pages for printing as shown in the example below. This process, called "imposition," requires positioning the pages on a signature so that each page will appear in the proper sequence after printing, folding, cutting, and binding.

A Sample Imposition of a 16-Page Signature

Side A

5	12	9	8
4	13	16	1

Side B

7	10	14	6
3	11	15	2

The exact imposition layout depends on your printer's equipment, but all signatures come in groups of at least four pages.

Applying Color

You or your publication's designer should understand your printer's imposition scheme, because it might affect decisions about where to use color in a publication.

For instance, if you put a four-color photograph on page one in the 16-page signature example just described, that whole side of the paper must run through a four-color press using colored inks. Therefore, you could put four-color images or ads onto all the other pages into Side A as shown above, without additional ink or printing cost. The figure below shows how the color would appear within the finished newsletter.

A 16-Page Newsletter Layout With Color

1*	2	3	4*	5*	6	7	8*	9*	10	11	12*	13*	14	15	16*

*Pages with color if you print only one side in color.

It's very likely that you can save on printing expenses by using color only on one side of the paper. But someone designing a publication who did not understand this printer's imposition scheme might unwittingly force a printer to use color on both sides of the paper by placing one color image on the first side of the page and another color image on the second. Avoid such extra costs by making sure that your printer explains its imposition requirements to those responsible for designing your publication.

Binding

Newsletters are always bound with staples or simply folded. But there are two ways to bind magazine pages together: with staples in the center, called "saddle stitched;" or glued to a spine, called "perfect bound."

Saddle stitched magazines are assembled by folding signatures and piling them on top of one another, with the covers on top, as shown in the image on the left of the illustration below. For perfect binding, the printer lines up the signatures beside one another, with the covers on the outside, and then glues them all to a spine, as shown in the image on the right, below.

Saddle Stitching and Perfect Binding

The illustration below shows folded signatures of pages ready to be saddle stitched (left) and perfect bound (right).

Perfect binding usually does not work very well for publications with fewer than 32 pages, depending on the weight of the paper you use. Conversely, saddle stitches or staples cannot securely hold together magazines with many pages, so magazines with more than about 64 pages are commonly perfect bound. Larger printers generally offer both binding methods, but smaller ones may offer only saddle stitching.

Both binding methods can accommodate inserts that may be added to the issues at the binding stage. Examples of this include subscription cards and cover wraps—printed forms that attach to the outside of a magazine, often used for renewal reminders and other communications with subscribers.

Generally, publishers buy promotion cards and wrappers from specialty printers, then have them delivered to the magazine printer for binding into the issues. Your magazine printer must provide detailed instructions to your insert printer, specifying when the inserts should arrive and what formats are acceptable. To be certain things work as expected, check to be sure that the instructions are communicated properly and that the inserts are delivered correctly.

As mentioned, after binding, the pages are trimmed around the sides to provide an even, clean edge to the final magazine.

RESOURCE

The books listed below provide all the technical details you'll need to understand before entering into negotiation with printing companies. And each one also includes tips about how to save money on printing.

- *Editing by Design: For Designers, Art Directors, and Editors—The Classic Guide to Winning Readers,* by Jan V. White (Allworth Press).
- *Getting It Printed: How to Work With Printers and Graphic Imaging Services to Assure Quality, Stay on Schedule, and Control Costs,* by Eric Kenly and Mark Beach (How Press).
- *Pocket Pal: The Handy Little Book of Graphic Arts Production,* by Michael H. Bruno (International Paper). This book is one of the few that is regularly updated as technology changes. For that alone, it's a priceless reference book. But readers will also appreciate how well the editor has translated technical information into accessible language.
- *Put It on Paper! Every Person's Guide to the Printing Industry,* by Margie Gallo Dana (Xlibris Corporation), available through the author's website at www.bostonprintbuyers.com.
- *Working With a Magazine Printer,* by Bert Langford (self-published) is available from *Folio* Magazine at www.foliomag.com or through the author's website at www.bnlconsult.com, but not from retail bookstores. This is a serious and comprehensive handbook for beginners and professionals alike that includes a great glossary of printing terms.

Getting Distribution Help From Printers

After printing, binding, and trimming, your publication is ready to be distributed to readers. Magazine and newsletters printers often help handle this process, too—using either paper labels or digital files that can be printed by laser directly onto the publication. You must provide distribution instructions to your printer along with the digital printing files. If you will need this labeling service from a printer, be sure to review the costs involved as you negotiate the printing contract. (See "Sample Publication Specification Sheet," below, for more.)

To save money on postage, subscriber names must be presorted by zip code. (See Chapter 9 for details on these and other postal requirements.) Some printers can help you save even more money on postage and distribution costs by bundling your publication with others that are headed for the same location. This process is called co-mailing, co-palletizing, or pool shipping—and it can save as much as 15% on postage and even more on retail distribution expenses. Printers are generally very astute about getting the most efficient and affordable distribution, so ask them for help and advice.

If you are sending copies of your publication to newsstands through a distributor, those shipping instructions must arrive at the printing plant before the presses start to run. As the copies come off the printing press, labels are applied or copies are bundled automatically for retail stores. The printer then gathers labeled copies into bundles or mail sacks and delivers them to the USPS or to your retail distributor.

Environmental Concerns and Paper Choices

Many nonprofit publishers are justifiably concerned about not using old-growth trees, not adding toxic chemicals to the environment, and not flooding landfills with old copies of their publications.

Unfortunately, the environmental issues surrounding printing and paper choices, discussed below, are complex and difficult to resolve. Take recycled paper, for example. If you learned that toxic chemicals are used to clean recycled paper or that milling recycled paper burns more energy than virgin paper, would you still use it?

A paper and printing consultant, Marcus Witte, offers some information and suggestions for publishers who want to make sensitive choices about controversial environmental issues.

Cut office wastes first. According to the Natural Resources Defense Council (www.nrdc.org), American businesses recycle only about 25% to 35% of paper they use. By contrast, magazine printers recycle nearly all of the paper spoiled during production. In fact, magazine printers reuse nearly 98% of the materials left over after the printing process. If your nonprofit is committed to using and reusing paper in an environmentally sound way, increasing the percentage of office waste that you recycle may actually have more impact than buying recycled paper for your publications.

Publish smaller issues. It is difficult to recycle perfect-bound magazines, because the glue leaves a gummy residue that won't break down in the recycling process. If your magazine is perfect bound, then your readers are probably clogging up their local recycling centers with your binding glues when they dutifully put old issues out on the curb. To avoid this problem, keep magazine issues to fewer than 64 pages, and stick to saddle stitch binding.

Avoid UV coating. The chemicals used for curing UV coatings, discussed below, render magazines unsuitable for recycling, too. Avoid UV coatings to keep these chemicals out of the recycling system.

⊘ CAUTION

Be sure to cover your postage costs. Printers don't pay postage for you, so you have to be sure to deposit enough money to cover the expense into your USPS account. If there are insufficient funds there, your distribution will certainly be delayed.

Choosing Paper

Newsletter and magazine paper comes in a dizzying array of weights, colors, and finishes, and it can account for as much as 40% to 50% of your total production costs. So it's especially important to do a little research before choosing the paper on which your publication will be printed.

All printers will buy paper for you. They make some money when providing this service by marking up the price slightly to cover their handling costs. You can also buy paper from a broker and have it delivered to your printer. Either way, be sure your paper costs are itemized separately so that you know exactly what they are.

Then ask your vendor—either the paper broker or your printer—to help cut the cost by suggesting less-expensive alternatives that won't reduce the quality of your publication. This section helps you evaluate their advice and may also prompt you to come up with a few cost-cutting ideas of your own.

Using a standard size and weight of paper often leads to bargain prices, because such paper is widely available at competing prices from many different suppliers. Some printers also buy huge quantities of standard types of paper and offer it at prices that are cheaper than anything you can buy elsewhere.

Sometimes, however, because of the sensibilities of your audience or your organization's mission, you may choose something other than the least expensive option.

EXAMPLE: One environmental group established a policy of printing all documents on recycled paper, including its quarterly newsletter. That publication is printed on a brand of uncoated 50-pound, 100% post-consumer recycled paper called "EcoOffset"—a paper that costs about 15% more than standard papers. The printer does not stock this paper; the nonprofit group has to buy it directly from the paper merchant. Because there is a 40,000-pound minimum order for this paper, the group buys enough for three issues at one time and pays a small handling fee to the printer for receiving and storing it.

Paper size and weight. The standard sheet size for magazine paper is 25" by 38," and it comes in weights ranging from 25 pounds to about 100 pounds basis weight. The "basis weight" of a paper equals whatever a 500-sheet bundle would weigh in the trim size of a magazine.

The type of paper you choose affects how your publication feels in the hands of your readers. Heavy paper adds more bulk to a publication with very few pages, but higher-weight paper is generally more expensive and also significantly boosts postage and distribution costs.

Newsletters are commonly printed on paper with a basis weight of 60 or 70 pounds to add heft to their scant number of pages. But many magazine publishers avoid such heavy paper except for covers. Nearly all magazines use paper in the range of 34 pounds to 50 pounds for inside pages. For comparison, consider that the bond paper you likely use on your home or office laser printer usually has a basis weight of 20 or 24 pounds, roughly equivalent to a 50-pound grade.

Paper grade. In addition to being categorized by weight, paper is graded from premium (#1) to standard (#5) according to ground wood content, which influences how well it holds ink. Most magazines are printed on standard grade #5 paper or the next best alternative, #4 grade.

There are scales for other characteristics, too—including opacity, brightness, gloss, and thickness. Brightness runs from 70 to 100, for example, and most magazines are in the range of 76 to 80. Only the most expensive publications chose paper above grade #3 or above 83 for brightness.

Dos and Don'ts for Buying Paper

Printers and paper brokers won't always volunteer information that might reduce how much you spend when buying paper from them. But these guidelines will help you ask questions to elicit those cost-saving ideas.

DO . . .

Get the best prices by choosing the stock your printer supplies. It will be readily available, and house papers are widely used and generally acceptable to most publishers.

Choose recycled paper if your readers will expect it, but recognize that you will pay more for it.

Ask for paper charges to be separated out from all other printing costs so that you can change to a different paper if yours suddenly jumps in price.

DON'T . . .

Choose a pricey paper just because it looks good. Make sure the extra expense of a high-grade paper is really necessary—and don't forget to budget for extra postage costs if the paper is heavy.

Choose a very low grade of paper that will turn away the advertisers because their ads do not look good on it.

Paper finishes. Paper also comes in different finishes and can be coated or uncoated and finished in glossy, matte, silk, satin, dull, or velvet textures. Some papers are coated with special enamel called UV coating that protects it from sun or light damage, just as sunscreens protect human skin. Finishes add to production costs because they can increase the weight of the pages—and therefore distribution charges—and also because printers charge a few cents per page for applying the coatings.

In addition to cost concerns, the type of finish you choose may depend on your nonprofit's mission and your readers' expectations.

EXAMPLE: *Mother Jones* is printed on a recycled paper that is not commonly stocked by the printer because recycled paper appeals to its audience. The paper is a strategic investment in the publication's relationships with its readers. For greater retail impact, the covers are coated with a clay-based glaze that increases the richness of colors.

Your printer or paper broker can supply paper samples and help you understand the differences in price and feel among all the various options. You can also show an example of a magazine or newsletter printed on paper stock you like and ask what a matching paper would cost for your publication.

Using Color

Just as the type of paper you choose can drive up costs or keep them down, the colors that you select to use in your publication can have a huge impact on its production costs. And the color decisions also affect which printing presses can be used. This section explains how color is applied to printed publications so that you can make color choices that fit your budget and publishing goals.

There are two kinds of color that you can use in your publications: spot color and process color.

Spot Color

Printers create spot colors by mixing colored inks together, the same way colors are created for house paint. The ink that results from the mix is applied in one pass through an inking station on the printing presses.

A two-color press can readily apply one spot color plus black. And you may pay as little as $25 extra to add a spot color—much less than the cost of process colors. That's why spot colors are so common.

Spot colors are also easier to control than process colors because once the inks are mixed together, you can see exactly what the color will be.

Spot colors are commonly referred to as PMS or Pantone colors, and individual colors are referred to by a numbering system according to a color guide that you can find in any art store.

Process Color

Process colors use four colors of ink that are applied individually at separate stations on the press. The combination of these four colors creates the impression of a full-color image. If you plan to include color photographs, then you have no choice but to use process colors. Many advertisers also want their ads to be run using process colors. The extra cost can amount to several hundred dollars per page. For example, a black-and-white magazine typically costs 8% to 10% less to print than the same magazine printed in four colors.

The four process colors are blue, magenta, yellow, and black. In printing shorthand, these primary pigments are referred to as CMYK: C stands for cyan or blue, M stands for magenta, Y is yellow, and K stands for black. The process of balancing colors to achieve the right full-color image is tricky, although printing computers are quite good at reaching the proper balance. As mentioned earlier, you can't get an accurate picture of how process colors will print from seeing them on a standard computer screen. Instead, you must either examine printed pages as they come off the press or use a specially calibrated monitor linked to your printer's proofing computer systems.

TIP

Beware of how paper affects color. The paper you choose to use will affect how colors reproduce in your publication. Brighter, higher-grade papers take color better to produce a more crisp and clear image than newsprint or unbleached recycled papers. Coated papers can improve the look of printed colors, too. And glossy paper takes ink differently than paper with a matte finish.

To obtain a specific outcome, you may have to make some trade-offs. For example, if you pick uncoated recycled paper to please your readers, you may lose some financial support from advertisers who feel that the paper doesn't hold four-color inks as well as virgin paper.

Additional Printing Charges

Printers often add charges to their proposals and invoices that may be unfamiliar or confusing to you.

For example, the work they do to set up the presses to run your job is called "make ready," and there is a charge for that labor. And extra charges will be added if you make plate changes—that is, you stop the presses and change something.

Make Ready and Running Charges

The term "make ready" refers to all the steps a printer takes to set up your magazine on its presses: making the plates, loading the ink, adjusting the colors, and so forth. Some printers show you the make ready items separately from the rest of the printing expenses. The make ready term is sometimes depicted with the initials M/R. For example, your bill might include a notation such as: "$2,900 M/R and $90 running charges per thousand copies." Other printers combine make ready with other items and show a single expense, as in the sample printer's bid below.

Plate Change Charges

Some charges are called "press stops" or "plate changes" because the presses will be stopped and the printing plates will be changed to accommodate essential changes you request. These are relatively rare in nonprofit publications.

If you have to change a printing plate midstream, then the make ready charges will be increased. Plate changes also affect the printing's timing: It generally takes from two to four hours to complete the make ready process for any change in printing plates, plus another four to eight hours of extra time on the bindery equipment when the plates change.

Sometimes, this extra cost and time is necessary because printers need different versions of a particular publication.

EXAMPLE: *Mother Jones* magazine has a distribution bar code on its newsstand copies that does not appear on its subscriber copies. To get these two versions, the printer sets up to print subscriber copies first, then stops and changes to a new plate for the cover of the newsstand copies and finishes up the job.

EXAMPLE: *Kentucky Living* is a magazine created for the members of a dozen local electric cooperatives across the state. Every month, the printer makes several plate changes so that some coops can insert unique pages into the issues going to their local membership. The cooperatives that use this service pay a few extra cents per copy for creating a customized edition to the statewide office that produces the magazine.

Sample Printer's Bid

In the sample below, notice that the printer is free to withdraw the bid after 30 days and that it does not include sales taxes. Contact your state's taxing authority, usually called the Board of Equalization, to check the rules governing sales tax charges on your printing bill. Don't pay any sales taxes that are not required in your state.

The sample bid below does not have any plate changes. And this printer is not helping the publisher distribute individual copies to members or subscribers; instead, this bid notes that the printer will put all the magazines into cartons and deliver them to the publisher's subscription fulfillment offices. Freight charges for this shipment are not included in this printing bid, and must be budgeted separately.

Quote Number	1234
Job Title	Doing Good Magazine
Description	52-page magazine printed in three 16-page signatures with a separate 4-page cover
Final Trim Size	8.5 X 11
Bleeds	Cover only
Paper	Inside pages: 40# uncoated recycled matte Cover: 60# coated recycled matte
Ink	4 color process / 2 sides
Inserts	None
Artwork Supplied	Electronic files with high-resolution images in position. Printer traps where required.
Proofs	Digital blue lines and contact proof
Bindery	Perfect
Packaging/Ship Instructions	Carton and skid-packed for bulk shipment to customer's fulfillment offices.
Quantity	49,000
Total Price	$37,000
Price per Unit	$.76
Terms of Sale	Net cash 30 days from the date of invoice on approved credit.
Comments	This bid is valid for 30 days and does not include sales tax. Customer is responsible for applicable taxes and freight charges.

Negotiating a Printing Contract

As one printing consultant says, "Every printing assignment is a custom job." That's because there are so many differences in paper, colors, page counts, quantities, trim sizes, and designs. This is a helpful thought to hold in your mind as you begin asking printers to give you bids. Another reality is that nobody can give you a decent bid unless you describe the publication that you envision in complete detail.

Here are some tips on how to negotiate the best printing contract for your publication.

- Start by locating three or four printers that have the equipment, expertise, and services that seem appropriate for your needs. Collect comparable samples from all the finalists and tell each one of them that you're going to be asking for a bid.

- Give each printer the same detailed specifications—for example, by filling out the Publication Specification Sheet, below. Even if the printers use their own specification sheets, giving them all the same requirements on one sheet of your own is the best way to make comparisons at this stage.

- Each printer should respond with a bid that is essentially an invoice showing what it would charge for the job that you specified.

- Read the bids carefully so that you understand the differences among them. You may learn that one printer is pricier than the others but more compatible or more flexible.

- If possible, visit the most favorable candidates. Try to meet the staff people who will handle your work and assess how well you can communicate with them.

- Check references. When you are close to picking a printer, ask for references. Then contact the references and ask questions such as: Have you been able to depend on this company? Does the printer communicate effectively? (For more ideas about questions to ask, see "When Money and Location Aren't Everything," below.)

- After you make your choice, keep the competing bids in your files in case your chosen printer washes out for some reason.

TIP

Look to your printer for training. Most printers offer onsite production training once or twice a year, and some paper mills also offer these programs. It may pay for you or people on the staff at your nonprofit who are dealing directly with printing to attend these programs. The more you know about production technologies, the more efficient your publishing operations will be.

When Money and Location Aren't Everything

People often routinely choose the printer that is closest or least expensive. But you should look deeper than that during the bidding process. Distance is not an issue when your work travels by email, anyway. And low prices sometimes signal desperation from a printer that can't keep its customers.

The following qualities are often more important than price and location when comparing bids from different printers.

- **No surprises.** Bids should accurately reflect what you requested. Those that don't could signal that the printer doesn't actually use the equipment or provide key services you need. Ask the printer to fully explain any deviations from your specifications.

- **Timeliness.** If the printer submits a bid late, that may signal larger management issues.

- **Communication style.** Pay attention to any information lapses or issues about friendliness that might affect your ongoing relationships. And note whether everybody with whom you needed to talk was easy to reach.

- **Comparable work.** Does the printer provide examples that are truly comparable to your publication, or is there really no match? You will always find it easiest to work with a company that specializes in publications similar to your own.

Sample Publication Specification Sheet

This example shows the information that you might provide to prospective printers when requesting them to make a bid. The column on the right explains the type of information you will provide for the topic listed in the left column.

Publication Specification Sheet	
Organization	Name of your organization and contact information
Publication Name	Name of the publication
Publication Mission	Who will read the publication, and what is its purpose?
Frequency	How many issues will be published per year?
Trim Size	The final size of the finished publication
Bleeds	Note whether the printing will extend to the edges of the pages or whether there is white space framing the pages. (See Chapter 6 for an explanation of this.)
Folio Pages	Number of pages in the issue; "folio" refers to page numbers
Signatures	Body: How many four, eight, or 16-page signatures will be included in the body of the publication?
Cover	Cover: Will there be a separate cover?
Color	Specify two-color or four-color
Plate Changes	Note any that might be required and explain what is needed
Paper Stock	Specify the sheet size
Cover	Specify the paper chosen for the cover
Book/Body	Specify the paper chosen for the body
Binding	What kind of binding do you need?
Inserts	Describe any inserts that will be required, such as subscription cards or donations envelopes
Ink	Specify what ink you want used
Quantity	Indicate how many copies to print
Scheduling	Note any specific deadlines, for example, if you must meet a newsstand distributor's dates
Prepress	Explain how your files will be prepared for printing and whether or not you need the printer to bid on this service
Delivery and Shipping	Explain how the copies will be distributed, for example, you might note: 80% subscriptions via USPS, jet labeled from our presorted files; 20% retail per distributor instructions

CD-ROM

This Specification Sheet is included as a spreadsheet on the CD-ROM that accompanies this book so that you can print it out and compare bids from a number of different printers.

Comparing Bids

Ask each printer to bid separately for presswork and paper, and provide at least one sample publication that shows them what you want. If you have not yet published any issues, then use someone else's publication as a sample. Choose one that matches the paper you want to use, binding, number of pages, and intended color.

CAUTION

Don't get bids until your plans are final. You should expect to revise the detailed specifications of a new publication during the planning stages. But beware that every time you change some detail, all the printers you consult will need to change their bids. Therefore, don't seek bids until you feel reasonably settled on the details, and allow enough time to get new bids if something big changes, such as you decide to use color or significantly increase or decrease the size of your publication, after receiving the original bids.

Ask the printers whether you would get any significant price breaks by changing the publication's specifications—for example, the use of color or the weight of the paper used for the publication. Also invite them to tell you about any services they can add to what you've requested, such as co-mailing, subscription database management, and prepress services.

According to one publishing consultant, "The single biggest mistake that consumers make with their print jobs is failing to involve the printer soon enough. Often the printer can make recommendations that will save you time and aggravation, but once the paper is running through the presses, it's too late for the printer to help you improve the job."

Emphasize to the printers that you welcome their advice about increasing the efficiency or reducing the costs of your job. Consider that the printer will become a central figure in your publishing endeavor, and learn to include your contact person at the printer in your planning and design process. If you ask, a printer may be able to streamline your work, save money, or add improvements that you didn't know were possible.

> **TIP**
>
> **It may pay to keep asking.** Printing technology is constantly changing. Every year, ask your current printer if there are any ways to shave time or money from your production process. And every few years, collect bids from other printers, just to see what new options or savings opportunities have become available since the last time you asked. You can even ask your current printer to provide an estimate for each issue as it goes to press, to help you stay on budget and to avoid surprises.

Troubleshooting the Printer Relationship

Many publishers experience problems in their relationships with printers, and it's not always easy to figure out why. Too often, a publisher does not have the staff or expertise to keep up with a printer's technical demands. This could be the case, for example, if you are constantly missing deadlines or sending mistake-filled files to your printer.

Some printers can be trusted to tell you how to shape up. But many of them are more likely to suffer in silence and jack up your bill by adding on late fees and other penalties.

If you are causing the problems—because you can't produce your publication without mistakes and on time—then switching to a new printer will not help. Instead, you'll need someone to help you get on top of your work. The remedy might include hiring more staff, training the people who now work on the publication, getting newer equipment, replacing a designer or a prepress vendor, or hiring a production consultant to troubleshoot. (See "Hiring a Production Consultant," below, for detail on this.)

Getting your house in order may save your current relationship, and if not, it will certainly help you develop a better one with a new printer.

Hiring a Production Consultant

A consultant brings an impartial, informed perspective that may be just what's needed when you're dealing with cleaning up a messy relationship with a printer. You can find production consultants in *Folio* magazine at www.foliomag.com.

Expect to pay $75 or more per hour for a production consultant. If you have trouble justifying that expense, calculate how much you could save in a year if the consultant is able to trim your printing bills by just 10%—a very reasonable goal—and then find a consultant willing to take on the job for that amount.

Fixing your systems. If your work procedures are the source of the problem, then a consultant should be able to help you better organize your side of the relationship to get rid of these kinks. Look for someone who knows how to train or evaluate your staff, upgrade your computer systems, refine your schedules, and negotiate terms with a printer.

Replacing your printer. Sometimes you're doing everything right but the printer still treats you badly. An outside consultant who has had experience with a number of different printing companies can quickly spot poor performance from your printer and help you find one that's a better fit.

If you think the printer is causing the problems—by not communicating well, adding lots of unexplained charges, or consistently failing to produce good work—then it's time to switch. Printers most commonly let you down because they're not really equipped to handle your publication or because they've failed to upgrade their equipment over time.

Start your search for a new printer by assessing what went wrong with the last one, and then go back through the bids you've received in the past from other printers to find a more suitable fit.

TIP

Be sure to ask about similar printing jobs. When starting your printer search over again, don't forget to ask each prospect about its track record in producing publications like yours. This is the single most important factor in finding a good fit.

CHAPTER

8

Producing a Website

Today, people expect almost all organizations, companies, and associations—even their neighborhood restaurants—to have a website. When in search of information, even something as simple as a telephone number, they'll often turn to the Internet instead of a telephone book.

If readers can't find your publication online, you miss an opportunity to get your message out to the public, and your organization may also lose credibility. Even with such high stakes, however, many print publishers have not yet succeeded in posting their periodicals on the Internet, perhaps because website publishing appears too daunting. Or the expense of posting free content may be too hard to justify. And many nonprofits that do maintain a website fail to fully capitalize on the strengths of the medium, leaving out some of the most popular interactive features, such as links.

But producing a professional website is easier, and can be less expensive, than you might imagine. This chapter briefs you on what you need to know to plan, develop, and maintain a functional website. It reviews many common Web features and also discusses a range of options for creating a website, from working within an existing institutional website to creating a standalone site on a tiny budget.

CROSS-REFERENCE

Nonprofits have many urgent reasons to connect with members, donors, and staff. A website is not always the quickest or most effective means to handle these communications, and many groups regularly send out email alerts or action campaigns to their mailing lists. Email can be powerful for bringing people quickly up to date on what matters.

This chapter primarily focuses on developing a website that people will come to visit, but the book also offers advice about creating electronic communications that you send out by email:

- How to write copy that works well in email formats (Chapter 5)
- Email design rules and formatting suggestions (Chapter 6)
- Mailing lists and broadcasting services (Chapter 9)
- Avoiding Spam (Chapter 9), and
- Getting financial support from sponsors (Chapter 10).

Strengths of the Web

Beyond the obvious savings in paper, time, and postage expenses, communicating on the Internet can offer unique advantages over print publications—but only if you capitalize on those advantages. In the same way that you would study common components of other magazines and newsletters before developing one of your own, you should focus on standard and popular website features, many of which are discussed in detail later in this chapter.

For now, consider the following core advantages that the Web has over print publications.

Immediacy. If you have a website, anyone with Internet access can find information about your organization 24 hours a day, seven days a week. Readers can find fast-breaking news stories or blog entries immediately after you post them. You can take advantage of this by including frequent updates of news items linked to current events or the affairs of the day. Posting frequent updates to your website helps train people to visit more often. You can also send out timely information in an email.

Community and interactivity. Even members or subscribers who live half a world away from one another can use email listservs, chat rooms, and Internet bulletin boards for networking among themselves and collaborating. Consider including these features in your site design, particularly if part of your nonprofit's mission is to promote community. (See "Chat Rooms, Forums, and Message Boards," below, for details.)

Economy. There is little additional cost for expanding and delivering in-depth material through your website once the basics are in place. For example, you may be able to print only a short excerpt of a conference session in your newsletter, but you could post the whole transcript to your website for those who couldn't attend. Publishers who can afford to print a magazine only quarterly can usually afford to update a website much more often. You can use the extra space and timeliness to expand on printed articles and update information in between issues of your print publications.

Linking content. One of the beauties of online content is that you can link to other information sources in your articles. Commercial website sometimes fret about sending potential customers off to other websites through links, but nonprofit publishers more often find that links provide a useful means for augmenting their sites with information from other credible sources. So add links wherever you can.

For example, if you are publishing a story about a piece of legislation that threatens to reverse clean air and water laws, you wouldn't likely publish the entire legislative history at your website or in your magazine. But for readers who have an interest, you can link your website article to other Internet sites that do. Similarly, you can link to interesting source documents or to other articles on your own site that would give readers a better context in which to understand this story.

Administrative activities. Members can renew a membership, potential writers can read your guidelines for manuscript submissions, and the public can make donations to your organization much more easily through a website than they can through the mail. Prospective advertisers, sponsors, and grant-makers can also get needed information more efficiently online than they can in print. If your staff is small, automating a website to perform these administrative functions can free them up to focus on more-complex work.

Search. Search engines help nonprofit organizations reach more people than is possible in print. As a result, people seeking help or information are much more likely to find your organization through a website than a print publication. Take time to learn how the search engines operate so that you can increase your visibility through them. (See "Making the Most of Search Engines," below, for details on this.)

How Websites Work

Much has been written in the attempt to demystify Web technology—and much of that is overly technical. Here is a bare-bones explanation that should give you a basic understanding of how websites work—essential if your nonprofit is contemplating conducting some of its publishing online. Many of these activities are also described in greater detail later in this chapter.

Servers hold everything. When you type a website address into your browser program and hit return, your computer goes looking for another computer where the information it is seeking is stored. Your machine is called the **client**, and the machine it's seeking is called the **server**.

Browsers request and interpret the files. Once it finds the server, your computer collects the information it needs and interprets the data into the pages that are displayed on your monitor using a browser program.

Pages are coded in HTML. Servers store data in a program called HTML, which stands for Hyper Text Markup Language. HTML defines how words and images will line up on a page when you use a browser program to look at it.

Web software builds HTML coding for website pages. Advancing technology makes it easy for nontechnical writers to convert text and image pages into HTML using software programs such as Dreamweaver. And a growing number of Web-based applications help create fancier and more-interactive features on Web pages than ever before, eliminating the need to learn HTML code.

Publishers upload HTML pages to a server. As an online publisher, you will need to get your content into an HTML format and upload the Web pages onto a server for your readers to access. You will likely also need to register your own unique URL, or domain name, so that your readers can easily remember what address to type in when they want to find you.

Internet Service Providers often host websites. Most very large institutions, such as universities, keep their own servers, but the vast majority of website owners "rent" server space from an Internet Service Provider company that hosts websites for a monthly hosting fee. Hosting companies can also handle the job of getting the Web address that you want to use.

> ### How Websites Work, continued
>
> **Designers sometimes develop a basic site.** Many new website publishers start out by hiring a professional Web designer to create the overall look and structure of a site, plus its programming, because these activities are not easy for an untrained person to manage. But once a site is set up properly, it is usually relatively easy to update. Therefore, many publishers handle the updates themselves either by contracting a freelancer or training someone on staff to do the job.

RESOURCE

For additional straightforward explanations of the Internet, see "How Web Servers Work" and "How Web Pages Work" at www. howstuffworks.com or the entries for "Web pages" and "Web servers" at www.wikipedia.org and www.about.com.

Web Programming Tools

A number of computer programs operate behind the scenes to provide the features most people have come to expect at websites—including email subscriptions, blogs, search features, and message boards.

Do-it-yourselfers who have some technical savvy can buy these programs off the shelf and assemble them into a fully featured website. If you hire a freelancer or an outside company to develop a website for you, most will include these features, often at no extra charge. For example, nearly all website hosting services automatically include free mailboxes for email and dozens of free templates for designing pages. If a specific feature such as a blog or a chat room is important to your mission, then be sure to find a hosting service capable of providing that feature.

What Features Do You Need?

Websites are capable of all sorts of nifty features these days, but more-complex capabilities often cost more money. Refer back to your organization's top goals for your website and determine the features it can offer. (See Chapter 1 for guidance on determining your publication's mission.) The list below will help you determine if you really need all the bells and whistles that are available.

Donation capabilities. If one of your website's goals is to increase donations, consider including a way for people to make contributions online.

User registration or member login. If you are interested in capturing information about your website users or wish to make certain content available only to members, consider requiring visitors to register or log in at your website to access premium content, such as Web-only articles or your publication's complete archives.

Search function. Offering users the ability to search your site is a fairly easy feature to include these days, as discussed later in this chapter. Publications that are issued frequently and offer a lot of content online have an absolute need for this feature, which will help users find information quickly.

Online store. If your publication or nonprofit runs a side business selling branded products, such as the human rights nonprofit Global Exchange, consider setting up an online store. Be careful, though. Online shopping capabilities can be a complex undertaking that involves not only creating a way for users to browse and purchase items online, but also securely processing payments. You'll need to choose a host or website designer savvy enough to include these features.

Blogs. If your publication features a prominent or popular writer or you seek to influence public debate on a topic with your organization's unique viewpoints, consider starting a blog.

Forums. If one of your website's goals is to foster community and allow users to connect and share information, online forums can be a great way to foster that.

Advocacy capabilities. If your website aims to activate your readers to do something, whether it's to forward something to their friends and family, write to a legislator, or sign an online petition, consider adding advocacy features to your site.

At large institutions, many of these features have already been programmed into the group's existing website. If you are launching a new publication based on an institutional website structure, check with the organization's Web technicians to see what features are available to you. (See "Options for Building Your Website," below, for more details about doing it yourself, hiring an outside vendor, or working within an institutional structure.)

Some of the resources described in this section are available as "freeware"—meaning that you can get them by paying a small license fee to the person who created them. And some are available as a "hosted" service. A hosted or licensed version means that the software runs on a vendor's computer that is invisibly linked to yours, and at your control. Instead of buying the program, you pay a monthly fee to use it.

The best way to find these programs is to ask for references from a knowledgeable friend or vendor. For example, if you hire someone to create a design grid for your site, that person will either include the best programs as part of the design, or advise you about choosing them. If you are going it completely alone, without access to a technical adviser, then your best hope is to search for product reviews in each category, using the names of the programs listed in this chapter, such as "Web page design programs" or "content management systems" as search terms.

RESOURCE
Start your search at these general sites, which provide blogs and forums as well as general information and links to specific website programs:

- Search Engine World, at www.searchengineworld.com, and
- Web Master World, at www.webmasterworld.com.

And you can read product reviews and comparisons at these sites:

- *PC Magazine*, at www.pcmag.com
- Cnet, at www.cnet.com, and
- Idealist, at www.idealist.org.

Web Page Design Programs

Today, the vast majority of people who create and maintain websites use Web page design programs that allow them to arrange text, images, and ads visually—just as you would with a program such as PowerPoint. The software converts your page layouts behind the scenes into HTML code, the language that allows a browser program to "read" Web pages correctly. (Chapter 6 contains more information about designing Web pages using these HTML editing programs.)

HTML editing programs define the look of individual pages in your website and also control how a reader can navigate among them. Each page is a freestanding unit within the overall design and navigation structure. As a website grows—perhaps to several hundred individual pages that are updated daily or monthly—then controlling all the material building up on the site can become burdensome. For example, if your nonprofit changes the name of one of its major programs, someone would have to update the name throughout the site, one page at a time, wherever the program name appears. With a lot of pages and a lot of updating, the most efficient solution may be to add a Content Management System for handling this activity, as described below.

Content Management Systems

Many publications deal with so much content that's posted regularly, taken down, archived, or moved that it becomes inefficient to handle pages individually. They turn to a Content Management System, or CMS.

CMS programs automate many of the steps you'd normally go through to create or update a Web page by adding an extra layer of information about every feature on the page and storing them all in a database. Using this added information, the CMS program is able to retrieve and republish the same article or photograph simultaneously at several different locations on your site. And if you edit the article later, the CMS updates it everywhere it has been posted. Many CMS programs also have user-friendly interfaces that do not require any coding or technical skills. Instead, users click buttons, fill out fields, and follow step-by-step prompts.

For example, imagine that you want to post an award-winning cover story from the most recent issue of your newsletter on several different pages of your website: on a table of contents page for that issue, in the editor's blog, in a section summarizing articles by subject, and on a page summarizing all the prizes you've won. As one website manager said about making a similar update to several Web pages at one time: "Our CMS program is just faster. And it doesn't require the person to have a lot of technical skill or know how to code HTML."

CMS programs are not cheap, though. Depending on the features and level of customization for your organization, they can cost hundreds to even thousands of dollars per month. While various open source applications are available free on the Internet, they often need to be tailored to work for your purposes, which is tough to do if you lack the requisite programming skills.

> **TIP**
> **Institutional publishers may already have CMS.** Smaller nonprofits rarely use or need a CMS system. But most large nonprofit organizations have them in place or are considering installing them. If you are launching a new website for a larger organization, check with the technology staff to see if a CMS is already under development, and ask those who run it to teach you how to use it.

Email Broadcasting

Publishers find that broadcasting an email draws readers onto a site after new material has been posted. As a result, email subscriptions have become a standard feature for websites and should probably be included at any site that you build.

Let people sign up online, and make it easy for them to be removed from your email list, too. (Chapter 9 lists emailing programs you can add to a website and discusses some of the ethical guidelines about spam.)

RESOURCE

Convivio's Get Active is one of the most popular and established suite of programs designed to help nonprofit organizations build community-focused sites. You can let the company host your whole website or use its products to complement other features on your site. Go to www.convivio.com for more information.

Ad Servers

Ad servers are the equivalent of CMS programs, but they concentrate on advertising content. If you are planning to sell any ads at your website, then you will need either a local ad server program or a remote one. Many publishers use both.

Local ad server programs run on the computer that hosts your website and supply ads to your Web pages, allowing you to control the ads' content and format. Remote ad servers run on somebody else's server computer and can serve ads simultaneously to the websites of multiple publishers. Similar to CMS systems, remote servers deliver ads from one central source. Consequently, advertisers and publishers can track and control the distribution of advertisements across the Internet.

If you don't have an advertising sales staff, you can still include ads on your site by joining an ad sales network. Many publishers join more than one network. And if you have a sales staff to handle the business, you may also need the capacity to manage those ads, outside of any networks. This would require a local ad server. (Chapter 10 contains details about advertising sales options for websites. The ad server program you ultimately choose will likely depend on the sales strategy you develop after reading that chapter.)

Remote Ad Servers

Google is the best known among remote ad servers, but it is far from the only one. Google offers what is called "contextual ads," meaning that the text-based or image ads are delivered to Web pages that include related content. For example, Google sends ads for digital cameras to pages about photography, but not to pages about child care.

Other networks may offer ads based on a different scheme, but all remote servers work the same way. If you sign up to accept network ads on your website, the network provides a few lines of programming that you add to your Web pages, and its remote ad server handles everything else: signing up new advertisers, placing the ads on specific pages of your site, tracking and reporting activity on all the ads, and collecting fees from the advertisers. You get your share of the advertising revenue every month from the network and never deal directly with the advertisers. And you never have to store any ads on your own server computers.

There are many advertising sales networks, and some publishers join several networks at the same time. Each network maintains its own remote ad server system that catalogs all the ads within the network. You don't need to buy any special software for your own site to participate in these remote ad networks, and signing up with them is easy to accomplish in a very short time. (See Chapter 10 for more information about advertising networks and how to work with them.)

Local Ad Servers

If you can't find a suitable advertising network to join, there are dozens of freestanding local ad server programs that you can buy and run on your own server computer to manage ads or license to use from someone else's website. Sometimes, a network is not an ideal option. For example, some networks might include advertisers whose products or ads conflict with your mission. And you can certainly keep a larger share of the advertising dollars generated by selling ads directly rather than through a network. For these reasons, publishers with a sales staff to manage the relationships with advertisers generally buy their own local ad server software.

Ad server programs that you buy and run on your own computers can cost between $300 and $15,000. Hosted services can cost as little as $30 per month or as much as $10,000 per year, depending on how much traffic comes through your site, how many ads you run, and how much control you exercise over the ads.

Blog Publishing Programs

Blog publishing programs are comparable to CMS programs used for entire websites, but for blogs. Blogs are an advanced iteration of the old email or Internet bulletin boards with discussion threads, where bloggers keep a running journal, posting information or viewpoints on a subject, and other users can respond and comment. In recent years, blogs, short for "weblogs," have grown very popular and ubiquitous on the Internet. They have evolved both in how they are displayed to readers and in their complexity.

Blog entries are shown in reverse chronological order and differ in sophistication, both in function and appearance—with the more ornate incorporating photos, video, and audio.

As you can imagine, for a publication with multiple blogs on its website, arranged either by topic or blogger, managing all of this content can become overwhelming. For example, without proper controls and monitoring systems, people can post inappropriate or incorrect information to your blog. Good blog publishing programs help you weed out offensive and unwanted content by allowing a staffer to edit submissions or by banning anonymous postings. And blogging programs are so easy to use that a staff member or freelance blogger does not need advanced technical skill to easily make entries and have all that material appear properly displayed and linked on the website.

TIP

Some guidance on the vernacular. Blog publishing programs have been springing up like weeds in the past few years and continue to evolve. Some programs are free, open-source applications. Others are proprietary and require you to buy a license to download and install the software, much like other software programs you run on your computer. And still others are "developer hosted," meaning that, for a fee, you do everything you need to do—add and edit entries, add graphics and podcasts, and archive—through the software developer's website and don't need to install any software.

Onsite Search Function Tools

These days, many people jump right past every carefully designed navigation tool and home page and go immediately to a website's search box to locate the information they need. If your site does not offer this common amenity, some visitors might simply leave. And since an onsite search feature helps people quickly find information that they need, you really ought to include it—particularly if providing public service information is a central part of your mission.

It's easy to add this function to a website. You just need to paste the HTML search box coding onto the Web pages where you want the search feature to appear. Google and the other big search companies let small websites use their search engine technology in exchange for placing the company logo on your pages and linking to their website. But you can also get the search feature from other software companies for a fee.

> **TIP**
>
> **Helping search engines find you.** Take note of the tips about making the most of the searchability of your site in "Making the Most of Search Engines," below. Taking these steps to help Google and Yahoo find articles at your site will also help people effectively use your on-site search feature.

Chat Rooms, Forums, and Message Boards

Chat rooms, forums, and message boards are all names for the same thing: a website feature that allows people to write comments, pose questions, or participate in a text-based "conversation" with other people on a website.

There is forum software that makes these "watering hole" features work smoothly. Some forums are moderated, which means that you can screen out inappropriate comments before they show up on your site. And some are open to all posters. Most forum software allows you to create more than one forum.

Forums either allow visitors to post anonymously or require people to register and post items in their own names. Although blog comment pages are not exactly the same as Internet forums, they often use the anonymous system for the sake of simplicity.

Forum software packages are widely available on the Internet and are written in a variety of programming languages. Choose one that is compatible with the language used to program other elements of your website. Each package offers a different variety of features, from the most basic, providing text-only postings, to more-advanced packages offering multimedia support and formatting code, usually known as BBCode. Many packages can be integrated easily into an existing website to allow visitors to post comments on articles. Some are available as freeware.

Traffic Analyzer Programs

Chapter 11 covers a range of nontechnical ways to measure the impact of your website, such as counting the donations that result from your articles, measuring attendance at rallies promoted on the site, and correspondence received as a response to it.

The Internet also offers technical tools, called Web analytics or traffic analyzers, for directly counting how many people look at each Web page, click on a link, or download a PDF file. You can obtain a remarkable array of information from these programs—ranging from the time of day when people visit most often and the search engines that send them to you, to the browsers they're using, to which of your pages they visited.

Advertisers generally demand some accounting of your site traffic, and that's where these analyzing programs become especially important. But they also provide a handy way for you to assess which articles draw the most interest from your readers. You might use the statistics they gather to give feedback to writers, plan for new content, or justify new investments at the site. Publishers also find traffic analysis very helpful during a major overhaul of a site, when trying to decide which features to retain and which ones to retire.

If you use an outside hosting service, or if your website is part of a larger institutional site, these tools may already be included. In that case, you need only to ask your site administrator how to access them.

If your organization is not using a server that provides these logs, you can get the same information from a remotely hosted program. These remote programs generally work by putting a small snippet of code onto your Web pages—code that invisibly links back to their own site. Human visitors never see the system operating, but every time someone opens a page or follows a link, the hidden code can record their actions.

Making the Most of Search Engines

According to recent Internet user surveys, 87% of every Internet visit begins with one of the leading search engines: Google, Yahoo, MSN, or AOL. Even people who know the name of a website they want to visit are likely to use a search engine to get there instead of going directly to the site. One publisher reported that only 16% of new visitors to its site came through a search engine in 1999, but by 2005, more than 65% of new visitors came to the site through the search engines.

Because search engines are so powerful and so popular, it is essential that every Web publisher understands how to accommodate them. Luckily, a few simple rules cover most situations.

Unfortunately, you can't automatically assume that a professional site designer will follow these guidelines. Some designers consider these search engine optimization steps to be the client's job, not theirs. Therefore, it's a good idea to check with your site designer to ensure that these steps have been taken, because overlooking them can drastically reduce the number of people visiting your website. All of these practices are relatively easy to include in your website updating procedures once you know that they are necessary.

Stick to plain text. Search engines cannot read images and animation files, so make sure that no important content such as the name of your organization is posted within an image file or an animation.

This problem can occur even in a well-designed, text-based site. For example, if you use an image of your logo to identify the site, rather than your name spelled out in plain text, the search engines may not recognize the site as belonging to you. Many publishers take care of this issue by putting their names and addresses in plain-text footers on every page.

A Basic Search Engine Visibility Test

To find out what any search engine already knows about your site, enter "*site:yourdomain.org*" into its search box. You'll get back a listing of every page from your site that has been viewed and indexed by that search engine. In other words, you'll learn which of your site's pages will be visible to the public through that particular search engine.

Example: Searching for their own website, one nonprofit organization found 15,600 pages from Yahoo and 11,000 from Google. There are about 16,000 pages on the organization's site, so these numbers indicate that most of the pages posted at this website have been indexed by the search engines and are therefore easy for people to find using Google or Yahoo.

If doing this check does not return any pages from your site, or only the home page, then there is a serious problem. Most likely, the search engines are not able to read through your interior pages. Following the steps described in this chapter may solve the problem. But if not, read one of the Search Engine Optimization (SEO) books recommended at the end of this section, and consider hiring an SEO expert to help.

Pick the right keywords. Search engines try to rank pages according to how well their content matches the words a visitor entered in their search. People call those search words "keywords" because they describe the key information a user is looking to find. (Chapter 5 contains more information about editing for websites, including the step of editing to add keywords.)

Another important step toward making your site visible to search engines is including plenty of keyword phrases within articles about those subjects. And it is important to note that keywords also come in phrases. One study reports that only 20% of all searches are for a single word. People use two-word combinations for 33% of searches, three-word phrases 26% of the time, and four or more words on 21% of searches. The experts recommend building multiple word phrases into your keyword research. The longer phrases bring back fewer results, but the results are likely to be more refined.

Checking Your Own Searchability

Do this simple test to find out where your site currently ranks with the search engines on critical keyword phrases.

Make a list of phrases or words, including the name of your organization, that represent the topics you cover at your site. Then search those phrases at Google or Yahoo. You can dramatically improve your search engine ranking by adding the right keywords into the articles at your website and following the other practices recommended in this chapter.

Example: Here's how a recent test went when using the Heifer organization, www.heifer.org. First, seven out of the first ten results were pages from Heifer's website when looking for its name, "heifer." That's about the best any webmaster could expect. But when searching the phrase "hunger," which is a major component of Heifer's mission, there were 144 listings from other websites at Google before finding Heifer.org (at listing #145).

A user would have to scroll all the way down to page 15 before finding Heifer when searching on the word "hunger," and research suggests that at the most, a typical user will only look through the first 60 search results for any keyword or phrase. If Heifer could move up into the first 60 search results for people Googling "hunger," or even the top 30 listings, there is no doubt that many more people would find it.

EXAMPLE: One nonprofit published a long article about new breast cancer treatments in a magazine. Before posting the article to the website, an editor took time to add some of the most important keywords, often substituting a keyword phrase for a less specific one—for instance, using the two-word phrase "breast cancer" instead of "disease" or just "cancer." Those modest word changes will help search engines locate the article, giving it the potential to reach many more readers.

Include meta tags. In addition to the keyword phrases they find within your articles or Web page contents, search engines rely on "meta tags," special coding in the HTML language to decipher what each page is about, as described below. Meta tags that most closely match keywords that users would type into a search engine to find information about that topic are best. Including keywords in the page title and description meta tags also boosts the visibility of your pages to the search engines.

Human site visitors don't see meta tags, and because of that, some webmasters simply forget to include them. But a site is nearly invisible to the search engines without meta tag coding on each of its pages. It pays to include them.

TIP

CMS handles tagging. CMS programs automatically add appropriate meta tags to Web pages. If your site is built around a CMS program, then it will be easier to ensure that every page is tagged correctly.

The most important meta tag is called a "page title." The tag itself is invisible to users, but the phrase that you write for it—40 to 60 characters in length—will appear in the top bar of a user's browser window as they view that page. The page title tag is useful for helping users understand the purpose of that page. But more important, search engines will *ignore* pages that don't have a unique page title tag, so be sure to put one on every page.

Search engines also appreciate finding a unique "description" meta tag on every page. Sometimes your descriptions will appear in the search results for that page, and therefore, it is always worth the effort of writing a description that invites people to read every page by explaining what's contained within. Use up to 250 characters, including spaces, in each description. Include your organization's name along with a compelling phrase about the page's content.

EXAMPLE: Here are the meta tags from one nonprofit's page about its service learning programs. The keyword phrase "housing for the poor" is contained in the description tag, along with other keyword phrases, such as "ending homelessness" and "rural America."

In HTML, the page title reads:

<title>Service Learning Programs | Help the Anti-poverty League build housing for the poor in rural America.</title>

In HTML, the description reads:

<meta name="description" content="Help us end homelessness and build housing for the poor in rural America by joining one of our Anti-Poverty League service learning programs.">

And if a searcher entered the phrase "housing for the poor" or "service learning programs," the search listing for this page might read this way:

Service Learning Programs | Help the Anti-poverty League build housing for the poor in rural America

---

Help us end homelessness and build *housing for the poor* in rural America by joining one of our Anti-Poverty League *service learning programs.* www.antipovertyleague.org/slp/housing.html - 18k - Cached - Similar pages

---

Give search-friendly names to links. Search engines can read plain text only. If your programmers used JavaScript , C++, Perl, or some other high-level programming language to create your website's navigation system, as many do, the search engines will find your home page but nothing else. The reason is that unless the links are in plain text, search engines cannot read any of those links within your site and therefore can't find any of your interior pages.

You can fix the invisible links problem by making sure your home page and other important pages are peppered with plain-text links. Even if the text links duplicate your fancy graphic ones, include them on any page you want the search engines to find.

Experts also recommend using your keywords in all of your links to help visitors appreciate the focus of your site. For example, instead of using the plain word "Links," you could say "Links to School Funding Information." The reason: Every extra time you use descriptive keywords within the content of your pages, you make it easier for search engines to classify the pages properly. And you also make it easier for the general public to appreciate the mission of your site.

Add a site map. To guarantee that search engines find every essential page of your website, give them a single page with text-based links to every important interior page. Programmers call this a "site map." The ideal site map looks like a book's table of contents: It lists every top-level item or chapter name and one or two layers of important features within each chapter.

Search engines use site maps to help find all the important pages inside a website, so make sure to map any pages you want search engines to find. And put a link to your site map on every page of your site.

> **TIP**
> **Pay heed if your intended audience is large and general.** "Search Engine Optimization," or SEO, is a term used to describe a series of steps you can take to make sure your site shows up prominently when people use a search engine. For most nonprofit websites, exhaustive SEO planning is not necessary; you can get by with the simple advice provided in this chapter. But for those who intend to reach a very wide audience among the general population, then SEO is absolutely essential and well worth mastering. You can actually double the number of people visiting your website by executing a thoughtful SEO campaign.

RESOURCE

A number of books provide helpful details about SEO.

- *Search Engine Optimization: An Hour a Day*, by Jennifer Grappone and Gradiva Couzin (Sybex): This book comes from experienced Web consultants who seem to understand the problems caused by limited budgets and staff time. These authors offer downloadable worksheets to make the process easier, at www.yourseoplan.com.

- *Search Engine Optimization for Dummies*, by Peter Kent (For Dummies): One of the first and most popular writers to cover this topic, Kent offers practical advice based on long experience with search engines. The author also has an informative website at www.ichannelservices.com.

Website Planning Tips

Now that you have an overview of what resources are available for developing and maintaining your website, figure out how much money you have to spend on the project and go comparison shopping.

Few people can afford all the features they'd like to have. Instead, decide what you absolutely must have to accomplish your top goals.

TIP

Paying less: It doesn't hurt to ask. Don't be afraid to try to negotiate a nonprofit price for products and services with vendors and contractors. Bruce McCurdy, webmaster for the Foundation for National Progress, says he always asks vendors to discount their services for his nonprofit organization—and many of them do. By asking, McCurdy estimates that he has saved several thousands of dollars annually.

If you are not technically savvy, but know people who can help with the technical aspects of the site, you might want to try searching for free or low-cost open source applications that could be adjusted to meet your needs.

Proceed cautiously when purchasing products and services or hiring contractors and consultants. Use common sense and screen vigorously before parting with your money: check references, talk with former clients, visit and use websites they have worked on. Many companies will offer a 30-day trial of their products before you must buy. If they don't, ask for it.

Here are some specific tips to follow when planning the services and features to include on your website.

Match the spending to your goals. Many of the latest and greatest features are not appropriate for every website. And trying to include all of them in the launch of your first website may overwhelm your budget. Instead, focus on the features most essential to your core purposes. For example, if providing public service information is a top priority, focus on building a site that helps people find what they need, with features such as search and navigation tools. Add blogs, chat rooms, and other features later, as the budget allows.

Keep it manageable. If you don't have technical experts to help, don't build a site that depends on them. It's much better to have a simple site you can manage on your own than to have one you don't know how to use. You should be able to post a new article, update a blog, or blast an email without having to call in the techies for assistance.

Segment the audiences. Create channels for different audience groups when their needs might not be exactly identical. For example, if members want to network, make a members-only section of the site that allows them unfettered access to one another, and put public information elsewhere.

Options for Building Your Website

The choices you make when building a website will largely depend on your circumstances and your budget. A tiny organization without access to technical experts may have only one choice: Find a good outside vendor to design and build a bargain site that you can manage by yourselves.

And the same organization could try to build a simple website from scratch if it's lucky enough to have a technically savvy staffer or volunteer available to help. But the do-it-yourself option is not practical for most nonprofits. Some publishers have to fit their work into the confines of an institutional website. Others need so many complex features that no volunteer or staffer could manage to include them all.

There are also website hosting services that make the job easy for some nonprofits. If your main goals are to have a no-frills website that makes your print publication visible on the Internet, post a few articles, and list basic masthead information—then maybe all you need is to register a domain name, buy a subscription from a hosting service, and post the content according to the instructions the host provides.

Some hosting services are suitable for individuals only, so be careful to look for one that already provides services to organizations rather than private individuals. Otherwise, you may quickly outgrow the capabilities of your host and be forced to move elsewhere.

RESOURCE
There are hundreds of website hosting services, so choosing one can be overwhelming. For information about picking the right hosting service, go to www.wikipedia.org/wiki/web_hosting_service.

Registering a Domain Name

An Internet domain name provides an address that readers can easily and clearly identify as the publication's online home when they type it into their browser. It's the name that looks like this: www.yournamehere.org. You will have to secure a domain name when you set up a website—and pay an annual fee for each domain name, about $40 per name.

You can also secure several different domain names and use them within one main website, and many organizations do just that. For example, a museum could have a unique address for its magazine, such as museummagazine.org, that can be programmed to deliver users into the magazine's section of a museum's overall website. And perhaps there are other domain names also pointing to the same overall site, including museumvolunteernews.org and museumeducationprograms.org.

TIP

Get all the permutations. As a nonprofit publication, you will probably want to buy a name ending in ".org." But many organizations these days are staking claim to all the iterations of a domain—.org, .com, .net—just so that competitors do not set up shop or to avoid confusion among users who may be unclear just what type of organization you are. You can arrange it so that regardless of which address ending users choose, they will always be redirected to the proper website.

Often, the same companies that offer website hosting on their servers will also help you to get a suitable domain name for your site. But the steps for registering a domain name are fairly simple. Start at www. icann.org, which is the website of the Internet Corporation for Assigned Names and Numbers, the agency that maintains and manages the international directory domain registrations, and pick from the list of accredited companies with which to register a name. Click on "Registrars" and then "Registrar listing." At these websites, you can type in possible names for your website to see what is available. NetworkSolutions.com, GoDaddy.com, and Register.com are just a few of the most popular places to register a domain name.

If the domain you want is already taken, you can come up with a slightly altered version by using abbreviations for some longer words in your ideal name, by adding a hyphen, or by adding the words "magazine" or "newsletter" at the end of the name. You can also approach the owner of the domain and ask him or her to transfer or sell it to you. But if the owner is demanding a hefty sum, you'll need to weigh just how important it is for you to have that specific domain.

Once you register a domain name, you are free to begin posting your website to that address.

Doing It Yourself

If your publication website will consist mainly of text and simple images and will not be updated more frequently than monthly, hiring a part-time or freelance person with website development expertise to create and update Web pages may suffice. Alternatively, if you don't expect you'll be constantly changing the structure of your website, you could hire a Web designer or developer to create Web page templates that you or someone on your staff could learn to use in just a few days, or even hours.

This option is possible only because so many of the required programming tools are readily available and relatively easy to assemble. But the main downside to going this route is that your organization may become completely dependent on the person who built your custom site. Every site needs ongoing technical support.

Save the headaches that can come up if your webmaster quits or leaves town by making sure he or she follows the steps described below.

Document the technical details. Write up a handbook that describes enough technical details about the programs and components added to your site so that another programmer could step in and manage the site if the creator is no longer available.

Stick to common components. Rather than creating programs that no one else knows how to use, ask your programmer to install standard, off-the-shelf programs that most other programmers probably know how to run.

Train a few back-up people. Make sure that several people know enough about the "guts" of your site to update it or repair it in a crisis.

RESOURCE

Do-it-yourselfers will appreciate the book *Building a Web Site for Dummies*, by David A. Crowder (For Dummies). And the book *Nonprofit Internet Strategies: Best Practices for Marketing, Communications, and Fundrais-*

ing Success, by Ted Hart, James Greenfield, and Michael Johnston (John Wiley & Sons), provides good advice about how to use the Internet effectively.

Working With an Established Website

If your publication is attached to a larger institution that already has a well-established and sophisticated website, that can both be a good and a bad thing.

On the plus side, you will not have to go out and buy many of the software programs or hosting services discussed here, because they will probably have already been purchased or provided by the organization. And you don't have to buy or build the infrastructure, just figure out how to plug in to use it.

On the negative side, you will probably have less flexibility in developing the site and will have to conform to the organization's overall website structure. For example, even though the title of your publication has no connection to the nonprofit's name and you'd benefit from registering your own domain name, the institution may not allow you to do so because it wishes to direct all user traffic to its home page, first.

To maintain consistency, your nonprofit may also insist that your Web pages look similar to the rest of the organization's pages, even though the logo and design of your publication is quite different from the institutional materials. The IT staff may not have time for you and may be opposed to some of the things you want to do that they aren't already doing, such as selling ads.

Here are some ideas for working within an existing institutional structure.

Make friends in IT. Bring them brownies or buy them lunch once in a while. Listen to them so that you understand their working conditions and how to relate to them. Meet with them so that you understand how they operate. Other parts of the organization must occasionally have similar needs or want tailored Web pages, so find out what process they follow.

Hire your own technical adviser. So that you don't make unreasonable demands and so that you can get maximum value out of the centralized system, hire a tech-savvy person to help you figure out what to do.

Include the IT department in your publishing plans. If you are going to depend on their support, be sure to include someone from IT in discussions about your publishing mission and its importance to the organization. For instance, ask the tech experts to help you obtain the most appropriate domain name for your new publication, as mentioned above, and to integrate your publication's pages with the organization's other pages.

Outsourcing

There are so many individuals and companies providing options for every aspect of creating and maintaining a website that it is quite feasible to outsource almost all of the work.

There are advantages to outsourcing: You get ongoing technical support and constant upgrades to the programming. Also, because the site is hosted elsewhere, it's automatically backed up by your host. And they guarantee to have it running 24/7, even when the nonprofit staff is on holiday.

EXAMPLE: Launching a nonprofit news website with less than $20,000 to spend, the Public Interest News Gate organization hired a website design firm to design and build its site, www.askquestions.org. The total cost for initial programming and design was less than $9,500. Monthly charges are $100 for hosting and email service.

Take time to do your research and beware of companies or individuals that are selling more than they can deliver. Again, it's a good idea to find or hire somebody knowledgeable about what's out there to help you sort through all the choices, because there are many and more are popping up every day.

Find websites that have capabilities you would like to emulate; then call them up and ask how they did it. Ask them what companies, services, or individuals they used. What problems did they run into? What would they have changed if they could go back and do it all over again?

Website Dos and Don'ts

While the Internet world is changing quickly, some commonsense advice has evolved and endured for those interested in Web publishing.

DO . . .

Translate print articles into searchable language. Eliminate metaphors and hyperbole that is likely to confuse a search engine. Translate a poetic headline such as "The Sky is Falling" into a practical one that will be easier for search engines to understand, such as "New Facts About Climate Change." (Chapter 5 offers additional advice about editing for websites.)

Gather reader feedback. Encourage people to add value to your site by posting their own comments and ideas when they visit. Content created by readers is an easy way to expand a site without busting your budget.

Explore free Google ads for nonprofits. Google has a Grants program that offers up to $10,000 per month in free search ads to qualifying nonprofits and community organizations. Learn more at www.google.org or www.google.com/grants.

Make your site searchable. It's easy to add a search function to every website, and many users go straight to a search rather than reading your index or contents pages.

Break long articles into multiple Web pages. Readers rarely scroll through a long article and may quit reading before the story ends. But if you break a long story into short pages, with a descriptive link to each one, they are more likely to follow the whole thing. (Find more editing tips in Chapter 5.) Advertisers also like shorter pages. And if you break a long article into three or four pages instead of one, you'll have that much more room to carry ads.

DON'T . . .

Leave out links. Putting links in articles adds value for readers. Linking also helps to forge strategic partnerships with other nonprofits and information sources. Trading links with other websites also helps to boost your visibility with search engines and your traffic.

Depend entirely on search engines. Try to list your site with every directory and website that covers your field so that people within the niche can find you, even if they don't use a search engine.

Forget to ask for nonprofit discounts. Ask every vendor to give your nonprofit site a price break. You'll be surprised at how often this tactic yields significant savings.

Testing Your Website

Though it may be cheaper and easier to fix mistakes on a website than in print, online errors can be no less embarrassing and reflect just as badly on your publication—perhaps they feel even more public because the material is available to the world instantaneously. Online publishers need to establish a process for proofing and testing their websites.

The proofing process for websites is similar to the process for print publications in that you need several people to review the site as it will appear and function to the world once you upload it to the Web server. Content that makes it to this production stage should already have been copy edited long ago for the usual typos. What you are looking for now is how Web pages are displayed, how long it takes them to get displayed, and whether all the links work properly.

The easiest way to do this is to upload the pages to a server that is but located at an Internet address, usually a subdirectory of the main URL, that only the proofers or testers know so that it's shielded from the public. Once you have it up, enlist all editors, the webmaster, and any other volunteers with a fresh set of eyes to review and use the site. Ask them to click on every link. Does it go to the right place? Does it dead end and produce an error page? If you're asking users to fill out a form, what happens when they omit fields? Reviewers can print out hard copies of the site, mark up any needed fixes, and route to the person designated to make changes. If your reviewers are working remotely, it's also possible to save screenshots as PDFs, mark those up, and email them back to the right person.

> **TIP**
>
> **Link check programs.** It's always preferable to have humans check your links, but if you are short staffed, consider using software to vet the links instead. Some HTML design programs have a link check feature built in, but you can also run your website through a variety of link checking programs. The downside is that most only search for dead or broken links and won't necessarily flag links that connect to the wrong place. The upside is that many are available free or offer free trials before requiring a purchase. You can find many of them by typing "link check" or "Web test tools" into any search engine.

If you have the time and money, some organizations test their website with potential readers by hosting a focus group. (See Chapter 11 for details about conducting focus groups.)

With complex websites, sometimes changing, adding, or removing one element will unintentionally affect other parts of the website. Changing the point size of a headline should not affect other pages, but adding a new login feature might. It's a good idea to routinely check whether all parts of your website function. If you accept online donations, go through the process of making a donation and see if it works. If you allow responses to blogs, post a response and see if it appears properly.

Website Production Checklist

This is a summary of the steps commonly needed to prepare each article or Web page for loading to your website. Taking them will ensure that every page includes all essential elements and that each article will be visible to search engines.

Optimizing the Page

- **Plain text.** Check to ensure that there is no important information in images or graphics files only; key facts and identity details also should be available in plain text

- **Keywords.** List ten to 12 keywords and keyword phrases that apply to the page.

- **Page title.** Define a unique page name for this article and put that name into a page title meta tag.

- **Description tags.** Put your keyword list into the description meta tag, along with any other language that you want the search engines to use when describing the page.

- **Links.** Add links to resources mentioned in the article or to other content available at our site, and make sure the links on this page are described so that readers want to follow them. Include keywords in the link names, if possible.

- **Site map.** If appropriate, add this page to the site map.

Uploading the Files

- **Graphics files.** Assemble any graphics files that accompany this article and make sure to upload those files with the article.

- **HTML check.** Do a test to see that the HTML page appears as expected when viewed in a browser program.

Distributing and Promoting Your Publication

This chapter describes how to deliver your publication to readers efficiently and without mishap. It covers the issues of pricing, promotion strategies, and postal regulations—including the rules for obtaining the favorable prices that the United States Postal Service (USPS) offers to periodicals and nonprofits. It also looks at a number of additional ways you might consider to distribute your publication—including through libraries, databases, newsstands and email.

Every tactic described here applies to both Web and print publications. For example, you can trade subscription ads with other nonprofits equally well for a print newsletter or an electronic one. And some of the same vendors described here help to distribute both printed periodicals and electronic ones.

The chapter also covers opportunities unique to the two different mediums: postal regulations that only apply to printed periodicals, and spam-busting guidelines that apply only to electronic publications.

Reading through this chapter, you should be able to make necessary decisions about how to distribute your publication. For print publications, that means deciding how many copies to print and how to distribute them and learning how much that distribution will cost. For electronic newsletters, it likely means determining how often to send emails and updates and what to include in each one, as well as knowing the cost of maintaining a spam-free email list.

Acquiring Readers

You have probably already decided who should read your publication. (See Chapter 1, "Defining Your Target Audience," for more on this strategic issue.) Now, the question is how to reach those readers so that you can establish ongoing relationships with them.

To make subscribing easy, every copy of your publication should be loaded with offers about how to become a member, buy a subscription, or sign up to receive more copies. Other publishers follow this practice because it works so well; that's why you find all those subscription cards, ads, and links embedded in most publications. But before you can make that all-important pitch to people, you have to find ways to get your publications into their hands or onto their browser windows.

There are a few basic methods used to acquire a reading audience:

- send free copies to people you already know—such as members, donors, or volunteers
- distribute free sample issues or free subscriptions to people keenly involved in your niche—including prospective donors, volunteers, or clients
- sell paid subscriptions to nonmember outsiders or the general public, and
- sell single issues through retail outlets—such as in bookstores or on the Internet.

Each method affects your publication in different ways. For example, you might generate some extra income if you sell subscriptions, and some nonprofits depend on subscription sales to support their publications. But forcing readers to pay for your publication might limit your opportunity to share your message with key supporters—and for that reason, some nonprofits fund their publications from other income sources.

Depending on your publishing goals and resources, you might decide on a mix of distribution methods. Several possibilities are discussed in detail below.

Free to Known Audiences

A magazine, newsletter, or website can be a very effective resource for deepening a nonprofit's relationships with current constituencies. In these situations, finding readers can be as simple as printing out a set of mailing labels from your current database and popping the publication into the mail or broadcasting an email.

But even in this simple scenario, there are important considerations to keep in mind. You might choose to send a publication only to certain groups of your members—your largest donors, for example, or your newest members—and your database may need an upgrade to handle those selections. You might also need to update your database to exclude members who elect not to receive your publication. (See "Tracking Readers Through a Database Program," below, for specifics on this.)

Free to Prospects

In addition to including people already in their databases, many nonprofits routinely include a sampling of prospective members or donors to receive a new or revamped publication. That helps draw new members or donors into the organization. The strategy involves the same considerations already described, plus some new ones.

The major new challenge is finding appropriate prospects and devising a way to convert them into members or donors.

> **EXAMPLE:** Only 35% of eligible parents were joining the PTA at one neighborhood high school. And yet the school depended heavily on volunteer support from parents for field trips, tutoring, and hosting events at the school. The PTA was able to increase participation significantly by mailing its monthly newsletter to the nonmember parents on the school's roster of families and handing out free copies to parents at school events.

Some people in your organization, perhaps in the membership department or development group, may already handle this prospecting activity. If so, consult them when deciding how best to reach new readers. They may also be able to help you assess what kinds of content are likely to appeal most to potential members. Work with them on timing issues and setting the editorial calendar (discussed in Chapter 2) so that the publication is smoothly linked to your organization's other activities.

If your publications are expected to recruit new members or donors, but there are no membership or development professionals in your organization, then consider hiring outside consultants or developing an advisory group to help build a recruiting function into your distribution plans.

And if none of those options is workable, then you might benefit from studying what other publishers are doing. Join a publishing association so that you can meet other publishers, attend seminars, or obtain expert advice. (See the resources listed in Chapter 12 for contact information.) Or simply contact some of the publishers whose publications you admire to make those connections.

Tips for Finding Prospective Readers

Consider some of the following ways to find and target new prospects to receive your publication.

- Rent commercial mailing lists or trade lists with other nonprofits, and send sample issues to appropriate prospects. For example, trade associations often send samples of their magazines to graduating seniors at related professional schools. You could also offer a free sample issue of your new magazine through the newsletters or websites of other nonprofits that address the same audience or subject area.

- Use your own database to revisit past relationships. Some lapsed donors or members may renew their interest if you send them a sample issue of your new publication as an incentive. For example, one nonprofit organization sends a special year-end issue of its magazine to people who gave money too little or too long ago to qualify for a current subscription—and a hefty percentage of them give a new donation as a result.

- Use your publication to develop new exposure for your organization through libraries or online databases. Potential members or donors may encounter your organization for the first time by reading material from your publications in research databases or libraries. (See "Libraries" and "Content Aggregators," below, for more details on these options .)

Paid Subscriptions to the General Public

Getting the general public to read your publication involves all of the considerations already described, plus the challenge of selling subscriptions. The work is vitally important for organizations that focus on "spreading the word" as part of their fundamental missions, such as those that concentrate on environmental concerns, health care, or social change.

But reaching out to the general public is infinitely more complicated than dealing with a targeted assembly of people such as members or current donors who are already familiar with your organization and who support its work. You can waste a lot of money trying unsuccessfully to sell subscriptions to complete strangers. For that reason, organizations that take this route generally hire experienced subscription marketing or "circulation" people either as full-time staff members or as outside consultants and advisers.

EXAMPLE: A quarterly magazine published by one nonprofit conservation group has formed partnerships with other local conservation groups to provide editorial content, outreach, and special events supporting that mission. Concerned about reaching more members of the general public, the group hired a circulation consultant two days per month to help develop a successful subscription sales program that included selling the magazine in local retail stores; selling subscriptions and back issues through a website store; and developing a host of marketing programs, including ads and direct mail.

RESOURCE
You can find circulation consultants through the trade publications *Circulation Management*, at www.circman.com, and *Folio* magazine, at www.foliomag.com. Both of them publish annual directories listing circulation consultants. The publishing associations listed in Chapter 12 can also help you find consultants with suitable expertise.

Selling Single Issues

Many paid subscription print magazines sell issues through bookstores and other retail outlets, as well as their websites.

An individual copy sold in this way can pack a double punch for the publisher by generating new paid subscriptions, donations, or memberships through the order cards packaged inside. Some publishers have learned that one enthusiastic reader can return two or even three new subscriptions by sharing the publication with friends. And single-issue distribution can also be a plus in the minds of advertisers who appreciate that a newsstand buyer is exhibiting an active and current interest that might lead him or her to buy products.

But selling issues in bookstores may place unworkable demands on your publication. For example, most retailers will reject magazines that have fewer than 64 pages in each issue and that are not published at least four times per year. And your design has to stand up to the glossy competition you find on newsstands. Before choosing retail distribution, spend some time in front of a retail magazine rack looking at the production qualities, design features, size, and content of publications that reach the same types of readers you want to reach. Also note the pricing. You'll have to conform if you want to succeed in this environment.

You can reach retail outlets through a network of distribution companies. But take note of the expenses involved: The distributor takes a share of the publication's cover price, and so does the individual retailer. You can expect to collect less than half of the cover price for the copies sold at retail stores. As many as half the copies will not sell at all, and you will collect nothing from unsold copies. You may even be charged a fee for reclaiming the unsold copies or recycling them. And it can take several months to collect the cash from retail sales, because distributors and retailers must first account for returns or unsold copies before they settle up with publishers. Planning ahead for these expenses and complications can help you set up a more realistic budget for your publication.

RESOURCE
As with subscription marketing, there are consultants who can help you set up a retail magazine distribution program. *Folio* magazine, at www.foliomag.com, and *Circulation Management*, at www.circman.com, list retail distribution consultants in their annual directory issues.

Pricing Your Publication

Pricing is another issue to consider and possibly discuss with a circulation consultant. Most publishers try to charge enough for subscriptions to cover nearly all of their publishing costs. But obviously, there are limits on how much you can ask people to pay.

Determining a Price

Get a ballpark estimate on pricing by considering what comparable publications in your niche charge.

Pricing structures vary dramatically among newsletters, magazines, and online publications. For example, email newsletters are generally free to members, donors, and even the general public, because funding comes from sponsors or advertisers. Print newsletter subscription prices vary according to the audience and subject matter. Websites sometimes have features that are available only to paying members or subscribers—and again, the pricing of these paid features depends on the publication's editorial mission and the market.

Sometimes you would best serve your mission by giving away your magazine or granting access to your website free, as noted below.

But if there are not enough donors, advertisers, or sponsors to cover their publishing costs, many nonprofits have no choice but to try and collect some revenue from readers. In such cases, the best option is to study how comparable publications are priced.

EXAMPLE: To remain competitive, *Bay Nature* cannot charge more than other local environmental magazines. Looking at a range of prices between $3.75 and $10 for a single copy, Bay Nature selected $5.95 as its price. To encourage subscriptions, it then offered subscribers a price per issue of about 50¢ lower than the newsstand price.

Pricing of Magazines in the Environmental Niche

Publication	Issues/ Year	Single Copy Price/Issue	Subscriber Price/Issue	Subscription or Membership Price/Year
Terrain—Berkeley Ecology Center	4	$3.75	$3.75	$15
Earth Island Journal— Earth Island Institute	4	$5.95	$3.75	$15
Bay Nature—Bay Nature Institute	4	$5.95	$5.49	$21.95
California Wild— California Academy of Sciences	4	$10.00	$6.00	$24 (individual)

Free Is Sometimes the Best Price

Many nonprofits opt to finance their publications through foundation grants or donations, rather than subscription sales, so they can reach the most people who need information and avoid the administrative obstacles presented by subscription sales.

A nonprofit that publishes health care information, for example, might raise funds from donors or sponsors to pay the costs of putting a magazine into every pediatrician's office or to finance the development of a robust website for cancer patients. Readers never have to pay for access to the website or to receive a copy of the publication when sponsors or foundations supply all the funding.

Postal Rules on Subscription Prices

SKIP AHEAD

If yours is a Web publication . . . This section applies specifically to printed publications that will be mailed through the United States Postal Service. Publishers with exclusively online publications can skip this section.

The United States Postal Service (USPS) encourages nonprofit publishers to set a subscription price for periodicals, even if the only so-called subscribers are your own members—and even if you actually distribute the publication free. This price establishes a value for the publication and helps to distinguish publications from other materials, such as brochures and marketing literature. Many membership nonprofits include a subscription to their publications as free benefits of belonging—and then allocate some share of dues to the publication.

While there are no set rules dictating how much of a nonprofit's dues should be allocated to a periodical subscription, there are some commonly accepted practices. One recent survey of more than 100 association publications found allocations ranging between $1.25 and $2.50 per copy. That amount translated to an average of $15 of annual dues assigned to the publication as subscription income. And that allocation is set whether or not the organization actually spends $15 per year per member on writing and printing and mailing the periodical. But establishing a reasonable price for a publication can help impress readers with some sense of its value. So don't skimp on the price.

You should also print the single copy price on the cover of the periodical itself and the subscription price on the masthead. Seeing the price helps readers appreciate the publication's value, even if they're actually receiving a free copy. The USPS requires publishers to include these prices in the identification statement on their masthead (see "Postal ID Requirements," below.)

Donor publications may establish a specific donation level that qualifies some people to receive a subscription and thereby encourages donations at that level or higher.

EXAMPLE: The Humane Society of the United States sends its quarterly magazine, *All Animals*, to any donor who gives $25 or more to the society in a single year.

Testing Your Market

No nonprofit has unlimited marketing money to spend, and every publisher has to make some trade-offs. Because you can't afford to give a free sample or mail a promotion letter to every person on the planet, you have to decide which prospects are most likely to become loyal, long-term supporters of your organization. Then you can focus your marketing dollars on appealing to them. The most efficient way to hone in on these hot prospects is to copy the concept of testing from the marketing experts.

Direct marketers use tests to help select the best marketing options: After making several different appeals to current and prospective readers and tracking what happens, they choose the most effective campaigns for future marketing efforts.

Marketers test prices, sales pitches, payment options, prospect lists, and the details of the order form—including color, type face, and design. They monitor the results for a selected sample of every campaign: which mailing list pulled in more new orders than the others that received the same promotion, for example, or which sales offer generated the most orders on the website. And then they concentrate the next campaign on the best performers.

Testing can become very complicated, but you'll have sufficient information to develop a simple testing program on your own if you record the origin of every new membership or donation in your database. (See "Tracking Readers Through a Database Program," below.)

For example, publishers who sell copies of their magazines in retail stores usually put a unique source code on the order forms inside of each issue so they can tell which issues generated the highest number of new subscriptions or donations. And they can compare bookstore returns from copies distributed in other ways—to paid subscribers, for example—because there are different source codes in those copies.

Your testing program is 90% complete if you use a unique source code for every marketing effort: one for the website, one for each email promotion, one for each outside mailing list that you use, and so forth.

RESOURCE
You can read more about testing and other tried-and-true direct marketing techniques in the classic reference book *Successful Direct Marketing Methods,* by Bob Stone and Ron Jacobs (McGraw-Hill).

Choosing the Best Promotion Strategies

These days, most nonprofit publishers use a mix of promotion strategies that include using a website, trying direct mail, trading ads, giving free samples to qualified prospects, and selling through libraries and content aggregators. All of these strategies are discussed below.

Promoting Print and Email Publications on a Website

Virtually all nonprofits offer access to their print and email publications through a website, either through paid subscriptions or as membership benefits. But there are lots of options available, depending on how complex or how simple your online sales activities will be. (See Chapter 8 for information on the technical issues of Web publishing.)

This section focuses on integrating your nonprofit's website into the overall marketing plan for your print and online publications. For example, if you sell a print magazine in retail stores or to paid subscribers, you cannot post the contents free online without undercutting print revenues of that issue. Similarly, if your website serves as a major member benefit, then making it available free to nonmembers might undermine your membership marketing strategies.

On the other hand, if your goal is to share information with the widest possible audience, then you should make it easy for the general public to read your articles online.

Your website may be able to support a paid subscriptions strategy by showing potential buyers selected articles, but not all the content, from your publication online.

EXAMPLE: *Mother Jones* magazine derives more than half of its income from paid subscribers and retail distribution revenues. Posting the entire print magazine online would diminish bookstore and subscription sales. Instead, the table of contents of the current issue is posted on the website, but just a handful of the articles. Later, when the issue is no longer for sale on newsstands, all the articles are posted on the website. The *Mother Jones* website at www.motherjones.com promotes paid subscriptions on every page. Subscribers can also renew, buy back issues, and buy a gift subscription through the site.

Many nonprofits sell discounted subscriptions or memberships to people who are likely to become members in the future. This tactic allows them to share information with prospective members that might encourage them to join when they become eligible.

EXAMPLE: The American Nurses Association (ANA) offers its magazine, *American Nurse*, only to members, whose dues range from about $25 to over $170 per year. Only members can read the magazine online and enter the members-only areas of the ANA website, www.nursingworld.org. But students and others who are not full-fledged members of the ANA can pay $10 per year to obtain a special password giving them access to the member areas of its website, or $20 per year for a subscription to the print magazine.

If you don't have paid subscriptions or memberships to protect, then posting every article to your website taps into a world of readers you could never afford to reach in print.

EXAMPLE: The Berkeley Ecology Center invests a great deal of effort producing high quality, in-depth articles about environmental issues for its quarterly print magazine, *Terrain*. The center prints only 10,000 copies of each issue but reaches at least 60,000 more people every year through its website at www.ecologycenter.org/terrain. Editors post the entire contents of every issue on the website, plus a searchable archive of articles going back six to eight years. Each article includes a link to the Center's home page, plus an invitation to subscribe to the print magazine and donate to the Center.

Direct Mail Sales

Direct mail involves renting somebody else's subscriber, member, or donor list and mailing or emailing membership, donation, or subscription promotion offers to those individuals on behalf of your organization.

Since these outsiders may know very little about your organization or its publications, direct mail can be a relatively inefficient way to sell subscriptions. Average response rates generally range between 1.5% and 3% in the publishing industry overall, meaning that 97% or more of the letters mailed to prospective subscribers fail to produce any new orders.

You can increase the efficiency of direct mail by sticking to mailing lists of organizations that are very closely related to your niche. But even so, many nonprofits eschew direct mail—especially the printed kind— because of the expense. It's not uncommon for direct mail subscriptions to cost $40 apiece, after dividing all the printing and postage expenses by the meager number of new orders generated. Email campaigns are much more affordable without the paper and postage expenses, but the $15 or $20 cost per order is still prohibitive for organizations on a tight budget. The nonprofits that succeed at direct mail promotions commonly have a full-time circulation expert on staff or hire a consultant on retainer to help generate a higher number of orders at a lower cost per order.

Some nonprofits also forgo direct mail because they don't need it. A college alumni association, for example, does not need to borrow or rent mailing lists from any outside group, because it already has the names of the school's graduates. But for nonprofits targeting the general public such as the national Audubon Society, which promotes wildlife, direct mail is an important vehicle for reaching new subscribers. The magazine *Audubon* employs a full-time circulation expert who conducts several sophisticated direct mail campaigns per year.

RESOURCE
For detailed information on marketing paid subscriptions, see *Starting & Running a Successful Newsletter or Magazine*, by Cheryl Woodard (Nolo).

Trading Ads and Links With Other Nonprofits

Trading ads with other nonprofits is a common tactic for generating new subscriptions and promoting your publications.

If you carry ads, it costs very little to run someone else's ads in your print or Web publication—and this is an easy favor for other publishers to provide, too.

EXAMPLE: The Buddhist Peace Fellowship trades ads in its quarterly magazine, *Turning Wheel*, with other Buddhist publications. And there is an entire section of links to other Buddhist publishers and resources on the website at www.bpf.org. Another Buddhist publication, *Tricycle*, takes this one step further by posting an online calendar that collects announcements from dozens of other Buddhist groups. The calendar is such a valuable feature that other websites link to it, adding significantly to the traffic at www.tricycle.com.

Make it easy for new readers to subscribe through your website, and then use your print ads in other publications and linking partnerships to direct people to your site.

TIP
Consider additional ways to cash in on trading. Book, magazine, and website reviews can serve the same function as ad trades. By creating these features on your own site, you can encourage other publishers to include a link to them from their sites.

Sampling

"Sampling" refers to a practice of putting a publication directly into the hands of people who are likely to buy a subscription. For example, nonprofits often distribute sample issues of their print publications at conferences and seminars and in the offices of their members to reach others who have not yet joined the association.

Another important resource for finding a particular population to sample is through a gatekeeper—that is, someone who routinely contacts your target readership. For example, a magazine for parents of premature babies might distribute sample issues in neonatal hospital wards. Or a website that describes assisted living options for aging parents might form a partnership with the professional association of eldercare counselors to trade articles, links, and email lists. At the same time, the website could give away a brochure through assisted living facilities that promotes resources posted on the website.

Libraries

Libraries commonly order subscriptions through two distribution agencies: Ebsco (www.ebsco.com/publish) and Swets Information Services (www.informationservices.swets.com). Both agencies handle print and electronic distribution of information from periodicals through public, academic, and business libraries.

It is worth your while to have a conversation with representatives at these agencies to learn whether your publication can be distributed this way. But recognize that libraries favor independent, in-depth information over membership news or self-promotion. Therefore, the agencies may choose only part of your publication to distribute to libraries, or none at all.

> ⓘ **TIP**
>
> **Get registered.** Obtain an International Standard Serial Number (ISSN) free from the U.S. Library of Congress at www.loc.gov/issn. In addition to making your publication easier for distributors and bookstores to find, the ISSN is used by libraries and interlibrary loan systems; by the USPS for special rates; and by researchers, scholars, abstracters, and librarians to assure accuracy when citing newsletters and magazines.

> ⓘ **CD-ROM**
>
> A copy of the ISSN Application Form is available on the CD-ROM included with this book. You can find additional information about it at www.loc.gov/issn.

Content Aggregators

Online distribution is also available through several content aggregators—database companies that compile articles from many different publications and resell the material to individual readers or to institutions. The major content aggregators are listed below.

When working through content aggregators, individuals and libraries pay for access to the articles, either through a subscription or as a pay-per-view option, and the publishers receive a small share of that revenue. Contact these aggregators to explore options. At the very least, you can expand awareness of your publications by including them in these directory services. And at most, you may generate some additional revenue from them.

RESOURCE

The following aggregators may help ensure that potential researchers, individual subscribers, and librarians are able to find your publications.

- LexisNexis sells legal, tax, and regulatory information to law and business researchers online at www.lexisnexis.com.
- Gale, at www.gale.com, publishes annual directories of periodicals and provides online access to them.
- The Online Computer Library Center, at www.oclc.org, is a nonprofit content aggregator that grew out of efforts of professional librarians.
- Project Muse, at http://muse.jhu.edu, is a project of Johns Hopkins University that focuses on aggregating scholarly journals.
- Ingenta, at www.ingenta.com, is a commercial aggregator.
- A division of the Stanford University Libraries, HighWire Press, at www.highwire.com, hosts a repository of free, full-text, peer-reviewed content.

Tracking Readers Through a Database Program

The primary resource for managing ongoing relationships with members, donors, and subscribers is a database program. Your organization may already have a member or donor database with categories and information that can be slightly modified to accommodate your publications. In fact, publications need pretty much the same customer service database features that nonprofits commonly build into their member or donor programs.

There are a few key features you will need.

- **Source codes.** For the sake of the testing activities described here, it's important to record which specific marketing effort generates which new membership or subscription. Then, you can track the response rate of every effort and compare it to others and to industry norms. Publishers commonly develop a matrix of source codes and assign one unique code to each promotion. For example, you might have a code series B that stands for bind-in subscription cards and a numbering system to identify each issue so that the new orders coming in from your first 2007 issue might bear a source code of B0107. Print that source code on the subscription cards in that issue, and then capture it with the database record for everyone who subscribed using that card.

- **Expiration dates.** In some nonprofits, all memberships expire at the end of the calendar year and the membership department schedules an aggressive year-end renewal campaign. But a six-issue paid subscription might end in March or June rather than December, depending on which issue was the first one sent to that subscriber. This discrepancy in expiration dates may require you to make some adjustments to your database program so that every subscription is associated with the correct expiration date—and so that you can automatically generate renewal campaigns at different times throughout the year.

- **Mailing labels.** The postal service provides steep discounts to organizations that can presort their mailings by zip code or even by carrier route. And these discounts are even steeper for periodicals than for other mailing classifications. (See "Mailing Through the U.S. Postal Service," below, for more on this.) Some organizations' databases are already programmed to generate presorted mailing labels, but some are not.

- **Website order processing.** Most periodical subscribers now assume that they'll be able to place a new order, change an address, or renew a subscription at a website. Your existing database may require an upgrade to allow these online transactions to feed directly into it.

- **Email addresses.** Generally, renewing a membership or subscription by email is much cheaper than any other method. Consequently, capturing email addresses has become a priority for many nonprofits. You can overcome the natural reluctance people have about divulging their email addresses by promising never to send them any emails they didn't ask to receive. Then be sure to keep that promise.

- **Multiple transactions.** Readers may interact with your organization in many different ways—as donors, volunteers, or members—and you should track all of these activities in one database. Each person may also receive more than one of your publications. Combining all these activities in one central database helps your organization be aware of its multifaceted connections to each person.

- **Opting out option.** As mentioned, some nonprofits exchange mailing lists with one another or even raise money by renting a member list to other appropriate entities. The law requires that you allow individuals the opportunity to "opt out" of these mailings, and your database must accommodate these requests whenever you generate labels or an email effort.

RESOURCE

The Privacy Rights Clearinghouse has a fact sheet for nonprofits about how to protect members' rights. It's available at www.privacyrights.org/fs/fs28-nonprofits.htm.

Getting Fulfilled

In the publishing industry, subscriber database management is called "fulfillment"—and there are dozens of independent companies offering these services.

The trade magazine *Circulation Management* (www.circman.com) conducts an annual survey of fulfillment services. It recently surveyed 36 companies and reported that all of the companies can do all of the tasks just described, and more. Its report noted: "The services offered by the fulfillment bureaus are increasing every year across the board. Each time we ask about whether a new service is being offered, we find that it is, and in abundance."

Even if your organization already has its own database capabilities, it is wise to interview a few of these magazine fulfillment services to see what they might add to your current database operations.

The nonprofit world also contains database service providers geared to handle activities other than publishing activities such as fundraising and membership development—and some of these vendors can also manage your publication databases. There are also consultants who specialize in helping nonprofits set up or update database systems. You can find two searchable online directories of nonprofit consultants at www.idealist.org and at www.allianceonline.org.

Since it's likely that your current database may need an upgrade to accommodate a new publication, you may need help from one of these consultants.

Mailing Through the U.S. Postal Service

SKIP AHEAD

This section applies to printed publications that will be mailed. Exclusively online publishers can skip it and go directly to "Distributing Emails," below.

The USPS gives substantial postage discounts to nonprofit periodicals, but there are some critical strings attached. Keeping track of the detailed regulations is a challenge because there are so many of them.

Not only that, the rules are always changing, often in response to political pressure. In 2004, for example, four of the largest American commercial magazine companies lobbied hard for revisions to periodicals postage rates that would cut their own costs and hike the rates for smaller publishers, including nonprofits. That specific change was averted, at least for that time, but postage rates are reviewed every year or so. And the lobbyists are always heavily involved.

RESOURCE

You can get updates on all postal requirements at the USPS website, www.usps.com. You can also find news about postal rate politics at a watchdog group called Postal Watch at www.postalwatch.org.

Nonprofit newsletter and magazine publishers have two different mailing options: Nonprofit Standard Mail and Periodicals Class Mail. Both categories offer first-class mail handling of "bulk mailings"—200 pieces or more mailed at the same time—at a discount from regular bulk mail prices. The rules for each class are outlined in the Domestic Mail Manual (DMM)—a massive document that you can read online, or download from the USPS website at www.pe.usps.gov. The application process for both classes can take a couple of weeks, and requires verification from a postal official. While reviewing your application, the USPS will charge regular rates for your mailings. But if your application is approved, you can claim a refund for the difference.

Postal ID Requirements

The U.S. Postal Service requires all publications that use the Periodicals mailing permit classes to carry specific identification information. An identification statement must appear within the first five pages of the publication, on either the masthead or the table of contents. It should include the following information: title, issue number and date, ISSN number, statement of frequency, subscription price, and mailing address to which undeliverable copies or change-of-address notices are to be sent.

In addition to the identification statement, publishers must submit an annual *Statement of Ownership, Management, and Circulation* to the USPS on Form 3526 no later than October 1st, and then reproduce the information from that form inside the issue of their publication that appears immediately after that date. On this form, publishers report how many copies were printed of that issue and how those copies were distributed. The USPS uses this information to confirm that a publication still qualifies for the Periodicals postage permit class discounts.

You can find these instructions in section 707.8.0 of the *Domestic Mail Manual for Periodicals* at the website www.usps.gov.

CD-ROM

The *Statement of Ownership, Management, and Circulation*, PS Form 3526, is available on the CD-ROM included with this book.

Magazine and newsletter printing companies can often help pick the proper postal class for a publication and can also set up the mailing to conform to all relevant rules. They may charge a nominal fee for this service or offer it free to regular customers. You can also expect this kind of support from a Fulfillment Service or an outside circulation consultant. In addition, you can get some help with these decisions from a Business Mail Entry (BME) Office of the USPS in your city. There is an online directory for finding the nearest BME at www.usps.com. What follows is a description of the basic rules for the two postal classes.

> **SEE AN EXPERT**
>
> **Get help from those in the know.** The basic rules and regulations for qualifying for the various postal rates are summarized here. But they can be somewhat tricky to apply. If you are confused about which rate to choose, talk with a postal official—and also ask your printer, fulfillment company, or circulation consultant—to help you choose which postal class is best for your circumstances.

Nonprofit Standard Mail

Nonprofit organizations can apply for a blanket Nonprofit Standard Mail permit. Once an organization is deemed eligible, then all of its bulk mailings that conform to the standards for this classification can be sent at that discounted rate. Under this rate, a letter that would cost 39 cents to mail first-class will only cost about 17 cents for comparable delivery service.

Some nonprofits are not allowed to use this postage classification. DMM 703.1 lists the nonprofit groups that do *not* qualify: business leagues, chambers of commerce, civic improvement associations, social clubs, hobby and automobile clubs, government bodies, trade associations, rural electric cooperatives, mutual insurance associations, and some political organizations. Those groups must use the Periodicals Class described below.

Nonprofits that have secured the right to mail at Nonprofit Standard rates use this discounted bulk mailing class primarily for their own direct mail fundraising, program marketing, or membership campaigns. But they can also use the discounted rate to mail newsletters and magazines. And in fact, publications get more leeway in terms of paid advertising content than other materials that you might mail.

Advertising Restrictions in Promotional Literature

To prevent commercial exploitation of the Nonprofit Standard Mail class, the USPS prohibits some kinds of advertising in the materials mailed under these rates. The USPS calls these "content-based restrictions," and materials that carry prohibited content will be rejected or charged a higher rate.

Only advertisers that would qualify for the nonprofit rates on their own merit should appear within your brochures, membership promotions, or fundraising campaigns—except when their activities are considered "substantially related" to your mission. For example, a commercial radio station can advertise its jazz programming in the course catalog of a nonprofit jazz school. And a church newsletter could sell ads for bibles in its membership directory.

But ads that are unrelated to your nonprofit's mission are strictly prohibited. A softball team can thank Jim's ice cream parlor for donating free sundaes to the team in its fundraising letters, but it can't accept a paid ad from Jim without violating the content rules.

The DMM in section 417.6 gives specific illustrations of advertising that would be allowed or banned in different situations. Advertising is defined broadly in DMM 417.6.3 to include any content promoting a product or service for which some fee or consideration has been paid: not just ads on pages, but also items inserted into a publication or attached to one. The nonprofit's own ads are counted as paid ads, too— even if no actual payment was made.

Different content restrictions apply to newsletters or magazines and to "advertising" materials such as member directories, catalogs, flyers, and fundraising campaigns. The USPS allows periodicals that qualify as "products" to carry ads that would be prohibited in other promotional literature. (See "When a Periodical Is a Product," below, for details.) For example, Jim's ice cream parlor *can* buy an ad in the softball team's newsletter but *cannot* insert a coupon in the team's annual fundraising letter. The newsletter is a periodical product, but the fundraising letter is not.

Because of this distinction, it's important for nonprofits to separate publications from other marketing campaigns and to follow the applicable rules for each of them.

When a Periodical Is a Product

By USPS standards, a periodical is a "product"—and therefore subject to fewer advertising restrictions—if it has the qualities described here:

- It has a title printed on the front cover page in a style and size of type that distinguishes the title from other information on the cover.
- It is formed of printed sheets rather than pages reproduced by stencil, mimeograph, or hectograph—which is a gelatin-based copying process rarely used these days.
- An identification statement appears on one of the first five pages of the publication that includes title; issue date; statement of frequency showing when issues are to be published—and this must be at least four times per year; name and address of the authorized organization, including street number, street name, and ZIP+4 or 5-digit ZIP code; International Standard Serial Number (ISSN); subscription price (if applicable); and issue number. Every issue of each publication must be numbered consecutively in a series that may not be broken by assigning numbers to omitted issues. The issue number may be printed on the front or cover page as well as in the identification statement.
- At least 25% of the matter in each issue must consist of content that is not advertising. Advertising is defined in DMM 707.4.12 and DMM 417.6 and includes any content promoting products or services for which some fee or barter consideration was paid.

Advertising Restrictions on Standard Nonprofit Periodicals

Periodicals can run ads that would be prohibited in other kinds of literature, such as a member directory, promotion letters, event calendars, or fundraising campaigns. But even within a nonprofit periodical, some types of ads are not allowed. These restrictions do not apply to publications that use the Periodicals Class, which is described below. For that reason, some nonprofit organizations decide to use the Periodicals rate for their publications and the Standard Nonprofit rate for their promotional materials.

If you choose to mail your publications under a Standard Nonprofit Mailing permit, a number of unique advertising restrictions will apply.

No credit or debit card ads. Publishing credit card ads will automatically disqualify a publication from this postal class, even if your organization has arranged special credit card terms for its members, such as the "affinity" cards that earn airline miles. You can describe an affinity card arrangement as a member benefit, but you cannot actually advertise one. Other financial services ads are acceptable, especially if the services are related to a nonprofit's mission.

EXAMPLE: Coop America runs dozens of ads for "socially responsible" investment opportunities in its quarterly magazine, which is mailed under the Nonprofit Standard Mail rates. In the eyes of the USPS, it helps that these ads are "substantially related" to Coop America's mission of "economic action for a just planet."

Insurance ad restrictions. Ads for insurance policies must meet all three of the following criteria:

- the insurance promoter itself must be eligible for nonprofit mailing status,
- the policy must be designated only for people associated with your organization—such as members, donors, or beneficiaries, and
- the coverage must not generally be available from commercial sources.

As with the credit cards, if your organization arranges special life insurance benefits for its members, you cannot run ads for that insurance, but you can describe it as a member benefit. There is an exception, however: Ads are acceptable if the insurer is also a nonprofit, the offer extends only to your members, and your members could not buy comparable coverage from a commercial insurance company.

Restrictions on travel ads. Travel ads must meet standards similar to insurance ads. For travel ads:

- The tour promoter must be eligible for nonprofit mailing status.

- The travel arrangements must be promoted for people associated with your organization—such as members, donors, and beneficiaries.

- The travel must contribute substantially to your mission; ads for tours of holy sites and retreat centers in Asia are acceptable in the Buddhist magazine *Turning Wheel*, for example, because they meet these criteria.

Some nonprofits do not accept any ads in their publications, or they accept ads from major donors only—a decision that rests on more than just postage costs. (See Chapter 10 for more on this strategic issue.)

TIP

Get advance approval. If you are confused about the rules regarding any specific ads that you want to sell, get clearance from a postal official—in writing—before placing those ads in your publication. You are entitled to an appeal if the USPS rejects one of your mailings over the ad content standards or demands the full commercial rate before accepting a mailing, but you will probably have to pay the higher rate while the appeal is pending.

Any ad-free periodical automatically qualifies for the nonprofit standard postage rate, as you can see from the following "decision tree."

Advertising Restrictions for Nonprofit Standard Mailing Rates

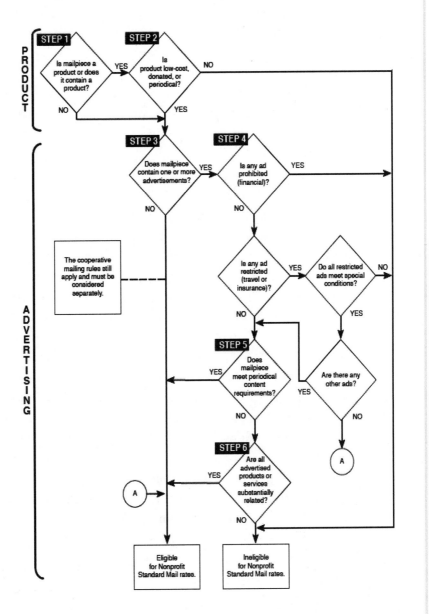

Source: The United States Postal Service, DMM section 417.6.3.

CD-ROM

The *Application to Mail at Nonprofit Standard Mail Rates*, PS Form 3624, is available on the CD-ROM included with this book.

Periodicals Class Mail

All periodicals, whether or not they are published by a nonprofit, can qualify for a set of postage discounts called Periodicals Class simply by automating mailings.

With this classification, publishers earn increasingly generous discounts according to how much presorting work they do before submitting their publications into the mail system. Big, commercial magazines sort their mailing labels down to the level of each carrier's delivery route; consequently, their magazines bypass the normal USPS sorting procedures and drop right into the carriers' bags. Some publishers don't have the capacity to sort their mailings to that level of detail, but there are vendors who can provide help with navigating the presorting rules to obtain the highest discounts. Most nonprofit publications have no trouble qualifying for a Periodicals discount based on some degree of presorting.

In general, Periodicals Class is a much more inclusive postage class in terms of who can use it. There are no advertising restrictions, and many nonprofit organizations choose Periodical rates for their publications instead of Nonprofit Standard Mail—particularly if credit card, insurance, or travel advertising is a significant source of potential income. In addition, almost all of the organizations that don't qualify for the Nonprofit Standard Mailing class can qualify for the Periodicals Class and enjoy similar discounts.

> ⚠ **CAUTION**
>
> **Be sure to explain changes.** The USPS rarely challenges the way a publisher calculates postage for any single issue, unless there is a significant change from previous practices—selling lots of ads after not selling any, for example, or showing a huge jump in readership. If your publication is about to make a sudden change that will affect your postage calculations, it's a good idea to warn the USPS in advance and add documentation to the forms for that issue. Otherwise, you risk holding up delivery while the USPS recalculates your postage.

Comparing Periodical and Nonprofit Standard Classes

As noted, there are some key differences between the Periodicals Class and the Nonprofit Standard Mail class.

- Periodicals rates are granted to publications, not to the organization that produces them. Therefore, many nonprofit organizations that would not qualify for the Nonprofit Standard Mail category can get a Periodicals discount.
- Periodicals rates are higher for advertising content than for nonadvertising content. So before handing a publication over to the USPS, publishers must submit a marked-up copy of every issue showing what percentage of that issue is advertising versus nonadvertising content.
- Nonprofits can save 5% off the Periodicals rate on content that is not advertising for one of their publications, so long as that publication also qualifies under Periodicals rules and is presorted appropriately.

Types of Publications Covered

Three main classes of publications in the Periodicals Class are relevant for nonprofits: general, requester, and institution or society publications. The USPS requires that publishers maintain records showing how their publications qualify to receive the Periodicals postage discount for the class they claim. These rules are described in DMM 707.8 and summarized here.

General publications. General publications are distributed mostly to paid subscribers or to people who receive their subscriptions as part of a paid membership. A paid subscriber is defined as a person who paid at least 50% of the nominal subscription rate—and, as publisher, you must have records to prove these payments.

Subscriptions may also be paid for with dues or contributions, as long as the dues or contributions and the subscription price are separated to show the amount paid for the subscription. For example, a membership order form must read something like this: "Annual membership dues of $[XX] include $[XX] for a one-year subscription to *[Title]*." A membership organization can also handle this requirement by passing a resolution that all membership fees include a specified amount for subscriptions.

You are allowed to send copies at this rate to people who have not yet paid or who have paid a rate below the qualifying subscription price, but at least half of the distribution of each issue must go to paid subscribers. In one year, a general publication can't have more than 75% advertising in more than half of its issues. So, in addition to keeping records about subscriptions, you must keep records about the ratio of ads to editorial content that appears in each issue.

Requester publications. As the name implies, requester publications must be requested by a subscriber. To comply with USPS regulations, every subscriber must have asked for the publication within the last three years. Such publications may have free subscribers, or a mix of both paid and free subscribers, but you must keep records showing that every one of them requested the publication. Requests can come through a website, by email, or by way of order cards bound into samples, as long as the request includes words similar to these: "Please accept my free subscription to *[Title of publication]* for a term of X [one to three] years and mail the publication to me at the following address."

> **TIP**
>
> **Making membership requests easy.** Membership organizations can take care of the "requested within three years" requirement by passing a resolution that every active member is automatically entitled to a subscription and then using their membership enrollment records for subscriptions documentation.

Requester publications can send only 10% of each issue's total distribution to people who are not requesters or subscribers under these rates. Anything above 10% will be charged at first-class postage rates. Each issue of a requester publication must contain at least 24 pages and may not contain more than 75% advertising.

Institutional and society publications. Selected nonprofit institutions and societies can send publications to their members at Periodicals rates.

The following groups qualify under this category:

- regularly incorporated nonprofit or state institutions of learning
- many state departments—including health, corrections, and conservation
- benevolent or fraternal societies
- trade unions
- professional societies
- literary historical and scientific societies, and
- churches.

There is no minimum issue size for this category, but the restriction on advertising applies: No more than 75% advertising in any issue. In addition, you must show that the publication is "originated and published to further the purposes of the qualifying organization." Circulation is limited to members, paid subscribers, or exchanges— meaning those copies organizations might have traded with each other. And there is an allowance for 10% as sample copies.

> **TIP**
>
> **An extra discount may be available.** Publications that meet any one of the previously described Periodicals Class standards can apply for an extra 5% discount if they are published by a nonprofit organization that may not have been included in any previous list—such as the rural electric cooperatives, for example, or a public radio station. Only one of your publications is entitled to this extra discount. These specific rules are described in DMM 707.10.

Mechanics of Paying Periodicals Postage

You need apply only once to obtain the appropriate classification for each of your publications, then follow the rules for presorting and submitting each issue. Since the regulations for your postal class won't change from issue to issue, you can develop a system for keeping records and delivering issues into the postal system that should proceed almost automatically.

Periodicals Class customers submit a tally of the issue's distribution by postal zone, along with a marked-up copy of the publication that shows how the ad and non-ad postage rates have been calculated. The USPS supplies a standard form for submitting this information, PS Form 3541-1. Along with the form, you must deposit enough money to cover the estimate of the mailing's cost.

> **CD-ROM**
>
> *Postage Statement—Periodicals: One Issue or One Edition*, PS Form 3541, is available on the CD-ROM included with this book.

TIP

Use a different provider for international mail. You can save money on copies you send outside of the United States by using an international mail provider other than the USPS. You can find information about this option from the International Mailers Action Group, a division of the Direct Marketing Association, at www.the-imag.org. Specific providers include: PDS, at www.internationalmail.com; Atlas International, at www.atlasintlmail.com; IMES, at www.intmail.com; and DHL/Global Mail, at www.globalmail.com.

CD-ROM

The *Application for Periodicals Mailing Privilege*, PS Form 3500, is available on the CD-ROM included with this book.

Distributing Emails

The decision to publish electronically versus print rests on your strategic goals rather than the desire to save on paper and postage. (See Chapter 1 for a discussion of those issues).

But it's also undeniable that email newsletters cost much less to publish than print ones—and for that reason, email has become a popular newsletter publishing option among cash-strapped nonprofit organizations.

In addition to saving money, email has several advantages over postal mailings: Email responses are typically much higher, publishing costs are much lower, and tracking is simple, as long as you set up your delivery systems properly.

Choosing a Delivery Method

Nonprofit publishers generally use three common email delivery strategies: engaging an in-house webmaster to generate new programming to handle emails, turning the job over to the outside vendor that manages the print publication subscriptions, and hiring a vendor dedicated to email processing.

In-house programming works only if you have someone on staff capable of handling the job. If so, then you may get a custom solution for very little money. It is wise to study all the services that dedicated email programs provide as described below and try to program them into your existing system.

Many of the vendors that handle print subscription fulfillment for periodicals will step in to create email fulfillment systems, too. This makes sense because of the crossover between print subscriptions or membership names and email mailing lists. Again, be sure to get a complete mix of services by comparing these vendors to the dedicated email services.

New and highly automated Internet services have become available to handle email publishing, and many publishers happily use them. Three of these services include Vertical Response (www.verticalresponse.com), List Box (www.listbox.com), and Benchmark Email (www.benchmarkemail.com). Check the Internet for other email marketing services that might be suited to your need.

You can easily transfer email addresses from your in-house database into the databases these services manage, and most services also provide simple coding that places an order form on your website feeding directly into a mailing list hosted on their computers. They also offer design templates for newsletters and extensive reporting packages tracking bounces, replies, cancellations, and orders or donations resulting from every email that you send. Costs depend on the size of your email list and the number of issues you send in a year, but the charges typically run less than $1,000 per year for most publishers.

Use the checklist below to compare and contrast available delivery options before choosing one.

Use this checklist to compare the features and prices of different email services.

Email Services Checklist		
Name of Email Service Provider:		

	Check if available	
Feature	yes	no
Easy set-up and management: plenty of instruction available online, without having to call for technical support	☐	☐
Capable of managing several different email and newsletter campaigns from the same database	☐	☐
Can easily upload your own contact list	☐	☐
People can sign up or unsubscribe from your website	☐	☐
Merge/Purge/Export list features are available	☐	☐
Automatically identifies and tags bad email addresses	☐	☐
Offers suitable HTML email templates	☐	☐
Allows you to create your own HTML email templates within the system	☐	☐
Allows you to upload your own HTML formatted emails created elsewhere	☐	☐
Offers a choice of text or HTML newsletters	☐	☐
Guarantees CAN-SPAM compliance	☐	☐
Marketing suggestions and consulting services are available if needed	☐	☐
Technical support: Full client support services are provided, by phone, live chat, or email	☐	☐
Real-time reporting of mail campaigns is offered	☐	☐
Reports include click-through rates, forwarding, bounces, and other responses to your emails	☐	☐
Allows you to save drafts and send test mailings before every campaign	☐	☐
Allows you to schedule when a campaign will be delivered	☐	☐
Cost per year for your mailing list capacity: _____	☐	☐
Recommendations from other publishers	☐	☐

CD-ROM

This checklist is also available on the CD-ROM included with this book, so you can print it out and compare the features offered by various service providers.

Avoiding Spamming

Whatever option you choose, marketing experts recommend some key features of your emailing system. And there are specific guidelines established by industry trade groups that you should follow. The guiding principle is: Don't spam.

The Federal Trade Commission (FTC) recently passed a law aimed at reducing or eliminating unwanted email. Called CAN-SPAM, the law is widely accepted by the direct marketing industry, and most mailing services are already complying. But to be safe, make sure you confirm CAN-SPAM compliance with anyone involved in mailing emails for you, as noted on the checklist above.

RESOURCE

The FTC provides straightforward guidance on CAN-SPAM at www.ftc.gov/bcp/conline/edcams/spam/business.htm and www.ftc.gov/bcp/conline/pubs/buspubs/canspam.htm.

The best advice offered by marketing experts and watchdog groups to avoid spamming boils down to three key things.

First, provide content readers will find valuable. Donations, subscriptions, and other reader responses fall off if the publication fails to offer a proper balance between reader-friendly content, such as news and how-to information, and self-serving or promotional information coming from their organization. Emails also draw higher responses when they're short and easy to scan. (See Chapter 5 for more information about providing compelling content.)

Next, get permission before sending anything. Even if you come across a prospect's email address by chance or good luck, ask before adding that person to your publication distributions. And even when a person subscribes via your website or in response to your emails, confirm the subscription by a return email. Always make it very easy for people to opt out of your emails, even if you've already obtained their consent in advance. Every issue must contain a link that lets people remove themselves from your email list.

Finally, use simple formats. Make sure your emails are formatted to read easily, no matter what kind of email program or Internet connection readers are using. (Chapter 6 includes details about email formats.) Recipients subsidize the cost of email by paying for their connection to the Internet, and some people don't want to or can't afford to pay for a high-speed connection. If you send HTML coding and fancy images that read well only on a high-powered computer with a fast Internet link, allow people with a slow Web connection to access a text-only alternative version.

RESOURCE

You can find guidelines for Proper Mailing List Management from the Mail Abuse Prevention System (MAPS), at www.mail-abuse.com/an_listmgntgdlines.html.

Direct Marketing Association, Council for Responsible E-Mail, offers guidelines at www.the-dma.org/councils/responsibleemailcouncil/index.shtml.

SpamCon.org is a nonprofit foundation working to reduce unwanted email. Its website includes a Best Practices section at http://spamcon.org.

Distribution and Promotion Checklist

Whether your publication is a magazine, newsletter, or Web publication, you can capture all your decisions about distributing and promoting it in this checklist.

- ☐ **Audience.** Define exactly who will receive the newsletter, magazine, or electronic newsletter, along with how many recipients you expect to have.
- ☐ **Pricing.** Decide on a price for a single issue and a year's subscription.
- ☐ **Promotion strategies.** Determine which promotion strategies are most promising for this publication and your organization.
- ☐ **Fulfillment plan.** Establish which vendor or programmer will manage your fulfillment needs.
- ☐ **Postal class.** Settle on a postal class if you will be mailing your publication.
- ☐ **Emailing options.** Determine which vendor will support emailing programs if yours is an electronic communication.

Selling Advertising

This chapter looks at the pros and cons of allowing advertising in your nonprofit's publication or website—a decision that rests in part on how you believe ads will reflect your organization's mission and affect your readers. For those who do opt to include advertisers, it gives tips on how to set prices and successfully manage your relationships with them. And it explains the specialized income tax rules and postal regulations that control advertising in nonprofit publications. For all readers, it points out other possible sources of revenue that may fit into your ultimate advertising plans.

SEE AN EXPERT

Getting tax advice before accepting ads. Before deciding to include ads in your nonprofit's newsletter, magazine, or website, discuss the unrelated business income tax (UBIT) rules with an accountant or lawyer. This chapter briefly covers this complicated area of law, but it is wise to get detailed professional advice about whether and how this federal tax law and other state tax laws may apply to your particular situation.

Deciding Whether to Sell Ads

Some nonprofit organizations do not accept advertising in their publications or on their websites—and for good reason. There is no doubt that advertisements create a distraction for readers and have the potential to overwhelm your carefully crafted messages. You have very little control over the look and feel of ads submitted by advertisers—and some ads will not appeal to you. And whether you intend it or not, readers often assume that your organization endorses the companies that advertise in its publications or on its websites. In addition, managing a successful sales effort will place extra demands on the publishing staff.

On the other hand, advertising can provide much-needed revenue that can be used to enhance the quality of your publications and Web efforts. Money you take in from advertising can mean the difference between being able to afford printing a magazine in color rather than just black and white, or being able to include fancier Web features. Advertising for closely related products or services can also help build community and further your mission by linking like-minded service providers and customers. Another plus is that some readers feel that an ad-rich publication is a successful one. That may also attract additional advertisers.

Keep in mind, though, that any income you earn from advertising is taxable, and that will cause you to incur added accounting and IRS reporting obligations. Make the decision about whether to advertise carefully, and be sure you have considered all the consequences of your choice. (See "Completing Your Advertising Plan," below, for a checklist of variables to consider.)

TIP

Get a reality check from your peers. Nonprofits are too often tempted to launch an ad sales program based on starry-eyed hopes about raising easy money. In reality, very few nonprofit organizations earn significant net income from publishing. A recent survey of 114 association publications found that about half (48%) earned net profits from their publishing activities, even with average advertising income of more than $370,000. If you don't know how much advertising income you can reasonably expect, this survey might be helpful. The complete survey is available from the Society of National Association Publications. (See Chapter 12 for contact information).

Another good idea is to check with organizations in circumstances similar to yours to see if your revenue hopes are reasonable. Experience differs widely from one situation to another. For example, small nonprofits have very different income patterns from large ones. Find people at comparable organizations who have more publishing experience than you do, and ask them to review your ad sales forecasts to see whether they seem reasonable.

Supporting Your Mission

Every interest group has a collection of nonprofit services, publications or websites, and cottage industries serving the unique needs of that community. Ads from these sources can be a boon to your readers and a significant support to the organizations serving the same community.

Consider whether your publication could provide valuable exposure for professional services, specialty products, or highly targeted information sources within your niche.

Recruiting Advertisers to Support Your Mission

If you worry that advertising will detract from your mission or that your readers will find it distracting or offensive, remember that you have complete control over who advertises in your publications and on your website.

Most nonprofit publications place some restrictions on what type of advertising they will accept, and you can always say no to an advertiser or type of advertising you don't like. In addition, you can actively *recruit* advertisers that you want in your publication: those that support and complement your mission and can help build community with your readers. (See "Composing a Wish List of Advertisers," below, for more on this.)

If you are concerned about the impact advertising will have, concentrate on mission-related advertisers and stay away from any type of advertising that might create a conflict or issue with your readers.

For example, *Terrain*, a quarterly ecology magazine published by the Ecology Center in Berkeley, California, actively recruits advertising from companies that share their same goals and interests. Every 40-page issue of *Terrain* includes about seven pages of ads. The publisher says, "We choose advertisers according to our values and screen prospects accordingly. Businesses that value a sustainable future and livable planet can reach readers who share those values through *Terrain*." By actively seeking advertising from companies that share their goals, *Terrain* is able to link readers and businesses within the same community.

EXAMPLE: La Leche League, which promotes breastfeeding, features a few pages of "Small Business" ads in every 52-page issue of its magazine, *New Beginnings*. The ads promote products and services—including breast-feeding coaches and handmade nursing clothes—that are difficult to find elsewhere. Often the small companies offering these specialized products and services cannot afford to advertise in more-commercial parenting magazines.

On the other hand, advertising can be seen to undermine the credibility of a publication such as *Consumer Reports* that strives to exercise objectivity regarding consumer products and the companies advertising them. Editors there don't want the temptation of favoring products from companies providing significant advertising support to the organization, so they do not allow advertising in the publication. And there are many other examples of advertising that creates mission conflicts: junk food ads in health magazines, for example, or ads for gas-guzzling cars on environmental websites.

Getting Revenue From Ads

Even if advertisers contribute nothing but cash to your publication, their participation can be extremely valuable. Extra revenue from advertising can be used to fund an upgrade to better paper, additional pages on your website, or a more colorful newsletter format. When advertisers foot the bill, the upgrades translate to reader benefits by beefing up the contents or making the publication more readable. With financial support from advertisers, your organization might be able to charge a lower price to readers overall or to send the publication for free to a larger number of people. (See the example of *Kentucky Living*, below, for a specific illustration of this.)

On the other hand, beware that advertising can cost more overall than it contributes and generate unwarranted stress for those responsible for tracking and managing it. Acquiring and publishing each ad page takes nearly as much behind-the-scenes effort as creating a page of articles or news items. In addition, billing, collecting, and accounting for ad sales money can eat up significant staff time. The postal service charges more for ad pages than for editorial pages, driving up your postage bill. (See Chapter 9 for more details on this.) And you may face demands from commercial advertisers that you are not prepared to handle—such as a request to favorably review certain products or provide an official endorsement for an item.

> **EXAMPLE:** One union magazine recently dropped its advertising program after discovering how much staff time was needed to handle the advertisers. The union was not earning enough ad revenue to justify hiring extra staff, but corresponding with prospective advertisers and collecting payments from current ones created much more work than the existing employees could comfortably manage. What's worse, commercial recruiting companies wanted to use the union's magazine and website to recruit for nonunion jobs—a practice that would likely lead to resentment among union members. The already overwhelmed publishing staff was especially unhappy having to deal with these union-busting advertisers.

Considering Your Readers

Nonprofits may decide to forgo advertising in their publications when reader sensitivities against ads are likely to outweigh the potential economic benefits.

Commercialization is the most common reader complaint, even when the ads are apparently related to your mission. Some readers may feel that consumer marketing just doesn't mix with charity, and they'll donate less money or volunteer less time when they perceive that your organization is catering too much to commercial interests.

> **EXAMPLE:** Donors to one disaster relief organization complained about the presence of online ads from companies such as construction supply retailers they perceived to be profiting from Hurricane Katrina, even though those same companies had also made significant donations to rebuilding the area. The nonprofit group did not wish to continue offending individual donors, so it pulled the corporate ads off its website.

In other cases, you may make production concessions for advertisers that conflict with other publishing values. Many advertisers favor magazines printed in four-color ink on glossy paper and websites covered with animated banner ads because that is what they are accustomed to getting from commercial publishers. But that high-impact format may conflict with the low-impact mission of your organization or the environmental sensitivities of your donors or volunteers.

On the other hand, readers often benefit from the presence of ads that link them to specialized opportunities they can't find elsewhere.

EXAMPLE: One nonprofit, the Fellowship of Intentional Communities (FIC), was organized 20 years ago as "an ecumenical clearinghouse for accurate and comprehensive information about North American intentional communities." Its 80-page quarterly magazine, *Communities*, maintains a robust section of classified ads linking interested individuals with the 700 or so cohousing communities across the United States seeking new members. And similar listings are provided on its website at www.communities. ic.org. The organization increases its social impact by including ads that help readers find suitable communities.

Deciding Whether to Sell Ads		
Consideration	Pros	Cons
Relation to Mission	Advertising furthers your mission; builds community and supports like-minded organizations.	Advertising detracts from your mission; introduces a potential conflict of interest between commercial goals and mission.
Revenue Potential Versus Costs	Advertising generates income and keeps publishing costs down; readers get more for less money.	Advertising costs more overall than it contributes; drives up production and postage expenses; creates burdensome accounting requirements.
Affect on Readers	Readers find ads useful for locating specialized services or products; ads may boost reader impressions that the organization is robust.	Readers find ads distracting or offensive; implies unwarranted endorsement; ads may repulse potential donors or volunteers.

Profile: Southern Hospitality in *Kentucky Living* Ads

The Kentucky Association of Electric Cooperatives' magazine, *Kentucky Living*, is distributed monthly to 500,000 households that belong to about 20 rural electric cooperatives in the state. The magazine's mission is "to create a community of people who take pride in thinking of themselves as Kentuckians and as knowledgeable electric co-op members, in order to improve their quality of life." The magazine has articles about local people, events, and places—and also includes cookie recipes, gardening tips, and photos of grandchildren submitted by coop members—giving each issue a neighborly feeling.

Advertising takes up less than a third of the pages in every print issue and less than 10% of the content on the magazine's website, but advertisers contribute more than 40% of the organization's total annual publish-ing costs. Print magazine issues typically run about 56 pages long, all in full color. Without the advertising cash to pay for it, the color would have to go and the nonprofit also might have to give up some of the more local, newsy items that contribute so much to the magazine's charm.

The Association follows strict guidelines in determining what ads to allow in its magazine. "We do not accept ads promoting the use of alcohol or tobacco, ads for firearms, or ads that guarantee medical results. We also do not accept ads for competing fuel sources, such as wood stoves or propane, or ads that attempt to influence the state legislature on a specific issue," says Paul Wesslund, the vice president of communications.

Furthering its pride-of-place and pride-of-membership mission, *Kentucky Living* gives a 33% discount to advertisers headquartered in Kentucky who are also members of the electrical cooperative. It also follows the American Society of Magazine Editors (ASME) advertising guidelines. (See "Ethical Standards for Advertising," below.) With clear guidelines in place, the Association can feel good about remaining true to its mission and readers while selling more than 200 pages of advertising per year.

Wesslund offers some advice about developing a successful advertising sales program: "Have a very clear statement of purpose and use it to guide both daily operations and strategy. View ads not just as a source of income but primarily as a service to readers or members: The ads should provide benefits the readers want. Know that advertising requires a large investment; have a solid business plan in place before you start. And remember to advocate for readers. Sometimes you will find yourself standing up to advertising income to protect your readers' interest. In the long run, holding reader interests above any other interest will increase your credibility with both readers and advertisers."

Tax Concerns

Under federal tax law, advertising income from periodicals is taxable, even if you are a nonprofit organization. The Internal Revenue Service (IRS) classifies advertising income as unrelated business income, and if profit totals more than $1,000 per year, you must report it and pay taxes on it.

The IRS defines advertising broadly. Any paid promotional message that you agree to include in your newsletter, magazine, or website counts as an ad. In most cases, the distinction is clear. But bear in mind that the IRS may view a corporate or business donation as taxable income, and not a deductible charitable gift, simply because you acknowledged the gift in your magazine and included the donor's logo or a photo of its products along with the acknowledgment.

RESOURCE
For more information on IRS rules about unrelated business income taxes, read IRS Publication 598, *Tax on Unrelated Business Income of Exempt Organizations*, available online at www.irs.gov or by calling the IRS at 800-829-3676. If your accountant is not familiar with this publication, be sure to give him or her a copy.

Mercifully, in figuring out your taxable advertising income, you can deduct any expenses directly connected with selling and publishing the ads, such as commissions and salaries plus printing and postage for ad pages, from any revenue you receive from advertisers. Because of this, many nonprofit organizations sell a lot of ads without having to pay any taxes.

When calculating your sales expenses, you can include commissions, travel, marketing, overhead, and salaries of any salespeople you hire, plus printing and distribution costs of the ad pages. If your advertising revenue still exceeds these direct advertising costs, you can also deduct the costs of providing the publication to readers. The IRS calls these "readership costs," and they include all of your nonad publishing costs: creating content, printing and mailing subscriber copies, editorial salaries—minus any membership dues or subscription revenues you've collected.

EXAMPLE: Like many other nonprofit publications, *Kentucky Living* has never paid more than a few dollars in unrelated business income tax on advertising despite its robust advertising sales program. Because subscribers pay only a few dollars per year to receive the magazine, it has never earned a significant profit in more than 60 years of publishing.

If you decide to accept paid ads, make sure there is someone on staff ready to handle the extra accounting requirements. For example, you must track all of your direct publishing expenses by issue, not just by month. You have to report the total number of pages in each issue and what percentage of pages carried ads. And you have to separate out every dollar related to advertising from everything else, including both revenue and expense dollars. (These accounting requirements are discussed in detail in Chapter 3.)

CD-ROM

IRS Form 990-T, *Exempt Organization Business Income Tax Return*, is included on the CD-ROM with this book.

Postal Regulations

Including ads in your publication will increase your postage bill. The postal service charges higher rates for mail that contains advertisements, and, depending upon what type of postal permit you have, it may also limit the kinds of advertisements you can accept. Magazines paying standard nonprofit postage rates, for example, are prohibited from accepting ads from financial, insurance, or travel companies.

Before selling any ads, check your postal permit to see what restrictions apply. If you find them too onerous, you can switch to a more accepting USPS postal class. (See Chapter 9 for more details about postal restrictions on advertising and different postal classes available for nonprofit periodicals.)

Ethical Standards for Advertising

Even ads from the most compatible companies can create ethical issues as you get your publication or website up and running.

For example, advertisers may demand certain placement or design elements that you don't want to go along with because you want readers to clearly understand the difference between your articles and material supplied by advertisers. Or an advertiser may ask you to feature its product in an editorial photograph or in an article. This practice, called "product placement," is common in fashion magazines and on television shows and movies, but uncommon in the nonprofit world—and is even shunned in many commercial publications. (This placement issue is covered by the ethical guidelines described below.)

Another problem arises when an advertiser produces material that looks like an article that appears in your nonprofit publication—a common dilemma on Web pages as well as in newsletters and magazines. For example, a pharmaceutical company may want to supply an article about menopause to your website that is designed to look just like the articles you produce but subtly promotes the advertiser's medications. Fortunately, this practice is also covered by the guidelines described below.

The American Society of Magazine Editors (ASME) publishes ethical guidelines for editors and publishers to follow to ensure that their editorial and advertising content operates independently and that the distinction between the two is clear to readers. If you follow these guidelines, you can avoid many potential conflicts with advertisers by having specific rules in place about what you can and can't do. Many advertisers are already familiar with the ASME guidelines and will respect your choice to adopt them. By following the guidelines, you are simply conforming to publishing industry standards.

The ASME print guidelines are organized into ten statements of principle and practice that cover issues related to design, covers, adjacencies—which means putting ads next to articles in such a way as to blur the differences between them—sponsorship, logos, product placement, advertising sections, editorial staff, and editorial and advertising review procedures.

The guidelines provide specific directives for each area. For example, in design, the guidelines state that advertisements must look different enough from editorial pages so that readers can tell the difference or must have "Advertisement" or "Promotion" at the top of the page to avoid any confusion. There are specific rules about advertising placement—for example, no ads on spines or covers, the advertiser's rights to control placement, and staffing issues such as not allowing sales staff to have titles suggesting they are editors, and not allowing editorial staff to be involved in producing ads. Every magazine, newsletter, and website editor should know and follow these guidelines. They are available online at www.magazine.org/editorial/guidelines/_guidelines_for_editors_and_publishers.

A few other recommendations:

- **Editorial review.** So that the chief editor can monitor compliance with these guidelines, that person must be able to see every ad page far enough in advance to make any necessary changes.

- **Advertiser review.** While advertisers can be informed about general topic matter of upcoming issues, they should not be permitted to review a specific article, layout, or table of contents in advance of publication.

- **Logos.** An advertiser's logo should not appear on editorial pages except in a journalistic context.

Internet practices have raised new ethical concerns for publishers. For example, when your organization can earn a small commission from selling books through an online book dealer, will your editors be tempted to review them more favorably? What if an eco-tourism company or a professional training program wants to pay big bucks for registering people through your website? Should your visitors know about these commercial relationships?

Fortunately, the magazine editors group has created standards for websites, too. Similar to the guidelines for print publications, these Best Practices for Digital Media are designed to guarantee that readers know whether advertisers or editors created information posted on your site and whether your organization has any commercial relationship with the products of companies you describe at your site. The ASME website

guidelines are posted online at www.magazine.org/editorial/guidelines/
best_practices_for_digital_media.

A few highlights from the website standards are summarized here.

- If any content comes from a source other than your editors, it should
  be clearly labeled.

- Hypertext links that appear within the editorial content of a site,
  including those within graphics, should be at the discretion of your
  editors. If advertisers pay for links, disclose that to users.

- E-commerce commissions and other affiliate fees should be reported
  on a disclosure page so users can see that the content is credible and
  free of commercial influence.

TIP

Taking a stand on ethics. You can significantly reduce the number
of outlandish requests or sticky issues raised by your prospective advertisers
by putting a copy of the ASME guidelines into your advertising sales
materials. You can also ensure that your editors don't have to waste time
fending off unethical suggestions by making sure every salesperson knows
what is and is not allowed, according to the standards you intend to follow.

Managing the Ad Sales Process

In a nutshell, the ad sales process begins when you decide to sell ads
and ends when advertisers pay for their ads. There are many steps and
sometimes dozens of people managing everything that happens in
between.

Some organizations have marketing people to research the market,
set prices, and develop a sales pitch; salespeople to communicate with
individual advertisers and close sales; production people to see that the
ads are in the proper form and format; and accounting people to send
invoices and collect payment for the ads. With some groups, this is all
handled internally by staff, while others use outside contractors or a

combination of both. In a small organization, one person may handle everything.

Various staffing options will be offered in the explanations of each step in the selling process. (And hiring staff and freelance salespeople is discussed in detail in Chapter 4.)

Composing a Wish List of Advertisers

Those running the publications at some nonprofits decide that they won't accept ads for certain types of products—tobacco, liquor, or firearms, for example—because they don't want to offend their membership or donor community.

Others use ad pricing to actively encourage advertising from specific companies.

EXAMPLE: *Dollars and Sense: The Magazine of Economic Justice*, concentrates on selling ads to other nonprofits and charges bargain prices so that nonprofits can afford to advertise in it.

Another tactic is limiting ads to companies that join as members.

EXAMPLE: Coop America accepts ads in its electronic newsletters, print publications, and website from its business members only, using its publications to boost membership.

One commonsense piece of advice: Don't waste time trying to sell ads to companies that have much better advertising opportunities elsewhere. For example, because people can sample digital sound snippets at websites, music companies have transferred nearly all their advertising budgets to online ads.

It's also wise to skip over advertisers that have a built-in objection to your publication. A vegetarian magazine won't have success trying to sell advertising space to local steakhouses, for example.

Focus instead on ads for products closely related to your cause, where your publication may actually enjoy a competitive advantage. *Audubon* magazine, for example, provides a much better marketing opportunity for bird-watching tour operators than a magazine such as *People,* even though *People* has a much higher circulation. *Glimpse* magazine, geared to college-aged people interested in traveling abroad, would enjoy a similar advantage selling advertising for foreign exchange trips and study abroad programs. But when it comes to selling soap and SUVs, *People* magazine—with millions of potential shoppers reading every issue— wins hands down over *Audubon* and *Glimpse.*

Develop a profile of the companies most likely to advertise in your publication and most compatible with your mission: a "Wish List" describing the companies you hope to convert into advertisers. New publishers often look to see who *might* advertise by combing through competitive magazines to see who already *does* advertise. There's nothing wrong with this; it's a smart practice. You can develop an accurate and up-to-date profile of each prospective advertiser by clipping ads from other publications. Make a list of the advertisers in other nonprofit print publications or websites that have similar audiences to yours.

Next, consult with your members and fundraising department about the wish list and any possible restrictions you are considering. If you have an editorial advisory board (see Chapter 4), it would be good to get its feedback at this stage, too. Discussing any advertising-related issues thoroughly with all interested parties ensures that you will make lasting decisions that are strongly supported within your organization.

Establishing Prices and Policies

Before approaching any advertisers, learn as much as you can about their expectations about cost. The best way to do this is to find out what other publishers are charging advertisers with similar products to reach an audience comparable to yours. You can then align your pricing policies with the standards in your niche.

Ad pricing is completely different in every publishing niche and often dependent on reader buying power, not just the number of people you reach. (See the list of publications in the ad pricing table, below, for a representative range of prices.)

EXAMPLE: A bandage manufacturer that will happily spend $100,000 per ad to reach an audience of hospital administrators might not spend even $1 to reach individual consumers. This is because administrators buy millions of bandages every month, while consumers may buy only one box per household per year. If yours is a professional association of hospital administrators, you may find bandage companies rushing to advertise in your magazine; many nonprofit organizations do have members that some advertisers are eager to reach. And their aggressive ad pricing reflects this advantage.

Cost-Per-Reader or Impression (CPM)

When comparing advertising prices among publications and websites with significant differences in audience characteristics and volumes, it is useful to calculate how much it costs an advertiser to reach 1,000 readers or website visitors—a calculation commonly referred to as CPM or cost per thousand readers—the "M" being the Roman numeral for 1,000.

Your CPM equals the price you charge to buy one ad page, divided by how many thousands of readers receive that issue or how many thousands of visitors view that Web page. If your publication charges $300 for a full-page ad and distributes 10,000 copies, then your print CPM is $300 ÷ 10 or $30. If 50,000 people download a page from your website and you charge $450 for a banner ad on that page, then your online CPM is $450 ÷ 50 or $9.

Publishers generally try to match the CPM of competitive websites or print publications. The chart below shows the ad price and the CPM for a full-page black-and-white advertisement in a sampling of a number of nonprofit publications. The CPM numbers range from about $20 to almost $550, reflecting the diversity of niches served by these publications. For example, the magazine printers, consultants, and service companies advertising in *Association Publishing* are willing to pay a relatively high CPM because 100% of the magazine's readers are prospective buyers spending many thousands of dollars on similar products per reader per year. But even with a much larger number of readers, *Audubon* charges significantly lower advertising prices per thousand readers because it reaches individual consumers, not people buying services for a business or nonprofit organization.

Ad Price and CPM for One Full-Page Advertisement

Publication Title	Circulation	Ad Price	CPM
American Journalism Review	27,900	$6,399	$229
American Libraries	66,000	$4,980	$75
American Music Teacher	24,000	$1,630	$68
Association Executive	17,900	$3,149	$175
Association Publishing (SNAP)	1,300	$698	$537
Associations Now	20,000	$7,030	$352
Audubon	400,000	$22,045	$55
California Wild	25,000	$2,150	$86
Communities	4,000	$275	$69
Community College Times	6,125	$1,875	$312
Coop America Quarterly	65,000	$2,150	$33
Diabetes Forecast	489,000	$15,810	$32
Dollars & Sense	5,000	$550	$110
Episcopal Live	289,000	$6,110	$21
Glimpse Quarterly	10,000	$1,495	$150
Kansas Alumni	45,000	$2,120	$47
Kentucky Living	505,004	$11,555	$23
Mother Jones	240,800	$12,245	$51
National Geographic	5,376,750	$157,660	$29
National Wildlife	669,000	$22,230	$33
New Beginnings (La Leche League)	30,000	$2,280	$76
People	3,691,167	$156,000	$42
Presbyterians Today	57,400	$3,170	$56
Rotarian	490,000	$10,500	$21
Tricycle: The Buddhist Review	50,000	$1,410	$28
ULCA Magazine	125,000	$4,450	$36

Source: Standard Rate and Data Service, Fall 2006

Online ad prices follow a similar pattern: Websites that attract a professional or business audience can charge a much higher advertising price than sites geared mainly for individual consumers. (See "Online Ad Pricing Methods," below, for more details.)

Classified and Marketplace Ad Prices

Most print publishers also include specialized advertising sections for small businesses or individuals. These ads are generally priced less than other ads, and the ads are usually grouped together in a special section, often called a "Marketplace" because the pages include nothing but these small ads. For example, *Mother Jones* created an advertising section for book publishers called "In Print." Every page in the section carries 12 book ads, and each ad includes the book's cover (in a standard size), plus about 40 words of description. Ads in this section run both on the website and in the print edition of *Mother Jones*.

Pricing of classifieds and Marketplace ads is linked to distribution, as with the other ad prices. For example, *Communities* magazine charges 25¢ per word for a classified ad and has about 4,000 paid subscribers. But with more than 240,000 paid readers, *Mother Jones* can charge $7.25 per word for a classified listing.

Readers generally love classifieds and Marketplace ad sections. However, setting up and maintaining either one is a lot of work. Each classified or marketplace advertiser spends less every year than a bigger advertiser, and some of them need a lot of help writing a successful ad. But the smaller advertisers may be extremely loyal, running their ads over and over again, year after year. Therefore, in niche communities with the potential for similar loyalty from small advertisers, classifieds and marketplace ads can generate a lot of income over time.

RESOURCE

For more information about competitive positioning, pricing, and marketing ads to commercial advertisers, see *Starting & Running a Successful Newsletter or Magazine*, by Cheryl Woodard (Nolo).

Advertising Rate Card

Ad prices are commonly summarized on a "rate card" such as Sample Magazine rate card shown below. The example shows advertising rates for a monthly magazine with 300,000 readers and a CPM of $50. An advertiser buying a half-page ad in every issue of this magazine will spend $77,220 in one year (12 times $6,435).

Sample Magazine Rate Card					
Prices per ad based on how often it runs					
Ad Size	1 Time	3 Times	6 Times	9 Times	12 Times
1 page	$ 15,000	$14,250	$13,800	$13,500	$13,200
2/3 page	$ 11,250	$10,688	$10,350	$10,125	$ 9,900
1/2 page	$ 9,750	$ 6,947	$ 6,728	$ 6,581	$ 6,435
1/3 page	$ 6,750	$ 6,413	$ 6,413	$ 6,075	$ 5,940
1/4 page	$ 5,250	$ 4,988	$ 4,830	$ 4,725	$ 4,620
1/6 page	$ 3,000	$ 2,850	$ 2,760	$ 2,700	$ 2,640

CD-ROM
The rate card in this example is included on the CD-ROM that accompanies this book, in a format that you can modify when designing your own rate card. The rate card on the CD also calculates frequencies other than the ones shown in this example, including four and eight times, which are common publishing frequencies at small nonprofits.

Online Ad Pricing Methods

The same print magazine pricing principles apply to ads on websites: There is a higher CPM for readers who have lots of purchasing power.

But there are significant differences in how Web ads are priced. Pricing on the Web potentially can be tied more closely to direct results, rather than to simple per-reader or per-impression pricing. And several other pricing schemes are also being used, including cost-per-click, commissions, sponsorships, and classifieds. There are also online advertising sales networks that will handle these ads for you.

Cost-per-click ads. Cost-per-click or CPC is a pricing model based on the number of people who interact with a specific ad. Normally, advertisers pay a few cents or a few dollars for every person who clicks on an ad appearing at your website. Advertisers like this plan because they pay only for results. No clicks, no fee. Publishers like it too because there are no expenses involved in running the ads. So CPC is rapidly becoming the most popular way to charge for online ads.

Your organization can sell its own CPC ads, and many nonprofits do sell these ads to the same companies advertising in print newsletters or magazines. And you can also hand over the sales job to a search engine company or a network sales agency. Both approaches are described below.

Google AdSense is currently the leading provider of CPC search ads, but Yahoo and MSN offer comparable services. After being accepted by one of the search companies, you paste a block of HTML to the pages of your website where you want ads to run. The search company charges advertisers a cost-per-click fee for matching their ads to keywords appearing on your site and handles all the cash dealings with advertisers. Although the exact percentage is a closely guarded trade secret at Google, outside analysts estimate that publishers get about a 50% share of the CPC search revenue generated at any site through Google, and comparable percentages from Yahoo and MSN.

Traffic levels determine how much clicking is likely to occur and, therefore, how much CPC revenue will result. For example, with traffic averaging about 140 visitors per day, the Publishing Business Group website at www.publishingbiz.com earns just over $90 per month from the Google search ads it carries on 40 of its pages. The nonprofit public interest website Ask Questions, at www.askquestions.org, earned just under $6,000 in 2006 from Google ads by including them on 370 pages of the site, which averages 1,100 visitors per day. And a newly launched website that gets only 30 or 40 visitors per day might earn only around $100 per year from CPC ads.

There are also several networks willing to sell CPC or CPM banner ads on your site and handle all the relations with advertisers in exchange for a share of the revenues. As with the AdSense program at Google, there are no out-of-pocket costs to participate in these networks. DoubleClick and other very large networks focus exclusively on sites that get at least 2 million page views or impressions per month, but other networks handle "specialty" sites that see only 3,000 impressions per month or fewer. Generally, the networks pay 60% to 75% of revenues to publishers.

Here are some advertising networks worth exploring.

Name of Ad Network	Minimum Impressions Per Month	Percentage of Revenue Share
AdBrite.com	Not specified	75
AdEngage.com	Not Specified	75
AdServingNetwork.com	2,500	60
BurstMedia.com	5,000	50 to 55
ExperClick.com	Not Specified	65
RealTechNetwork.com	25,000	70
ValueClickMedia.com	3,000	Negotiable

Classified ads. Online classifieds are sold by the amount of time that they appear on your site rather than the number of words in the ad. Costs are normally a few dollars per day, again depending on traffic levels. Some of the same networks that handle display ads (listed above) will also handle classifieds for a share of the revenues.

You can also install software to handle this function on your own. Some classified ad sales software vendors to consider include USANetCreations.com, E-Classifieds.net, and GeoClassifieds from GeoDesicSolutions.com.

EXAMPLE: One alumni association charges $12.50 per month for online classifieds and leaves each ad up for two months at a time. The online classifieds are generally from individual association members advertising vacation rentals or personal items for sale.

Commissions and pay-per-performance ads. A commissioned transaction, also called pay-per-performance advertising, gives your organization a share of the revenue generated when someone buys a product or service through your site. For example, you can add a bookstore to your site and collect a few cents each time someone buys a book from the retailer that manages your store, such as Amazon.com. Sometimes called affiliate programs, you can set up these ads yourself through your favorite online retailers, or you can join a network that handles the affiliation agreements for you. CommissionJunction.com is one example. Performics.com is another. Typically, commissions range from 5% to 10% of sales.

Sponsorships. Sponsorships are usually flat fees negotiated directly between your organization and your key advertisers for a specific period of time, similar to a classified ad, or for a specific issue of your email newsletter. The fee is normally calculated based on how many people will see the ad, similar to the CPM model. Fees range from $1 to $200 CPM. For example, an alumni association might collect several hundred dollars per month from an employment website that sponsors a monthly column of career advice on the website. (See the discussion of sponsoring email newsletters in "Other Revenue Opportunities," below, for more on sponsorships.)

Marketing to Advertisers

The primary way you market and sell to advertisers is with a media kit. This is your all-in-one information guide designed to encourage companies on your wish list to become advertisers in your publication or website.

The media kit should include any important restrictions or requirements you have for advertising. And it should provide a clear, succinct description of your website or print publication's editorial mission; its calendar and circulation; and the demographics of your readers. This is also your opportunity to highlight the strengths of your publication and the advantages it offers over competitors. Post the media kit on your website and mail it to every company on your advertiser wish list.

A Media Kit Checklist

Your media kit should include everything a prospective advertiser needs to assess the value of your publication or website as a marketing vehicle compared to others the advertiser is considering. The essential elements are listed below.

- ☐ Name, mission, and charitable status of your organization.
- ☐ Editorial mission statement and an editorial calendar that highlights the value of your content. (See Chapter 5 for details on editorial calendars.) For example, *Kentucky Living's* editorial mission statement highlights the magazine's deep roots in the state, saying, "Through vibrant profiles of Kentucky's most colorful personalities, handy and informative guides to events and attractions, and fact-driven features on business and social trends, *Kentucky Living* has reflected the culture and character of the Commonwealth for nearly 60 years."
- ☐ Circulation details. Number of copies distributed and to whom.
- ☐ Demographic information about your readers that highlights their marketing value. For example, *Glimpse* magazine notes that 89% of its readers are college students and 95% of them are planning to travel abroad in the next 12 months. *Audubon* includes information about the median household income among its readers, which is 50% higher than the national average. And *California Wild*, the magazine of the California Academy of Sciences, markets successfully to restaurants in the neighborhood by reporting that its readers typically dine out six evenings per month, based on a simple reader survey. (See Chapter 11 for a detailed discussion of reader surveys.)
- ☐ Advertising rates—by size, frequency, and type of ad, commonly produced on a grid called the rate card, such as the sample provided earlier.
- ☐ A description of your online advertising options and any newsletter sponsorship opportunities.
- ☐ Advertising requirements and restrictions. Publishers often use this generic statement to cover any potential problems: "The publisher reserves the right to refuse any advertisement for any reason."
- ☐ Mechanical requirements, including the dimensions of ads you will accept and the formats in which ads can be submitted. Some of this information may be supplied by your printer or website designer.
- ☐ Contact information for sales and editorial staff.

Look at the media kits of other organizations, including your competitors, often posted on their websites. You can also request a media kit from a competitor's sales team. By doing this bit of investigating, you will gain useful information about media kits in general and you will also learn how competitors describe their own strengths. Then you can tailor your media kit so that it addresses what your competitors are saying about themselves.

Here are some good examples:

• *California Wild*, the quarterly members magazine of the California Academy of Sciences, accepts ads for the print magazine but not the website. The media kit is beautifully designed and reflects the overall look of the print publication, a very good practice. Find it at www.calacademy.org/calwild/standard/ads.html.

• *Kentucky Living* has good information for different kinds of ads and different pricing according to ad type. There are "direct response" prices, for example, that apply only to products sold exclusively by mail order or on the Internet and not to products sold through retail outlets. There are special discounts for companies located in Kentucky. The group's online media kit describes all the options at www.kentuckyliving.com/advertise/index.asp.

• *Glimpse* has a media kit that promotes both a print quarterly magazine and a unique online sponsored link and referral option. With sponsored links, an advertiser can target specific regions and countries where it is more likely to reach interested viewers. The referral program forwards contact details for people who register with the Glimpse Abroad site and request information about a specific region. Find out more at www.glimpsefoundation.org/advertise.php.

Send your media kit to every advertiser on your wish list. Then keep reminding each one of them about upcoming opportunities to advertise with a postcard or email message. Tell them if you update your online media kit. And let them know when you have a special issue coming out or a convention or conference at which there will be extra distribution.

If you get new information about your readers, keep advertisers posted on that, too. Finally, always send a free copy of every issue of your publication to all the prospects on your wish list.

> **TIP**
>
> **Finding ad prospects.** You can find new advertisers by listing your publication in the Standard Rate and Data Services (SRDS) magazine advertising directory, online at www.srds.com. Most large advertisers and advertising agencies use the SRDS directories if they are looking for new publications. Since the listings are free, you shouldn't overlook this opportunity to find new advertisers.

Closing the Sale and Getting Paid

A salesperson follows up with advertisers on your wish list to learn about their needs: what products or services they're advertising, how much money they can afford to spend, and what kinds of ads they're running in other publications or websites. (Chapter 4 contains detailed information about hiring the right people to handle this work.)

Using what they learn in these discussions with advertisers, publishers offer an advertising proposal and budget detailing ad sizes both in print and online, prices—including any negotiated discounts—and schedules. For example, after negotiating these terms with an advertiser, a salesperson would write a letter or an email summarizing the agreement, such as: "Based on our conversations, we agreed that you will run a quarter-page ad in our monthly magazine for the 12-time discounted rate of $450 per issue, plus a 12-month listing in our online directory for $120 per month, and a 80-word sponsorship listing in our March email newsletter for $120. The total budget is $6,720 for the year, and we will break that amount into monthly billings of $560."

Once you have reached an agreement such as this one with the advertiser, you both sign a document called the insertion order or advertising space reservation form. This is the contract that spells out what ads it is running, when and where the ads will run, the prices you've negotiated, and a payment schedule. It includes the name and contact for the person at the advertiser who can handle any problems with the ad and indicates where to send the bill. It also provides the publication's deadlines and instructions for submitting ads in the proper format. This document is often the key to smooth production and billing.

CD-ROM

There is a sample insertion order that you can tailor to your own needs on the CD-ROM included with this book.

Advertisers are usually billed monthly for website ads. But for a magazine or newsletter, the bills go out when an issue comes off the printing press. Sometimes publishers ask for advance payment, and this is an acceptable practice. Classified ads are nearly always paid in advance, for example. Publishers commonly send invoices asking advertisers to pay within 30 days, but it can sometimes take longer. To avoid late payments, some publishers give a discount of 2% or more to advertisers that pay within 30 days.

Advertising sales management software can help you keep track of all of your advertisers—an otherwise difficult and cumbersome task. (See "Help With Managing the Sales Process," below.) Some of these programs can be integrated with your accounting system so that you can collect the data required for IRS tax reports and postage statements.

Automate as much of this process as you can—even if you have to write new database programs from scratch. Keeping track of all advertisers, how much they spend, and what kind of ads they bought can become overwhelming when you start producing a lot of issues or Web pages that carry a significant number of ads.

Help With Managing the Sales Process

The resources described below incorporate the lessons learned by publishers over many years—and they're a quick, cheap way to access all that expertise.

- Magazine Manager is an Internet-based program for maintaining a database of advertising prospects; recording contacts with them; and tracking their ads, bills, and payments. The program also has the capacity to manage editorial workflow and circulation. It costs about $1,500 to set up and $200 per month to maintain (www. magazinemanager.com).

- Sequel Ad Sales Management Software is another Internet-based program delivered on a subscription basis and priced so that smaller publishing companies can afford to subscribe (www.publish2profit. com).

- Smart Publisher is another integrated, Internet-based suite of programs to manage advertising contacts, ads, and editorial workflow (www.pre1.com).

- Fake Brains has a program called Account Scout that handles the same general features online (www.fakebrains.com).

- Ad2Ad is a program specifically designed to handle classified ads in community publications and on websites (www.ad2ad.com).

- You can also search the websites of database programs to find templates developed for managing ad sales. For example, look at one called AdSails for Filemaker Pro (http://solutions.filemaker.com/fsa/partner_results.jsp?).

- QuickBooks Nonprofit Accounting Software also provides tracking through its invoicing functions (http://quickbooks.intuit.com/product/accounting_software/nonprofit_industry).

Other Revenue Opportunities

Once you have a system in place for selling ads and friendly relationships with a significant number of advertisers, consider what other products you might sell to them.

Here are some additional potential revenue-producing ideas.

Sponsoring email newsletters. "Sponsoring" normally involves including a few lines of text inside the emails that your organization sends to its subscribers, in exchange for a promotional fee. Many nonprofits do not allow outsiders to sponsor newsletters, believing that even small text ads are a distraction—and that can be an important consideration. Before accepting ads in your emails, consider how much value they produce for you in other ways: donations, traffic to your website, new or renewal memberships. Coop America, for example, carries a lot of ads in its print magazine, but the only "ads" included in its weekly emails are its own fundraising appeals and promotions for its own programs.

When sponsorships are allowed, the advertiser commonly puts its logo or a text message toward the top of your email message, which links back to the advertiser's website. Sometimes, the advertiser can also put up to 75 words of additional text in the body of the newsletter. Prices for this type of sponsorship in the commercial world range from $20 CPM to $100 CPM.

Grant-funded articles or Web content. Foundations and other donors will sometimes finance the cost of reporting and writing a specific article if it meets their criteria for public service news or education programs. For example, the Fund for Investigative Journalism (www.fij.org) is a nonprofit that offers grants ranging from $500 to $10,000 for articles written by freelance investigative reporters. A listing of other journalism grants programs is available online at the journalists resources on NewsWise at www.newswise.com/resources/j_grants.

Renting names on a member list. The term "list rentals" includes any occasion when your organization allows another party to mail or email something to the people in your databases in exchange for a favor or a fee. Renting or trading mailing lists is a common practice among commercial publishers. But there are a limited number of circumstances when this may be an appropriate moneymaker in the nonprofit world, and the bylaws of many nonprofits explicitly prohibit the commercial use of their membership names.

"Chaperoning" is an interesting alternative to list rentals recommended by Michael Gilbert at Nonprofit Online News (www.news.gilbert.org). In this noncommercial exchange, Nonprofit A promotes Nonprofit B in its emails to members with an introduction such as: "Because you're a loyal supporter of our group, we thought you might be interested in also supporting this organization." No money changes hands, and the lists are not released to the other group, so this practice avoids many of the objections people make to a commercial rental agreement.

Business memberships. Consider allowing businesses to join your organization as an associate or business member, provided the business serves your same community of interests.

EXAMPLE: The Society of National Association Publishers (SNAP) invites organizations that offer products and services to publication members to join as associate members. Associate dues range from $195 to $495 per year, depending on the gross annual revenues of the business. Associate members receive a listing in SNAP's printed and online membership directories, plus a 15% discount from nonmember advertising rates in its magazine, *Association Publishing*.

EXAMPLE: Coop America has 3,000 business members who pay dues from $75 to $3,000 per year based on a sliding scale of business revenues. Business members must agree to the statement that: "As a member of the Coop America Business Network, my company conducts business according to standards that reach beyond contemporary practices in addressing the needs of consumers, employees, the community and the environment. I certify and can demonstrate that we strive to operate in a socially just and environmentally sustainable manner."

Special issues. Sometimes you can boost ad revenues by creating a special issue focused on a single topic. Your quarterly magazine could publish a fifth issue focusing on continuing education, for example, stocked with ads from professional development schools in your field. Or your environmental website could create a new section about eco-travel and invite a whole new group of travel companies to become regular advertisers. These single-topic issues are great for testing both your readers' and your advertisers' tastes for coverage on selected subjects.

> **EXAMPLE:** Coop America publishes an annual *Financial Planning Handbook* about socially responsible saving and investing that generates lots of extra advertising revenue. The *Handbook* is free to members and $11.95 for others.

Directories. Nearly every nonprofit niche can use an annual directory of products or services unique to that niche. Coop America, a nonprofit dedicated to "economic action for a just planet," publishes the *National Green Pages*, an annual directory of "screened and green" businesses. Companies apply to be listed in the directory, and applicants are screened to determine whether or not they fall within Coop America's "green" criteria. *The National Green Pages* accepts print and online ads from companies that pass the screening for $2,100 per page in print and $1,500 per year for an online banner ad.

Books and booklets. A professional association might publish "technical manuals" providing in-depth information on a specific topic for members, such as career advice or background information about industry trends. These manuals might be constructed by repackaging articles from a magazine or website about a specific topic. Or there could be a lighter side to this business—whatever is appropriate to the niche. *Kentucky Living* publishes a cookbook for $12, for example.

And some nonprofits offer booklets or books for online downloading. For example, you can download packages of current news about breast feeding research and policy issues for $3.50 per report from the website of the La Leche League at www.lalecheleague.org.

Completing Your Advertising Plan

Use the following questions to help develop a plan for including ads in your publications or websites. The questions can help you gather comments from people who might influence the decision: board members, key donors, staff. And the plan will help you communicate effectively with salespeople and prospective advertisers about what ads are acceptable. Finally, answering these questions will help everyone understand how much work goes into a successful sales program.

- **Mission fit.** Are there certain advertisers or advertising subject matter that is not acceptable to your organization? Do you want to establish guidelines for acceptable advertising or advertisers? What requirements and restrictions will you have for placing ads in your publication—for example, ruling out political ads, liquor, junk food?

- **Your wish list.** What companies would be most suited or desirable as advertisers in your publication or on your website?

- **Competition and pricing.** What do competing publishers offer those same advertisers—at what prices and with what restrictions? How much will you charge for ads, both online and in print?

- **Marketing.** How will you find advertising prospects? Who will manage the marketing effort? And how much money will you spend on it?

- **Staffing.** Who will be in charge of ad sales, how much will you pay them, and what territories will they cover? Who will manage the advertising production process? Who will handle billing and collections? Who will monitor IRS and postal regulations, file necessary paperwork, and keep abreast of changes in law and policies?

- **Revenue potential.** How much can you earn from advertising, based on your wish list of companies and comparable revenues at other nonprofits?

- **Total selling costs.** How much will you spend on marketing, sales tools, commissions, and staff?

- **Other revenues.** Are there other products or services you can sell to the same companies that advertise? ●

11

Connecting to Readers

There is never enough time or money to publish every article or Web page you would like the public to read. Instead, you will have to make trade-offs and compromises because of staff or money constraints. And sooner or later, every cash-strapped nonprofit will expect its publication to prove that it can justify the money budgeted to it. If you hope to increase the publishing budget or to launch a new publication, you must be prepared to prove how well the publication connects with readers to justify the expenses involved. You must also evaluate its potential for fulfilling the organization's larger mission. This chapter describes how to accomplish these feats.

Starting with the most basic consideration—whether or not readers are using the information you provide—this chapter sets out several options for understanding your readers and obtaining their feedback. Then, it helps you document how your publication is fulfilling any other purposes it may have, such as recruiting members or raising money. This kind of documentation is essential at budgeting time and easier to collect and present than it may seem.

The chapter also provides step-by-step guidance for adopting the most common methods for gathering reader feedback, including reader polls and surveys. And it offers some benchmark data that you can use to compare your efforts to other publications.

Finally, it includes tips about reporting your publishing successes to board members, staff, and other decision makers at your nonprofit.

Profiling Your Readers

Before you can influence those who read your publication to join up, donate to, or volunteer at your nonprofit, it helps to understand who they are and what other activities they customarily pursue. For example, do your readers already belong to other associations? Do they generally donate money—and if so, to what causes? Are they already volunteering in community service activities? Are they engaged in political activities related to your mission? That information can help you ensure that your publication matches readers' needs and expectations.

In addition, nonprofit publishers sometimes want to know what other publications their readers use for information and how much they already know about the organization's work. For example, do they avidly read related information sources? Are they likely to understand the social problems the organization is working to solve, or must they be educated? Do they have any misconceptions that need to be corrected? Do they know the full range of the organization's activities and programs?

Among the dozens of reader surveys nonprofits use to find out such information, there are two common forms: one that develops a profile of readers and their habits, and one that invites feedback about a specific publication or website. (Feedback surveys, also called reader satisfaction surveys, are covered in the next section.)

A profile survey of members, donors, or constituents asks for personal information such as age, gender, income, education, occupation, and job title. It also commonly seeks information about activities related to the organization's work: belonging to clubs or associations, donating, volunteering, engaging in political activities, serving on committees, or attending conferences, for example. And to complete the profile, organizations commonly ask those taking the survey for general information related to the organization: Do they use its services? How long have they belonged? Do they visit the group's website—and if so, why?

You can use all of this information to help plan editorial features. For example, if your nonprofit is made up of unionized nurses, and 64% of them report that they're regularly required to train less-experienced nurses, it signals you could help meet readers' needs by running articles about training in the magazine or opening up a training forum on your website.

Foundations, donors, and advertisers may also value the information in your basic member profile. For example, if members report that your website is their only reliable source of information about an important social issue, then your organization could use that feedback to raise funds from donors for expanding the website.

If your organization has not developed a profile of its members, donors, or volunteers, consider starting the practice. A large organization would likely conduct a profile survey either online or through the mail. Both methods are described later in this chapter. A small organization might gather the same information by interviewing each targeted reader individually.

EXAMPLE: A newly formed trade association profiled its members by conducting personal interviews with one person from each of the 500 businesses that had already joined the association. Working for more than a month, the association staff interviewed each member about business activities, staffing, and sources of income using a questionnaire and interview guide. They learned that although every member intended to set up an employee retirement program, only a small percentage of them had actually done so. As a result, the association hosted a conference about retirement plans tailored to small businesses. And in turn, the conference helped the association to attract dozens of new members.

RESOURCE
The Web survey companies listed later in this chapter all provide sample surveys for various purposes and templates that you can adapt to your own use. You can find more samples and tips about conducting surveys in the book *Designing and Using Organizational Surveys: A Seven-Step Process*, by Allan H. Church, Janine Waclawski, and Alan Kraut (Jossey-Bass Business and Management Series).

Gauging Reader Interest

When you thoroughly understand the nature of your audience, the next obvious question might be: Are your print and online publications valuable to them? You can monitor who is reading your publications—and why—by conducting reader satisfaction surveys and developing performance benchmarks, as described below. In evaluating websites, you can also use traffic monitoring programs to keep tabs on reader likes and dislikes by noting which pages on your site are getting the most attention.

The data you collect about reader interests may be valuable in persuading board members and executive staff that your investment in these publishing activities is justified. For example, if you are campaigning for enough money to hire professional writers rather than volunteers, you might strengthen your case by comparing how articles from the two sources stack up in your feedback surveys and website traffic studies.

Likewise, surveys documenting the kind of articles readers have rated favorably in the past may provide helpful ammunition when board or staff members have untenable suggestions for the kind of stories you should include.

Using Reader Satisfaction Surveys

It's hard to know how readers are using your print publications unless you ask them. You can get direct what-did-they-read feedback from a website, but you must ask readers of print publications to report their likes and dislikes in a feedback survey.

Specifics of creating surveys are discussed later in the chapter. (See "Creating Surveys and Other Feedback Tools," below.) But for now, know that publishers commonly ask four basic questions about reading habits in editorial feedback surveys:

- How many of the last year's issues do you recall reading?
- How much time did you spend reading the last issue?
- Do you commonly share the issues with any other people?
- How many other people have read your copy?

These four questions address the simple issue of whether or not people are reading and sharing the publication—and you could include all four questions in every survey.

In addition to these questions, you can tailor editorial feedback surveys to find out whether the content you offer is meeting your publishing goals. To get at this concern, publishers commonly ask readers to make a number of specific assessments, as described below.

- Rate the overall contents, on a scale of X to Y, on qualities important to the editorial mission or strategy. For example, if your publishing mission is to teach people about world hunger, living with cancer, or choosing environmentally sustainable products, you would ask readers to rate how well you delivered on that promise.

- Rate how well your publication comes across to readers on a similar X to Y scale about communication issues such as clarity of writing, timeliness, accuracy, scope, authority, usefulness, balance, comprehensiveness, technical depth, or value.

- Ask readers about actions they have taken in reaction to the publication—especially ones linked to your publishing mission, but also general ones such as calling or writing to a politician; making a donation; discussing issues with friends, students, or colleagues; attending a meeting; writing letters to the media; changing personal behavior or consumption choices; buying a new product or service; or renewing a membership. For example, you might ask: On a scale of X to Y, how much does the nonprofit's magazine, newsletter, or website contribute to your decision about renewing your membership?

- Ask readers to weigh in about any new publishing technologies or formats the organization might develop, such as email newsletters, podcasts, digital editions, or downloadable documents.

- Ask for open-ended feedback. This gives readers a chance to surprise you with feedback you weren't expecting. (See "Creating Surveys and Other Feedback Tools," below, for more on this.) A few common open-ended questions include: Do you have any suggestions for making this publication or website more useful? Any complaints, comments, or other suggestions?

- Evaluate particularly important or mission-critical articles, Web features, or departments that appeared in the past year. You might, for example, use a chart such as this one:

Please indicate which of the following articles you recall reading and how you would rate the ones you read:			
Article or Department Name	I read it (Check here.)	I didn't read it or don't remember reading it. (Check here.)	On a scale of 1 to 5, how much did you like this article?
Article 1			
Article 2			
Article 3			

TIP

Link demographics to other questions. It's a good idea to ask a few demographic questions in your editorial feedback surveys so that you can analyze how different groups are responding to your publication or website. Are you a hit with women, but miss the mark with men? Are higher-income readers getting your message, but not the others? Do newer members appreciate the website better than old-timers? The only way to make comparisons among segments of your membership is to ask the demographic questions in the body of your survey.

Benchmarking

Publishing success ought to be judged over the years, not by a single month's website traffic or response to a single newsletter issue. That's why it's a good idea to conduct editorial surveys regularly to develop a baseline of statistics that will help assess reader satisfaction over time and in context. A single study may have some value, but to judge the true feelings of most readers, it is better to conduct several studies, one at least every other year. (See "Creating Surveys and Other Feedback Tools," later in this chapter.)

"Benchmarking" usually means comparing your performance against some external standard—for example, how one baseball player's batting average stacks up against the league average. But you can also establish your own internal benchmarks by averaging out over time any performance levels you find important. For example, knowing that last year, an average of 32% of your subscribers read any article in your magazine establishes a performance standard for individual articles, allows you to assess how many articles beat the average, and establishes a reasonable goal for overall performance in the future.

Common editorial benchmark statistics include:

- **average readership**—the percentage of survey respondents who recall reading the average article
- **reader ranking**—the average score surveyed readers give to articles
- **page views**—the average monthly number of page views the articles on your website receive, and
- **referrals**—the number of people who visited a website feature because it was mentioned in your print publication.

RESOURCE

A useful book about benchmarking in general, and nonprofit performance issues in particular, is *Benchmarking for Nonprofits: How to Measure, Manage, and Improve Performance*, by Jason Saul (Amherst H. Wilder Foundation).

This editorial benchmark data can help you weed out unpopular writers and subject areas. But give the readers—and your publication—time to settle into a comfortable relationship before responding to jumps and jerks in the data. A new publication might conduct a first survey after a year or so, but it is wise not to put too much faith in the results for a couple of years. In practice, it usually takes about three years before you can be sure that your feedback data accurately reflects the audience's feelings.

As mentioned earlier, it helps to include demographic information in your editorial surveys so that you can develop unique benchmarks for segments of your audience, if necessary. For example, if you're trying to reach younger readers, or wealthy ones, then you can separate responses by age and income, but only if you ask age and income questions in your editorial feedback survey.

It also helps to use the same wording on questions year after year. Otherwise, it becomes impossible to make comparisons over time. For example, if you start out with a five-point scale in your article rating system, then stick to it.

Monitoring Web Traffic

Like Hansel and Gretel, website visitors leave a trail of crumbs as they wander through the pages of your site. Technically, this occurs because every visitor's computer has to request the pages each person visits while surfing through. As your computer responds to these requests, it captures information about the visitors, including details such as what kind of computer system they use. (See Chapter 8, "Traffic Analyzer Programs," for more information about the software you can use to read and interpret these markers.)

You may not need to know what computers or browser software visitors are using, and there is a great deal of additional technical information routinely captured from visitors that only programmers would want to know. But you will probably appreciate learning what articles people have accessed, whether or not they read every page of every article, which links they followed, what materials they downloaded from the site, and how much time they spent at the site during a visit. All of this information and more is readily available if your site has the proper tools to capture and report it.

A number of common indicators are used to measure website traffic.

- **Page hits or downloads.** Every request for a file or page from your site is called a "hit." A single page with five small images on it such as your logo and a few graphs or photographs, plus a column of Google ads, plus the text itself, would count as seven hits—even though there was only one visitor reading one page. Because of this technical way of counting, people use page views or visitor counts rather than hits to measure readership.

- **Page views.** When a visitor downloads a whole Web page, it counts as a page view. This is a valuable statistic because it allows you to rank every article or page according to its popularity with visitors.

Advertisers often pay for ads based on page views, too. (Ad pricing is described in Chapter 10.)

- **Unique visitors.** Every individual who visits your website at least once in a fixed time frame, typically a 30-day period, counts as a unique visitor. This number is commonly used to measure the total number of people visiting your site during that time.

- **Visitor paths.** As a single visitor moves through your site, your monitoring program can record what pages were viewed and how much time was spent on each page.

- **Visitor lengths.** This number tracks the average length of time people are spending at your site in a single visit. One of your primary goals should be to persuade visitors to hang around long enough to do whatever you want them to do, such as make a donation, take a poll, subscribe or renew a membership, or click an ad. The challenge is that the average visitor length at many sites is less than 30 seconds.

- **Returning visits.** Each unique visitor has a unique bread crumb or "cookie" that counts every time he or she returns to visit your website. Having a lot of return visits means that people like the site's content.

CAUTION

Avoid mistakes in doing the math. Website monitoring programs need a small snippet of code installed on every single Web page, and if you overlook any of this coding, your statistics will be corrupted. If you get a discouraging statistic—for example, if it appears that 90% of your visitors spend fewer than five seconds at your site—check to see whether it's the coding rather than your content that's the culprit.

Every organization will have its own goals regarding these website statistics. For example, a general interest startup organization will likely aim to attract lots of first-time visitors. But a close-knit, well-established association or community site would expect to draw mostly repeat visitors. It takes some interpretation to make these statistics useful to you and to your organization.

At the simplest level, you can determine which articles visitors like best by constructing a table similar to the one shown below. But you can also combine Web statistics with other information to dig deeper. For example, you might track articles by author or topic to determine which writers and subjects appeal most to your visitors.

Rating Articles by Traffic	
Name of Article or Web Page	**Number of Page Views**
Article One	
Article Two	
Article Three	

You might also track which articles lead the most visitors to make a donation or subscribe—or any other activity linked to the website's mission.

Rating Articles by Donations or Dues Generated	
Name of Article or Web Page	**Dollars of Dues or Donations Generated**
Article One	
Article Two	
Article Three	

Is Your Publication Fulfilling Its Purpose?

Once you get people reading the articles in your publication, you may still have the problem of inspiring them to donate to, volunteer for, or join your organization. As described in Chapter 1, every organization has unique reasons for publishing. As a result, there are many different ways to define a publication's success. This section helps you evaluate whether your publishing efforts are paying off in terms of the goals you have set.

Recruiting and Retaining Members

When your organization is conducting a number of different campaigns to recruit or renew members, it can be difficult to isolate whether a specific issue of a newsletter, magazine article, or website feature delivered particular results.

For example, even though everyone understands that a publication usually helps increase membership, most organizations do not put income received from members into their publishing budgets. And often, nonprofit publishers do not draw a direct link between what they spend on a publication and how many new members the organization has acquired. This common accounting practice potentially robs a publication of its most significant measure of impact: changes in the number or type of members.

It is probably not wise to lobby to change your nonprofit's long-standing accounting practices by moving membership income into the publications budget. But you can make this link on your own, in your planning and assessment activities, simply by calculating your net publishing costs per member, as described below.

Beyond simply calculating the net publishing costs per member, you can examine how much your publication figures into readers' decisions to join or renew a membership by surveying them. And many publishers also measure whether renewals increase in response to changes in publications or websites.

Monitor the renewal statistics at your organization and consider how your publishing activities affect them. Perhaps the renewal response rate increases if you bundle the magazine with a renewal letter in the same envelope, for example.

Or you may need to change the type of content your publication offers to better beckon readers to read and renew.

Net Publishing Costs Per Member

Dividing your total publishing expenses by the number of members gives you a gross publishing cost per member. You can go a step further and include any publishing revenues into the calculation to get the net publishing costs per member.

Take, for example, a nonprofit association that spends $145,000 per year to publish a magazine and website for its 6,500 members and earns $15,000 per year from advertisers, reprints, and other direct publishing activities. The association's net publishing costs are $130,000 per year, or $20 per member.

Depending on the politics and economics of your organization, people might view $20 as a bargain compared to other member acquisition costs or as an indulgence compared to spending on other programs.

Either way, you can use the $20 as a benchmark: a number to beat in your quest to sell more memberships through your publishing efforts. For instance, if you are convinced that hiring professional writers for your magazine or website will cause members to renew in higher numbers, then even though the total publishing budget may have to stretch to cover the higher writers' fees, the publishing costs per member could actually decline as you bring in more of them.

EXAMPLE: One editor at a professional association significantly revamped his magazine and website when he learned that younger, newly recruited members were not renewing at the same rates as older ones. By adding more content to the magazine related to early career issues rather than fixating on retirement planning and putting more interactive content on the website, including a salary calculator, this editor was able to boost the renewal rate among younger members. Before he started working on the problem, only 39% of first-year members renewed for a second year. Two years after he revamped the magazine and website, the first-year renewal rate had increased to 48%.

> **TIP**
>
> **Set the right renewal goals.** Renewal expectations vary widely among different kinds of organizations. At unions or professional associations, renewal rates can hover close to 90%—and a typical member remains involved for decades. But renewal rates are below 25% at many organizations in which members come and go frequently, such as parenting and student groups. Consider these realities in setting your publishing goals. There is only so much your publication can do to influence renewals where people have transitory interests.

Creating a Sense of Community

When your goal is to make readers feel good about belonging to a community rather than trying to recruit new people to join it, it can be a bit more difficult to measure your success.

The publications that are best at building communities take pains to establish an effective two-way communication path with readers. They include features that encourage people to contribute ideas through letters or submissions to a magazine or website, offer message boards or blogs on a website, and conduct opinion polls. They then keep track of how many people are participating in these communications.

You can track whether or not a substantial number of people are taking advantage of those opportunities by tallying reader interactions. For example, you might monitor:

- how many letters or emails come in from readers every month
- how many people responded to a poll, submitted an article, or asked a question on the website, and
- how the response levels compare from month to month or year to year.

You might also measure how effectively your publication has established a sense of community by monitoring whether members are interacting with the organization: Are they attending meetings? Responding when you ask them to volunteer?

EXAMPLE: When a midwestern teachers union called for volunteers to travel to New Orleans in response to Hurricane Katrina, the magazine editor went along and documented the trip so that all members could share in the experience. She also asked individual participants to contribute their thoughts and photos to her article about the trip. And then she posed a question to the general membership in the article: Did we do enough, or could we do more next time? Over the following months, readers wrote to the magazine in record numbers with thoughts and suggestions about how they could respond as well or better to the next disaster.

Educating About Issues

If, by using the surveys and tallies mentioned earlier in this chapter, you have already established that people read your newsletter, magazine, or website articles, then you can measure your educational impact in two ways: First, you can simply count how many people you are reaching. And second, you can ask readers what actions they've taken in response to the information your publication provided to them.

Calculating your reach. The simplest way to measure educational impact is by counting how many paid or free copies you distribute. As your distribution increases, it is likely your impact will, too.

With a print publication, you can extend your reach by encouraging readers to share it, taking it to work or passing it to a friend or colleague when they're finished reading. This is the offline equivalent of the "email this to a friend" link, which has become a common and familiar feature on Web pages and email newsletters. Online sharing of this sort is relatively easy to measure electronically through the website traffic monitoring software. (This software is mentioned earlier in this chapter and described in detail in Chapter 8.) But you have to ask print subscribers how many other people read their copy of the publication in a survey. Then you can use that "pass-along" number to measure your total audience.

Calculating your impact. The effectiveness of your publications can't be measured in numbers alone, however. Imagine that you learn from editorial surveys that 2.5 people read every copy of your magazine, and therefore the 10,000 copies you sent to subscribers have actually reached 25,000 people. While that's useful information to share with colleagues and advertisers, you still have the problem of determining whether any of those people were moved by what they read. Did they take any actions in response? Did they change their behavior or try to change someone else's behavior in reaction to information they read? For example, did your article about the dangers of second-hand smoke persuade them to stop smoking or to ban smoking in their homes?

Sending readers to a website makes it easier to track exactly how they reacted to a printed article by counting how many signed the online petition, responded to a poll, made a donation via the link you gave them, or downloaded a sample letter to Congress. You can also measure these activities with a reader survey, as described earlier.

Conducting before-and-after surveys is another way to measure what people know about an issue. This is a good idea, particularly when your organization is planning to invest major resources in a specific education campaign. If your goal is to reach a particular audience with a targeted message—teaching college kids how to avoid credit card debt, for example—you can conduct surveys or focus groups ahead of time to find out what they already know and don't know about the issue. Then create articles that fill in any information gaps you find. After you publish the information, repeat the surveys to see what information "stuck" with the audience and what might need repeating. (Another way to assess this impact, through using focus groups, is discussed later in this chapter.)

TIP

Promote to the media. Most established publications maintain a database of reporters and producers in the mainstream media companies and send them free subscriptions. While these reporters rarely credit the nonprofit sources openly, they come to depend upon the publications as trusted resources and often do follow-up on stories that expose the issues to a much broader audience. This allows a small publication to reach millions of people beyond its direct audience. To track these echo effects of your own stories, you can subscribe to a media monitoring service such as NewspaperClips.com, CyberAlert.com, or BurrellesLuce.com. Some groups also appoint a staff person to do this monitoring informally.

Boosting Contributions

Nonprofits whose publications have the main goal of raising money seem to have it easy. To learn whether their publications are effective, they need only count how many dollars came back after sending out each issue or posting each new solicitation.

You may assume it is simple to do the math to measure this impact: You spent $1 on the publication and it raised $5. End of story. But wiser heads of fundraising publications will keep asking themselves whether or not that $5 could be $6 or $8—or even $10. Use some of the same feedback channels discussed in this chapter, such as surveys and website traffic statistics, to learn what kinds of information inspires donors to give the most. And, as mentioned earlier, surveys can tell you about information gaps you can fill that will lead to higher rates of giving.

EXAMPLE: One editor of a nonprofit publication learned during a donor focus group that people mistakenly assumed his organization only helps elderly people. Donors knew nothing about the group's programs serving others, including people who care for the elderly and their families. Looking back over the prior year's magazine issues and website feature articles, the editor realized that he had given very little coverage to these programs. So over the next few months, he remedied that misconception by beefing up coverage of family and caregiver programs in the group's publications and eventually started to raise significantly more donations for these programs.

Targeting Underserved Readers

If your mission is to publish information that no other publisher provides for a group that earnestly needs it, then measuring your impact may be as simple as counting how many people you have reached.

For instance, if you know that 500,000 premature babies are born in the United States every year, and your publication's goal is to reach their parents with targeted information, you might evaluate your success by tracking what percentage of them read your magazine or visited your website. Tell your donors and sponsors what percentage you hope to reach—25%, for example—and then report whether or not you achieved that goal. By surveying the people who read your publication, you can also measure how valuable it is to them and help persuade donors to finance it.

Creating Surveys and Other Feedback Tools

A whopping 90% of the association publishers who responded to a recent benchmarking survey indicated that they regularly conduct some type of reader research, and 79% of them had done at least one reader survey within the past five years. Given the ready availability of help with such surveys (see "Finding Survey Experts," below), nearly every publisher can afford to poll readers in this way. And there is no better way to assess your impact than through an appropriate survey.

To avoid making costly mistakes in the process, however, it is wise to organize your research by taking the steps described here.

- **Establish goals.** Every good survey starts with a clear, simple statement of its purpose and what you intend to do with the information collected. Here's an example: "Renewal rates are falling and we don't know why. A survey will help us find out why some people choose to renew and others don't, so that we can act to increase membership renewals."

- **Select and qualify respondents.** Some opinions are more important to you than others, and the people you select for any particular survey should reflect its purpose. If renewal rates are falling, for instance, you might select people who *have* renewed along with a comparable selection of people who *have not* so that you can compare their opinions. Always design a sampling technique that captures the most critical people and properly classifies respondents so that you can distinguish among them.

- **Make a research plan.** Research usually has one of three goals: It helps define a problem, tests a specific hypothesis through direct research, or leads to a new strategy or program. Different methods work better for these different goals, and possible approaches are discussed in detail below. Write a research plan that defines your goals for a study and explains what methods you've chosen and why. The research budget, methods, and schedule of your study should match your goals, and the entire plan should include specific outcomes.

- **Get consensus.** If the research results will bear on political considerations within your organization, such as whether to divert funds from your marketing programs to your magazine or what topics to address on your website, be sure to preview your survey plan with everyone who will ultimately decide what to make of the findings.

- **Conform to norms.** When you want to compare your results to some outside measures, such as national income or education breakdowns, use consistent wording on questions that relate to them. For example, when survey respondents are asked for their ages, they are typically prompted to specify a range such as: under 18, 18 to 29, 30 to 49, 50 to 64, 65 or older.

- **Get professional help.** Many professional researchers maintain a database of demographic questions, with the latest national measures for comparison. Asking a professional researcher to help ensure that your research conforms to industry norms can significantly boost its value. In the same way that a professional graphic designer can design better-looking magazines than you might be able to on your own, a professional researcher can develop better surveys. If you're not sure you can afford full professional services, ask for a breakdown of fees so that you can select only the services you need. For example, you might pay someone a few hundred dollars to design or edit a questionnaire you've drafted rather than pay that person several thousand dollars to conduct, tabulate, and analyze the survey. A professional can usually add the greatest value during the design stages of a study rather than the execution.

Finding Survey Experts

You don't have to hire an expert to help with every survey. Instead, find someone to design projects and teach you how to run them so that you can later manage the task on your own. Professional researchers familiar with nonprofits and publications generally charge from $75 to $250 per hour for their time.

A number of resources, including those listed below, provide more detail about research services, along with targeted information for finding help that best suits your needs.

- *Quirks Marketing Research Review*: A print magazine that covers surveys and provides useful articles, including information about how to conduct research and hire researchers at www.quirks.com.

- *The Green Book*: Online at www.greenbook.org, this is a print and online directory of research firms and focus group facilities.

- The American Marketing Association: This group provides articles and tutorials about conducting surveys and working with researchers at www.marketingpower.com. The site includes a searchable directory of researchers.

- The Market Research Association: This group publishes a directory of researchers called the "Blue Book" at www.bluebook.org—and also offers research tutorials, including an ethical code of standards for researchers, at www.mra-net.org.

Mail Surveys

Surveys conducted through the mail are generally convenient, efficient, and inexpensive—but also subject to a number of pitfalls.

The minimum response rate for producing statistically valid results is about 60%, but many mail surveys achieve less than 30%, even when they offer respondents cash incentives. And results come back slowly from mail surveys: The shortest time between sending out letters and receiving completed questionnaires is about a month. Finally, if you pose a leading or misleading question—asking nondonors about their donations, for example—then you won't get useful results.

There are a number of steps you can take to help increase the success rate of mail surveys:

- **Target respondents.** Survey people most likely to respond because they already have a relationship with your organization: heavy users of your services, for example, or major donors. Surveying avid supporters will yield the best response rates of all.

- **Use short questionnaires.** Make it easy for people to respond by asking a limited number of questions and keeping the questions tightly focused. People who do not understand the logic of a questionnaire will bail out if there doesn't seem to be a reason for asking something.

- **Solicit ideas.** Open-ended questions can provide valuable and unpredicted insights; include one or two when appropriate.

- **Jog memories.** Prompt people if you think they won't remember something and to make it easier for them to respond. For example, list the programs mentioned in your fundraising campaign if you want to ask which ones respondents selected for a donation.

- **Do a road test.** Test the questionnaire with five to ten strangers to make sure every question is clear before sending it out to your target group.

- **Use honest flattery.** Write a cover letter that explains why the survey is necessary, how survey takers were chosen, and how their responses will be used to improve your programs. Telling people that you're contacting them because of their import to the organization will often motivate them to respond to the survey. It may give an added boost if someone the respondents are likely to recognize, such as the president of your association, signs the cover letter.

- **Include simple instructions.** Include a postage-paid reply envelope and give a firm deadline for responding—no longer than two weeks.

- **Send reminders to stragglers.** Send a follow-up letter to those who don't respond with a second copy of the questionnaire and a second postage-paid reply envelope.

• **Offer an incentive for responding.** A crisp dollar bill is the most widely used incentive among commercial publishers. But for some nonprofits, money would not be a good incentive; for them, a contest or an emotional appeal might be more fitting and effective.

When a random sample of the population is selected for a mail survey, and 60% or more respond, then you can safely assume that your results accurately reflect the feelings of the general population, not just the people who responded. In other words, the results are statistically reliable. That's why the Gallup organization can interview only 2,000 people and report that "Americans feel such-and-such." You can aim to meet the same standards in your surveys, but in practice, publishers rarely meet the highest standards in reader surveys. There are many instances in which statistical reliability is too high a standard or is really not necessary. Response rates closer to 40% can be acceptable when you have limited time or money.

You can also boost the reliability of your survey by picking a larger sample. Even with modest response rates, the validity of your results increases the more people you include. For example, if 62% of survey respondents express a certain opinion, you can assume that the result is accurate for the whole population within the percentage described in the table below, based on the number of people you sampled.

Projected Accuracy of Survey Results		
Number in the Sample	**Chance of Error in Results**	**Possible Accuracy Range for a 62% Response**
100	10%	56% to 68%
300	6%	58% to 66%
500	5%	59% to 65%
1,000	3%	60% to 64%

Source: *Look Before You Leap: Market Research Made Easy,* by Don Doman (Self-Counsel Press)

Web Surveys and Opinion Polls

Web surveys and polls are so easy to do that the biggest potential mistake is doing them too quickly or too often. Because you can put a questionnaire together and get the results within a few days, you may be tempted to skip crucial steps such as making a plan, drawing a useful sample, and testing the questions. But bear in mind that the more effort you put into planning a survey, the greater the value that will result.

RESOURCE

WebSurveyor.com is a company that offers survey software, and its robust site offers ideas and free information about conducting Web surveys and polls, as well as survey templates.

Before launching a Web survey or opinion poll, take time to define its purpose and specify how you will use the results obtained by each question. Obviously, a survey linked to some key strategic decisions that you're considering bears more consideration than a quick opinion poll that you plan to post on your website.

Web surveying vendors offer a common batch of features, including the ability to screen out people who might be trying to manipulate your findings or people who don't qualify for your target respondent group. Most also allow you to tabulate results easily and quickly. And, most can provide professional-looking design templates and sophisticated cross-tabulations of the results so that you can determine if one group is behaving differently from the others.

RESOURCE

Each of these Web survey providers offers a similar bundle of services for the annual prices listed here.

- Keysurvey.com: $800
- Questionpro.com: $400
- Surveymonkey.com: $200
- Zapsurvey.com: $200
- Zoomerang.com: $350 for nonprofits

> **TIP**
>
> **Sometimes you need a warm body, not software.** All of the Web survey companies can use their software to import your mailing list, generate and distribute your questionnaire, and tabulate the results for a much lower fee than a professional research company would charge. But beware that you will usually get better results if you ask a professional— someone who knows how to word questions for the strongest impact and how to design questions truly responsive to your decision-making needs—to help develop a research plan. So if a survey has a critical importance to your nonprofit's mission or your publication's viability, consider asking a seasoned professional to help you design the study.

Focus Groups

A focus group brings together from six to 12 people to discuss issues and concerns about your organization's mission, activities, or publications. It's a discussion rather than a personal interview, and the group interaction is an important element of the dynamics.

Focus groups are valuable for testing new ideas, checking your assumptions against reality, and evaluating your publishing products. They can be used alone or as a complement to other research methods. The main purpose of focus group research is to elicit attitudes, feelings, beliefs, experiences, and reactions in a way that would not be feasible using a survey.

Focus group sessions, which commonly last from one to two hours, are often videotaped. And it normally takes about six weeks to plan and execute a successful focus group meeting.

Nonprofits commonly run their own informal focus groups, and there are advantages to a do-it-yourself approach. For example, staffers might take notes in an informal group instead of hiring a professional to make a video. Staffers might also benefit from direct access to participants and may be able to ask more-targeted questions about publications or programs than a professional facilitator would think to ask. Also, focus group members often appreciate the cherished "insider" feeling they get from such an experience, which will prompt them to respond more honestly.

But many publishers hire a professional facilitator to conduct focus groups. Facilitators have experience leading a group to engage in a meaningful discussion, and they often offer facilities designed specifically to allow the sessions to be unobtrusively videotaped.

Whether you hire an outside service for help with a focus group or conduct it yourself, here are some tips for getting the best results:

- **Keep it simple.** Do not be lured into trying to get a little information about a lot of topics. Instead, determine a single issue and ask questions directly related to it—five or six questions at the most.

- **Recruit carefully.** Success depends mostly on who participates, so be careful to recruit people with enough knowledge and experience to provide meaningful ideas and reactions. Rather than a random sample of your membership, you might purposely pick people who represent a relevant segment: new members, for instance, or members serving on committees. And choose people who have an emotional interest in the topic, those most likely to eagerly engage in the discussion.

- **Choose a savvy moderator.** Use a moderator who knows how to lead a productive discussion and to encourage balanced participation from everyone—someone who can silence a know-it-all, open up a wallflower, and mediate among opposing viewpoints. The neutrality of the moderator often helps participants freely express their views.

- **Encourage diversity.** Hold focus group meetings in a number of different locations if you think people have widely diverging opinions in the suburbs versus the city, for example, or in different parts of the country.

RESOURCE

For help planning focus groups, see *The Wilder Nonprofit Field Guide to Conducting Successful Focus Groups,* by Judith Sharken Simon (Amherst H. Wilder Foundation). You can also find articles about nonprofit focus groups in the magazine *Nonprofit World,* and at the Society for Nonprofit Organizations website, www.snpo.org.

Getting Virtual Feedback Through Cyberfocus

It is possible to save both time and money by holding "virtual" focus groups on the Internet. People can save travel time by participating from their own desks rather than gathering in a central location. And a cyber focus group may cost less than half what a live one costs.

But there is some controversy among professional researchers about the effectiveness of this practice. Some believe that people don't participate as fully or as honestly when they're responding through a computer keyboard instead of face to face. Also, without being able to observe the faces and body language of participants, you might draw incorrect conclusions about their feelings.

On the other hand, using the Web makes it possible to include people from all over the world, as well as disabled people and others who may be unable or unwilling to participate in a live focus group session. And an online focus group would seem to be the ideal method for discussing your website. Finally, if your audience is a particularly Web-savvy group, such as teenagers or college kids, then a virtual meeting might be more suitable than a live one.

Online Discussion Groups and Feedback Panels

Recent studies show that 40% of Americans routinely refuse to participate in surveys, which means that any survey you conduct will usually fail to reach a certain segment of the population. But you can often overcome the resistance of the chronically unresponsive by inviting them to serve on a panel or advisory group. A personal invitation to join a feedback panel makes many people feel like honored experts rather than hectored survey respondents.

Many publishers routinely gather feedback from a body of people who agree to participate in a "Publications Advisory Panel" or "Member Advisory Group." Invite people onto such a panel if they match the profile of your key audience segments or if they have unique expertise to offer. (See Chapter 4 for details about editorial advisory boards.)

EXAMPLE: One health care nonprofit invites three groups of people to advise its magazine's editorial staff: publishing experts, including business and editorial consultants; medical experts from outside the organization who are knowledgeable about treatment trends and the nonprofit's health care education work; and program staff from within the organization familiar with its strategic goals and programs. This group as a whole meets once a year to critique the magazine and offer content suggestions.

Your group might include academics, working professionals in your field, or journalists who cover it. The goal is to find people who can give valuable guidance to your publishing work and provide critical feedback about the current publication.

Many advisory groups provide input through online message boards, email lists, or virtual discussion groups—although you can also meet with your advisors in person, too. Publishers generally meet once or twice yearly with publishing advisers. During the meeting, the group plans an editorial calendar for the coming year and offers recommendations about potential authors or topics that would add value to the magazine, newsletter, or website.

Feedback panels work best when you recruit specific individuals to participate and restrict access so that those without a suitable background cannot chime in uninvited. As with other opinion surveys, it helps to tell people why they've been selected to participate, how you'll guard their privacy, and what level of commitment you'll expect from them. You may require something as simple as answering a monthly email questionnaire or as complicated as previewing articles ahead of publication. Either way, telling folks the ground rules in advance makes it easier for them to fulfill your expectations over time.

Using Performance Benchmarks

After asking readers and other qualified outsiders for feedback on your publications, you can also make your own internal evaluations based on how much bang you deliver for your publishing bucks.

At budget time, when people want to know exactly what they're getting for the money spent on publications, you can be ready to show how your publication stacks up against others in the field or how it compares to historical averages. And these comparisons may be important negotiating chips in a climate in which nonprofit staff members are being asked to take on more work without additional staff or resources.

Everyone will know whether you are meeting your budget for revenues and expenses. But beyond that basic accomplishment, you should also expect that your publishing efforts will become increasingly efficient over time. For one thing, printing costs per copy always decline as you print more copies. In addition, as you develop management systems and procedures, and after you settle into comfortable relationships with vendors and advertisers, you can expect that other efficiencies will surface. Every person who works on the publication is likely to become more productive with experience, too. For example, editors will likely be able to produce more pages each year as they fine-tune relationships with writers, learn systems for converting print pages to Web content, and develop reliable information sources within the organization.

You can usually track this increasing efficiency by monitoring the benchmarks highlighted in Chapter 3: cost per editorial page, revenue per ad page, and so forth. In addition, the tables below show some benchmarking data from a recent survey of 114 association publications that you can use to assess your performance over time.

This data is presented by organization size because there are significant differences among small and large groups. Notice, for example, that smaller organizations, with bare-bones staffing, generally publish fewer and smaller publications. As the organization size increases, there is a corresponding increase in the publishing volume: 83.3% of the largest organizations publish monthly, while only 16.7% of the smallest ones do.

In these tables, "employee" includes part-time and freelance workers that were reported in the survey. The abbreviation FTE stands for "full time equivalent," a figure used to translate the activities of several part-time or freelance contributors into employee numbers.

Pages Published Annually Per Publishing Employee				
Organization's Total Annual Revenue	Median Number of Issues per Year	Median Number of Pages per Issue	Median Number of Publishing FTEs	Annual Pages per Publishing Employee
$100,000 or less	6	28	1	168
$100,001 to $500,000	8	51	2	204
$500,001 to $1 million	8	69	3	188
$1 to $5 million	10	91	9	101
$5 million or more	12	97	20	58

Source: Angerosa Research Foundation, 2005 Association Publishing Benchmarking Study, www.strattonpub.com/angerosafound.html

According to the study, one editor can produce about 168 pages per year and two editors can produce an average of 204 pages each—about 20% more than a single person working alone. As the publishing frequency increases, the organizations add more editors and each one appears to produce fewer pages. But these productivity measures do not include Web pages, books, or other publications a nonprofit may produce, so they may not track all of the work for which these employees are responsible. For instance, 54% of respondents in this survey reported that their publications staff also has responsibility for the association website, and 76% of the organizations with $1 million or more in total publishing revenue also publish books.

Publishers in the survey also reported how much they spend on writing and design. Editorial and design costs included staff expenses as well as money paid to freelance writers, illustrators, photographers, and designers. As you can see from the table below, larger organizations spend more per page than smaller ones. It is likely that smaller organizations rely more heavily on volunteers than larger ones and therefore spend less creating pages. For example, it's a common practice at smaller organizations to run digital photographs taken by staffers or freelance writers rather than paying professional photographers.

Editorial and Design Costs Per Page			
Organization's Total Annual Revenue	Median Annual Editorial and Design Costs	Median Annual Number of Pages	Median Cost per Page
$100,000 or less	$29,665	214	$139
$100,001 to $500,000	$88,503	427	$207
$500,001 to $1 million	$163,224	643	$254
$1 to $5 million	$374,995	1,087	$345
$5 million or more	$1,028,266	1,142	$900

Source: Angerosa Research Foundation, 2005 Association Publishing Benchmarking Study, www.strattonpub.com/angerosafound.html

The study's authors caution: "As you make comparisons with these findings, consider your own publication's unique variables and make appropriate adjustments. For example, associations where nearly all editorial content is contributed free by members will have lower overall editorial costs than publications where paid staff or outside freelancers write the majority of articles."

If you plan to use a study such as this one for budget negotiations within your organization, then buy the full report, which breaks down responses by publication type and organization size, and make the appropriate head-to-head comparisons. Editorial productivity is different for monthly magazines versus quarterlies, for example—and for publications that must produce a profit versus ones that don't. And in the smallest organizations, 67% of the print publication editors also manage the website, but in 66% of the largest organizations, someone else has this responsibility. All of these distinctions affect the benchmark readings for workload and productivity of editors.

Getting Additional Feedback and Training

Attending publishing conferences and seminars puts you in a prime position to get feedback from outsiders, hone your skills, and meet your peers.

For example, many of these conferences offer the opportunity to have an experienced designer or editor review your publication. Others offer the chance to discuss your circulation or ad sales strategy with publishing experts on the business side. All of these programs provide excellent training for employees, as well as the opportunity to meet other people involved in publishing and learn how your peers are managing their publications.

Below are some sponsoring organizations; their Web addresses; and names of the conferences, courses or seminars they customarily hold.

- *Folio*, a trade magazine (www.folioshow.com), sponsors the Folio Show, held in New York City every year. The conference covers a range of publishing topics, from ad sales and accounting to production and circulation. The focus is mostly on print magazines.

- The Magazine Publishers of America (www.magazine.org) offers classes and seminars throughout the year in New York City. Many classes are full-day or half-day programs on a specific issue, such as website design, and every program offers the opportunity to meet other publishers.

- The Society of National Association Publishers (www.snaponline.org) hosts a Publications Management Conference in Washington, DC and Chicago. The focus is on teaching management skills for people who work for nonprofit association publications.

- Stanford University (www.publishingcourses.standford.edu) provides several courses for mid-career publishing professionals. The Stanford summer course is a ten-day residential program that draws publishing people from all over the world. Stanford also offers a three-day Web publishing conference in the fall.

- The Western Publications Association (www.wpa-online.org) hosts a two-Day Publishing Conference that covers many publishing topics and includes both online and print publishing. The WPA conference is mostly for commercial publications: You won't meet many of your nonprofit peers at this conference, but you can learn the basics of editing, design, production, ad sales, and many other topics.

Using Feedback to Win Support

Information is the key to winning board and staff support for a publishing budget and program. Share the feedback from readers, benchmark data, and the other measures described in this chapter in a simple-to-read format that reminds everyone why your publications and websites are so valuable.

If strategic decisions are afoot—for example, if your nonprofit is debating whether or not to revamp the website, expand the publishing staff, or launch a new publication—then you can gather and report information specifically designed to help make those decisions.

But even when no major change is planned, it helps to keep people within the organization informed about your publishing activities and tell them what the publications deliver for the money spent on them. Unless you provide this information, your successes will surely go unnoticed.

Experienced publishers provide board members and the staff with a publishing performance report at least once a year. Sometimes these reports come more often. Yours should include any of the following information that is relevant to your current conditions. For instance, if your organization is growing rapidly, then everybody will want to see rapidly rising readership measurements. But if budgets are being squeezed, then you might emphasize how well you made do on a small budget by highlighting your productivity.

The following is some of the information you might report to your organization's decision makers to help them understand your publishing activities.

- **Readership measurements.** How many people are reading the print publications or visiting the website this year versus last year?
- **Content ratings.** Based on website traffic patterns or print publication readership surveys, what subjects are most popular with readers? And do they show a preference for specific writers or departments?

- **Mission impact.** What measurable results from publishing activities—such as increased membership renewals, donations, or volunteer activism—can you demonstrate? How do these results compare to previous years?

- **Productivity assessments.** How many articles were produced this year versus previous years? How does that output compare to other organizations? How does it compare to your spending levels this year versus last?

- **Outside recognition.** Did you win any prizes or editorial awards? Did any readers or outside reviewers offer special praises or complaints?

- **Editorial initiatives.** Are you planning new coverage or new strategies that people should know about? Have you made changes to fix or improve any problems from the past?

Keep performance reports brief and focused on only a handful of key points you want people to remember. Always link your work to the overall and current goals of the organization—for example, how you can help recruit younger members or how you are building awareness for specific programs.

Finally, don't forget to use feedback to change your ways if that's what readers seem to be asking you to do. You'll get bad news sometimes; everybody does. A cherished article will bomb with readers, or a Web initiative will fail. When that happens, don't panic and don't try to hide the news. Instead, use critical feedback as an opportunity to freshen your perspective and improve your connection with readers, then ask your advisers to help assess it. And finally, share your revamping ideas in your next performance report.

Resources

This chapter includes organizations, websites, books, and other resources that are valuable to those involved in publishing at nonprofits.

Accounting

These groups help recruit accountants specializing in nonprofit accounting who may offer special rates or free services to qualifying organizations:

- Accountants for the Public Interest, at www.geocities.com/api_woods/api/apihome.html
- Clearinghouse for Volunteer Accounting Services, at www.cvas-usa.org.

Budgeting and accounting issues for nonprofits are well covered in these books:

- *Bookkeeping Basics: What Every Nonprofit Bookkeeper Needs to Know*, by Debra L. Ruegg and Lisa M. Venkatrathnam (Amherst H. Wilder Foundation)
- *Bookkeeping for Nonprofits: A Step-by-Step Guide to Nonprofit Accounting*, by Murray Dropkin and James Halpin (Jossey-Bass)
- *Not-For-Profit Accounting Made Easy*, by Warren Ruppel (Wiley) (not as easy as it claims, but still a useful reference book).

Copyrights

All publishers should understand how to protect their own content and how to avoid violating the rights of other copyright holders. You can find useful guidance from:

- *The Copyright Handbook: What Every Writer Needs to Know*, by Stephen Fishman (Nolo)
- Copyright Information Center, at www.copyright.cornell.edu

- *Getting Permission: How to License & Clear Copyrighted Materials Online & Off*, by Richard Stim (Nolo)
- Media Law Resource Center, at www.medialaw.org
- *The Public Domain: How to Find Copyright-Free Writings, Music, Art, & More*, by Stephen Fishman (Nolo).

Designing

A growing number of resources are available for those interested in editorial and graphic design for magazines, newsletters, and websites. A number of books offer good help and advice on editorial design for magazines, newsletters, and websites, including:

- *Design It Yourself Newsletters: A Step-By-Step Guide*, by Chuck Green (Rockport Publishers): The author uses simple explanations of the newsletter design process and offers more than a dozen templates of different design styles so that readers don't have to start from scratch.

- *Editing by Design: For Designers, Art Directors, and Editors—The Classic Guide to Winning Readers*, by Jan V. White (Allworth Press): Covers everything from fonts, to appropriate line spacing, to how to evoke different reactions from readers through page layouts. Includes many visual examples of everything, often drawn in the author's whimsical style.

- *Homepage Usability: 50 Websites Deconstructed*, by Jakob Nielsen and Marie Tahir (New Riders Publishing): These website experts review their 113 guidelines, grouped by topic area, for the most usable websites and the reasons behind those rules.

- *Learning Web Design: A Beginner's Guide to HTML, Graphics, and Beyond*, by Jennifer Niederst (O'Reilly Media): Niederst leads Web design virgins step by step through the entire process, from explaining what the Internet is, to editing web graphics, to purchasing server space and getting files uploaded; for those who want to delve further, look up another of her books, *Web Design in a Nutshell: A Desktop Quick Reference* (O'Reilly Media).

- *Magazine Design That Works: Secrets for Successful Magazine Design*, by Stacey King (Rockport Publishers): A good overview book with many examples of successful magazine design; not much technical information about creating layouts.

- *Newsletter Design: A Step-by-Step Guide to Creative Publications*, by Edward Hamilton (Wiley): Walks readers through every step of the process in designing a newsletter; offers standard styles and lots of tips, but examples look dated since it was first published in the mid 90s.

- *Producing a First-Class Newsletter: A Guide to Planning, Writing, Editing, Designing, Photography, Production, and Printing*, by Barbara A. Fanson (Self-Counsel Press): Fanson takes readers through every stage of the process in creating a newsletter, from how to pick the right title to writing catchy headlines to designing on a grid.

- *Professional Web Site Design From Start to Finish*, by Anne-Marie Concepcion (How Design Books): While this book leaves the details of writing HTML to other volumes, it delivers other important aspects of Web design such as setting site goals, deciding the site architecture, managing the process, trafficking files, subcontracting, and analyzing Web log data.

- *Surprise Me: Editorial Design*, by Horst Moser (Mark Batty Publisher): A comprehensive guide to editorial design with many examples.

- *The Non-Designer's Design Book*, by Robin Williams (Peachpit): A practical, nuts-and-bolts guide to good editorial and graphic design for people with no design background.

- *The Non-Designer's Web Book*, by Robin Williams and John Tollett (Peachpit Press): A basic book for someone who doesn't know the first thing about designing a website; even if you'll be outsourcing the job, this good primer on the process will tell you what should be happening and what to expect from your site manager.

- *Webworks: eZines: Explore On-Line Magazine Design*, by Martha Gill (Rockport Publishers): A book that covers just the niche of online magazines. Gill discusses every aspect of starting, designing, and growing an electronic magazine; she collects advice and tips from e-zine staff and analyzes about 50 of the best ones.

Government Agencies

Nonprofits intersect with the government at several points, and fortunately, these government websites are well-organized and easy to use:

- Internal Revenue Service, at www.irs/gov/charities: The website explains the tax rules for nonprofits, particularly the rules regarding advertising sales profits; the IRS also offers online tax exemption workshops at www.stayexempt.org

- United States Library of Congress (LOC), at www.loc.gov/issn/is: The place to obtain an International Standard Serial Number (ISSN), which is required by the U.S. Postal Service, the IRS, periodical distribution companies, and libraries, and

- United States Postal Service, at www.usps.gov: Provides access to all current postal regulations and forms; for an independent analysis of rate changes and other USPS activities, go to Postal Watch, at www.postalwatch.org.

Hiring Artists, Writers, and Designers

Use generic job hunting websites, such as HotJobs and Monster.com, as a backup, but a more focused search can be conducted using these resources, which can help you locate and hire the specialized staffers or consultants—including editors, artists, writers, advertising salespeople, and designers—you need to publish a newsletter, magazine, or website.

Books

The following books help find creative people you will need for a publishing project. They often offer tips about standard fees and contracts—and you can generally search through them to see what other publishers are doing:

- *Artist's and Graphic Designer's Market* (Writers Digest Books): This book covers design, illustration, and photography.

- *National Writers Union Freelance Writers' Guide*, by James Waller (National Writers Union): A broad compendium by veteran freelance writers and publishing experts.
- *Writers Market*, an annual directory from Writers Digest Books, with a companion website at www.writersmarket.com; Widely used by freelance journalists and writers who are looking for work.

These are also a number of useful books about hiring employees or independent contractors:

- *Working With Independent Contractors*, by Stephen Fishman (Nolo)
- *The Employer's Legal Handbook*, by Fred Steingold (Nolo)
- *Job Description Handbook*, by Margie Mader-Clark (Nolo).

Websites

Publishing job descriptions and current salary levels are available from the following sources:

- *Folio* magazine, at www.foliomag.com
- The Society of National Association Publisher, at www.snaponline.org
- *Nonprofit Times*, at www.nptimes.com
- The Vault, at www.thevault.com.

Use the sites below to find staff and freelance editors, writers, artists, and designers.

- The Detroit Free Press Jobs Page, at www.freep.com/legacy/jobspage: A website that acts as a big portal to many other job websites.
- Editorial Freelancers Association, at www.the-efa.org: A membership organization of editors, writers, designers, proofreaders, researchers, translators, and other self-employed professionals in the communications field.
- Journalism Jobs, at www.journalismjobs.com: A well-organized and extensive national database of media jobs.

- The Journalist's Toolbox, at www.journaliststoolbox.com/ newswriting/jobs.html: The job bank of the American Press Institute.
- University of California at Berkeley's J-Jobs, at http://journalism. berkeley.edu/jobs: Linked to UC Berkeley's graduate school of journalism, J-Jobs is free for posters and draws employers and job seekers from across the country.

Use these sites for locating writers, artists, and photographers:

- Alternative Pick, at www.altpick.com: A jobsite for artists and Web designers.
- American Showcase, at www.americanshowcase.com: A directory of designers, artists, and photographers.
- American Society of Media Photographers, at www.asmp.org: Features photographers with publications experience.
- The Black Book, at www.blackbook.com: Includes a creative industry directory and portfolios online, and also publishes multiple catalogues of photography, illustration, and mixed media.
- Creative Hot List, at www.creativehotlist.com: One of the leading websites where designers go to post their portfolios.
- Directory of Illustration, at www.directoryofillustration.com: Illustrations searchable by style, technique, and subject.
- Workbook, at www.workbook.com: A national resource for the graphic arts community.

And search for outside advertising sales support at:

- National Association of Publishers Representatives, a trade association, at www.naprassoc.com.

Nonprofits, Generally

These associations, publications, watchdog groups, and websites provide valuable general information about starting and managing nonprofits.

Associations

A number of trade and professional associations offer training, publications, and other support for members. And your organization might already belong to them, including:

- American Society of Association Executives (ASAE), at www.asaecenter.org
- National Council of Nonprofit Associations (NCNA), at www.ncna.org.

Books

These books offer insight about what it takes to run a nonprofit successfully:

- *Effective Fundraising for Nonprofits*, by Ilona Bray (Nolo): A primer on nonprofit fundraising.
- *Starting & Building a Nonprofit*, by Peri Pakroo (Nolo): This book explains how to start a new nonprofit organization and gives a basic introduction to fundraising.

Periodicals

Subscribe to or check out the websites for these useful magazines and newsletters, which address a broad range of management issues for nonprofit organizations. This is where you'll find good reviews of products and services, statistics and surveys—including some salary and employment information—and practical advice. Among the most helpful are:

- *Associations Now* magazine, published by the American Society of Association Executives, at www.asaecenter.org

- *Association Publishing* magazine, published by the Society of National Association Publishers, at www.snaponline.org
- *Chronicle of Philanthropy*, at www.philanthropy.com
- *Nonprofit Quarterly* magazine, at www.nonprofitquarterly.org
- *The Nonprofit Times*, at www.nptimes.com, and
- *Nonprofit World* magazine, published by the Society for Nonprofit Organizations, at www.snpo.org.

Research

Surveys sometimes provide useful insight about the nonprofit organization activities.

- This study questioned associations about their publishing activities: 2005 *Association Publishing Benchmarking Study*, by the Angerosa Research Foundation, available from the Society of National Association Publishers at www.snaponline.org. This study reports common staffing and spending habits among association publications.

Watchdog Groups

These groups track how nonprofits are raising and spending their funds. You can study what other organizations are doing—and how they are rated—by visiting these sites:

- American Institute of Philanthropy, at www.charitywatch.org, a general nonprofit watchdog group
- Charity Navigator, at www.charitynavigator.org, helps donors assess nonprofits
- Guidestar Database, at www.guidestar.org, reports tax data from nonprofits, and
- Wise Giving Alliance of the Better Business Bureau, at www.give.org, monitors nonprofits.

Websites

- The website at www.idealist.org is a clearinghouse for consultants who work with nonprofits, and the site also publishes articles and FAQs for nonprofits seeking to find and work with outside experts.

- The website at www.compasspoint.org publishes general information about managing nonprofit organizations, including some excellent articles about budgets, tax returns, and audits.

- The Nonprofit Financial Center, at www.nfconline.org, is an Illinois nonprofit group offering financial advice and information to other nonprofits in the state. The site has articles and reports useful to nonprofits nationwide.

Printing

Helpful books about printing include:

- *Getting It Printed: How to Work With Printers and Graphic Imaging Services to Assure Quality, Stay on Schedule and Control Costs*, by Eric Kenly and Mark Beach (How Press).

- *Pocket Pal: The Handy Little Book of Graphic Arts Production*, by Michael H. Bruno (International Paper): The book is regularly updated and has current information about technologies used by publication printers.

- *Put It on Paper: Every Person's Guide to the Printing Industry*, by Margie Gallo Dana (Xlibris Corporation): A reference book about printing newsletters and magazines written by a printing consultant.

- *Working With a Magazine Printer*, by Bert Langford (blnconsult.com): Written by a production consultant, this book provides an excellent overview of the process, plus specific tips about saving time and money.

Publishing Courses and Seminars

- Folio Show, at www.folioshow.com
- Magazine Publishers of America, at www.magazine.org
- Society of National Association Publishers, at www.snaponline.org
- Stanford University, at http://publishingcourses.stanford.edu, and
- Western Publications Association, at www.wpa-online.org.

Publishing, Generally

A great many groups and publications support and inform the work of the publishing industry.

Associations

Trade groups often provide statistics about the publishing industry. Some also offer classes and training programs and list job openings. Through their membership directories, you can also find other publishers. The most relevant include:

- AIGA, at www.aigadesignjobs.org, a professional association for designers
- American Society of Magazine Editors (ASME), at www.asme. magazine.org; ASME publishes ethical guidelines for magazine and website editors at www.magazine.org/editorial/guidelines/_ guidelines_for_editors_and_publishers and www.magazine.org/ editorial/guidelines/best_practices_for_digital_media
- American Society of Media Photographers, at www.asmp.org
- Graphic Artists Guild, at www.gag.org
- Magazine Publishers of America (MPA), at www.magazine.org
- National Association of Publishers' Representatives (NAPR), at www. naprassoc.com

- National Press Photographers Association, at www.nppa.org

- National Writers Union, at www.nwu.org

- Specialized Information Publishers Association (SIPA), at www. newsletters.org

- Professional Photographers of America, at www.ppa.org

- Society of National Association Publishers (SNAP), at www. snaponline.org, and

- Western Publications Association (WPA), at www.wpa-online.org.

Books

The following books cover the whole range of publishing issues, not just a single topic, such as website design or accounting, which are addressed in other sources:

- *Publication Advertising Source* (several different editions, including Business, Consumer, and Health Care), annual directories from Standard Rate and Data Service (SRDS), at www.srds.com. Advertising agencies refer to these directories. Listing a publication or website is free, and if yours will carry ads, you should list it with SRDS. The many different SRDS reference directories are also useful one-stop resources for doing research about other publications.

- *Guide to Periodicals Publishing for Associations*, by Frances Shuping, (ASAE): Not available from retailers, but from the American Society of Association Executives website, at www.asaecenter.org/marketplace/bookstoredetail.cfm?itemnumber=15250.

- *Starting & Running a Successful Newsletter or Magazine*, by Cheryl Woodard (Nolo): Written for all publishers, this book covers the business side of publishing, especially selling subscriptions and ads.

- *Successful Direct Marketing Methods*, by Bob Stone and Ron Jacobs (McGraw-Hill): For publishers who sell subscriptions or memberships by direct mail.

Periodicals

There are a handful of magazines that report on trends, review products, and describe common practices in the publishing industry, including:

- *Circulation Management* magazine, about selling subscriptions, maintaining subscriber databases, and dealing with the U.S. Postal Service, at www.circman.com

- *CMYK*, about design and digital production, at www.cmykmag.com

- *Editor and Publisher,* for the newspaper industry, online at www. editorandpublisher.com

- *Folio*, for magazine management, at www.foliomag.com; its website has publishing job descriptions and salary surveys, and

- *How*, about graphic design, online at www.howdesign.com.

Websites

A number of websites focus on providing help for commercial and nonprofit publishers alike.

- Journalism Next, at www.journalismnext.com: A website geared to helping journalists of color find jobs and helping employers find diverse candidates, the site allows job seekers to post resumes and receive automatic notification and delivery of matching jobs

- Magazine Publishers of America provides a great deal of useful information about publishing, at www.magazine.org, and

- Publishing Business Group, at www.publishingbiz.com: Website by Cheryl Woodard, co-author of this book, links to additional online publishing resources, FAQs, and articles.

Surveys and Other Feedback

Geared specifically to help nonprofit organizations gather feedback from constituents, these books are highly recommended:

- *Benchmarking for Nonprofits: How to Measure, Manage, and Improve Performance*, by Jason Saul (Amherst H. Wilder Foundation)
- *Designing and Using Organizational Surveys: A Seven-Step Process*, by Allan H. Church, Janine Waclawski, and Alan I. Kraut (Jossey-Bass Business and Management Series), and
- *The Wilder Nonprofit Field Guide to Conducting Successful Focus Groups*, by Judith Sharken Simon (Amherst H. Wilder Foundation).

Website Construction

For nonprofit publishers who are new to producing a website or e-newsletter or who need help with a flagging effort, there are a burgeoning number of resources to consult for help with concerns from production, to getting the best search capabilities, to avoiding being a spammer.

Production

- *Building a Web Site for Dummies*, by David A. Crowder (For Dummies)
- *Nonprofit Internet Strategies: Best Practices for Marketing, Communications, and Fundraising Success*, by Ted Hart, James Greenfield, and Michael Johnston (John Wiley & Sons).

Search Engine Optimization

- *Search Engine Optimization for Dummies*, by Peter Kent (For Dummies): Highly recommended by nonprofit webmasters; the author also has an informative website at www.ichannelservices.com.

- *Search Engine Optimization: An Hour a Day*, by Jennifer Grappone and Gradiva Couzin (Sybex): Written by experienced web consultants who seem to understand the problems caused by limited budgets and staff time, they also offer downloadable worksheets to make the process easier, at www.yourseoplan.com.
- Search Engine Watch, at www.searchenginewatch.com, also includes information about Search Engine Optimization.

Start your search for website tools at this general site, which provides blogs and forums as well as general information and links to specific programs:

- Web Master World, www.webmasterworld.com.

Aviod accidentally sending spam or violating laws governing junk emails by checking with these sites for the latest rules and information from:

- Direct Marketing Association Anti-Spam Resources, at www.the-dma.org www.the-dma.org/antispam
- Mail Abuse Prevention, at www.mail-abuse.com
- SpamCon, at www.spamcon.org.

Writing and Editing

From style guides, to books offering writing inspiration, to manuals on the craft of editing for print publications and websites, there are a number of resources to which you can turn for help.

Books

If you looked at the bookshelf of a top website or magazine editor, you would find many or all of these books, the standard references and guidebooks for people in publishing.

- *Art and Craft of Feature Writing: Based on the Wall Street Journal Guide*, by William E. Blundell (Plume): This is a great little volume teaching nonfiction feature writers how first to better craft an interesting angle to a story and then go about reporting, organizing, and writing it; Blundell uses excerpts from real news stories to deconstruct the thinking and writing process.

- *Associated Press Guide to News Writing: The Resource for Professional Journalists*, by Rene J. Cappon (Peterson's Guides).
- *Associated Press Stylebook, and Briefing on Media Law* (Basic Books).
- *Bird by Bird: Some Instructions on Writing and Life*, by Anne Lamott (Anchor): Lamott offers less nitty-gritty writing advice than other books, but is so empathetic about the challenges of writing—writer's block, jealousy of others' success, anxiety at being discovered a fraud—that it's still a worthwhile read.
- *Chicago Manual of Style*, by University of Chicago Press Staff (University Of Chicago Press): This classic is also available in an online edition at www.chicagomanualofstyle.org.
- *Editing by Design: For Designers, Art Directors, and Editors—The Classic Guide to Winning Readers*, by Jan V. White (Allworth Press): This book explains how to assemble content in well-designed formats so that readers can easily digest it.
- *The Editor in Chief: A Practical Management Guide for Magazine Editors*, by Benton Rain Patterson and Coleman E.P. Patterson (Iowa State University): Editors of both print and Internet publications will also find this book helpful, as it explains how to acquire content and manage an ongoing publishing operation.
- *Elements of News Writing*, by James W. Kershner (Allyn & Bacon).
- *The Elements of Style*, by William Strunk, Jr. and E.B. White (Allyn & Bacon).
- *Follow the Story: How to Write Successful Nonfiction*, by James B. Stewart (Simon & Schuster): A Pulitzer Prize winner teaches nonfiction writers how to use the narrative devices of fiction to improve their writing, with chapters covering topics such as leads, dialogue, description, and humor and pathos.
- *Garner's Modern American Usage*, by Bryan A. Garner (Oxford University Press).

- *The Journalist's Craft: A Guide to Writing Better Stories*, by Dennis Jackson and John Sweeney (Allworth Press): A collection of essays by writers, editors, and writing coaches, this book focuses on what makes good storytelling, in addition to covering other basic topics such as how to generate good ideas and the mechanics of language.
- *Merriam-Webster's Collegiate Dictionary*, by Merriam-Webster (Merriam-Webster).
- *Melvin Mencher's News Reporting and Writing*, by Melvin Mencher (McGraw-Hill).

Writing for the Web

You can find advice about tailoring writing for website and email audiences in these books and other resources:

- *Hot Text: Web Writing that Works*, by Jonathan Price and Lisa Price (New Riders Press).
- "The Web Content Style Guide," by Gerry McGovern, an online source at www.gerrymcgovern.com/guide_write_01.htm.
- "Writing for the Web," an online article by Daniel Will-Harris, www.efuse.com/design/web_writing_basics.html.
- *Writing for the Web*, by Crawford Kilian; the author also has a blog about the subject at http://crofsblogs.typepad.com.

How to Use the CD-ROM

orms and other resources are included on a CD-ROM in the back of the book. This CD-ROM, which can be used with Windows computers, installs files that you use with software programs that are already installed on your computer. It is not a standalone software program. Please read this appendix and the README.TXT file included on the CD-ROM for instructions on using the Forms CD-ROM.

Note to Mac users: This CD-ROM and its files should also work on Macintosh computers. Please note, however, that Nolo cannot provide technical support for non-Windows users.

How to View the README File

If you do not know how to view the file README.TXT, insert the Forms CD-ROM into your computer's CD-ROM drive and follow these instructions:

- **Windows 2000, XP, and Vista**: (1) On your PC's desktop, double click the My Computer icon; (2) double click the icon for the CD-ROM drive into which the Forms CD-ROM was inserted; (3) double click the file README.TXT.
- **Macintosh:** (1) On your Mac desktop, double click the icon for the CD-ROM that you inserted; (2) double click on the file README.TXT.

While the README file is open, print it out by using the Print command in the File menu.

Three different kinds of forms are on the CD-ROM:

- Word processing (RTF) forms that you can open, complete, print, and save with your word processing program (see "Using the Word Processing Files to Create Documents," below).
- Forms (PDF) that can be viewed only with Adobe Acrobat Reader 4.0 or higher (see "Using Government Forms," below). These

forms are designed to be printed out and filled in by hand or with a typewriter.

• Financial planning spreadsheets in Microsoft Excel format (XLS), which you can use with Microsoft's Excel or another spreadsheet program that can read XLS files (see "Using the Financial Planning Spreadsheets," below).

See the end of this appendix for a list of forms, their file names, and their file formats.

Installing the Form Files Onto Your Computer

Before you can do anything with the files on the CD-ROM, you need to install them onto your hard disk. In accordance with U.S. copyright laws, remember that copies of the CD-ROM and its files are for your personal use only.

Insert the Forms CD-ROM and do the following.

Windows 2000, XP, and Vista Users

Follow the instructions that appear on the screen. (If nothing happens when you insert the Forms CD-ROM, then (1) double click the My Computer icon; (2) double click the icon for the CD-ROM drive into which the Forms CD-ROM was inserted; (3) double click the file WELCOME.EXE.)

By default, all the files are installed to the \Publishing Forms folder in the \Program Files folder of your computer. A folder called "Publishing Forms" is added to the "Programs" folder of the Start menu.

Macintosh Users

(1) If the "Publishing Forms CD" window is not open, open it by double clicking the "Publishing Forms CD" icon; (2) select the "Publishing Forms" folder icon; (3) drag and drop the folder icon onto the icon of your hard disk.

Using the Word Processing Files to Create Documents

This section concerns the files for forms that can be opened and edited with your word processing program.

All word processing forms come in rich text format. These files have the extension ".RTF". For example, the form for the Art Memo discussed in Chapter 5 is in the file ArtMemo.rtf. All forms, their file names, and their file formats are listed at the end of this appendix.

RTF files can be read by most recent word processing programs including all versions of MS Word for Windows and Macintosh, WordPad for Windows, and recent versions of WordPerfect for Windows and Macintosh.

To use a form from the CD-ROM to create your documents you must: (1) Open a file in your word processor or text editor; (2) edit the form by filling in the required information; (3) print it out; and (4) rename and save your revised file.

The following are general instructions. However, each word processor uses different commands to open, format, save, and print documents. Please read your word processor's manual for specific instructions on performing these tasks.

Do not call Nolo's technical support if you have questions on how to use your word processor.

Step 1: Opening a File

There are three ways to open the word processing files included on the CD-ROM after you have installed them onto your computer:

- **Windows users can open a file by selecting its "shortcut" as follows:** (1) Click the Windows "Start" button; (2) open the "Programs" folder; (3) open the "Publishing Forms" subfolder; (4) open the "RTF" subfolder; (5) click the shortcut to the form you want to work with.

- **Both Windows and Macintosh users can open a file directly by double clicking it.** Use My Computer or Windows Explorer (Windows 2000, XP, or Vista) or the Finder (Macintosh) to go to the folder you installed or copied the CD-ROM's files to. Then, double click the specific file you want to open.

- **You can also open a file from within your word processor.** To do this, you must first start your word processor. Then, go to the File menu and choose the Open command. This opens a dialog box where you will tell the program (1) the type of file you want to open (*.RTF) and (2) the location and name of the file (you will need to navigate through the directory tree to get to the folder on your hard disk where the CDs files have been installed).

Where Are the Files Installed?

Windows Users: RTF files are installed by default to a folder named \Publishing Forms\RTF in the \Program Files folder of your computer.

Macintosh Users: RTF files are located in the "RTF" folder within the "Publishing Forms" folder.

Step 2: Editing Your Document

Fill in the appropriate information according to the instructions and sample agreements in the book. Underlines are used to indicate where you need to enter your information, frequently followed by instructions in brackets. Be sure to delete the underlines and instructions from your edited document. You will also want to make sure that any signature lines in your completed documents appear on a page with at least some text from the document itself.

Editing Forms That Have Optional or Alternative Text

Some of the forms have check boxes before text. The check boxes indicate:

- **optional text,** where you choose whether to include or exclude the given text
- **alternative text,** where you select one alternative to include and exclude the other alternatives.

When using the Forms CD-ROM, we recommend that instead of marking the check boxes, you do the following:

Optional text

- If you don't want to include optional text, just delete it from your document.
- If you do want to include optional text, just leave it in your document. In either case, delete the check box itself as well as the italicized instructions that the text is optional.

Alternative text

- First delete all the alternatives that you do not want to include.
- Then delete the remaining check boxes, as well as the italicized instructions that you need to select one of the alternatives provided.

Step 3: Printing Out the Document

Use your word processor's or text editor's "Print" command to print out your document.

Step 4: Saving Your Document

After filling in the form, use the "Save As" command to save and rename the file. Because all the files are "read only," you will not be able to use the "Save" command. This is for your protection. *If you save the file without renaming it, the underlines that indicate where you need to enter your information will be lost, and you will not be able to create a new document with this file without recopying the original file from the CD-ROM.*

Using Government Forms

Electronic copies of useful forms from the US Government are included on the CD-ROM in Adobe Acrobat PDF format. You must have Adobe Reader installed on your computer to use these forms. Adobe Reader is available for all types of Windows and Macintosh systems. If you don't already have this software, you can download it for free at www.adobe. com.

All forms, their file names, and their file formats are listed at the end of this appendix. These form files were created by the US Government, not by Nolo.

These forms cannot be filled out using your computer. To create your document using these files, you must: (1) Open the file; (2) print it out; (3) complete it by hand or typewriter.

Step 1: Opening Government Forms

PDF files, like the word processing files, can be opened one of three ways:

- **Windows users can open a file by selecting its "shortcut" as follows:** (1) Click the Windows "Start" button; (2) open the "Programs" folder; (3) open the "Publishing Forms" subfolder; (4) open the "PDF" folder; (5) click the shortcut to the form you want to work with.

- **Both Windows and Macintosh users can open a file directly by double clicking it.** Use My Computer or Windows Explorer (Windows 2000, XP, or Vista) or the Finder (Macintosh) to go to the folder you created and copied the CD-ROM's files to. Then, double click the specific file you want to open.

- **You can also open a PDF file from within Adobe Reader.** To do this, you must first start Reader. Then, go to the File menu and choose the Open command. This opens a dialog box where you will tell the program the location and name of the file (you will need to navigate through the directory tree to get to the folder on your hard disk where the CD-ROM's files have been installed).

Where Are the PDF Files Installed?

- **Windows Users:** PDF files are installed by default to a folder named \Publishing Forms\PDF in the \Program Files folder of your computer.
- **Macintosh Users:** PDF files are located in the "PDF" folder within the "Publishing Forms" folder.

Step 2: Printing Government Forms

Choose Print from the Adobe Reader File menu. This will open the Print dialog box. In the "Print Range" section of the Print dialog box, select the appropriate print range, then click OK.

Step 3: Filling in Government Forms

The PDF files cannot be filled out using your computer. To create your document using one of these files, you must first print it out (see Step 2, above) and then complete it by hand or typewriter.

Using the Financial Planning Spreadsheets

This section concerns the files for the financial planning spreadsheets that can be opened and completed with Microsoft Excel or another spreadsheet program that "understands" XLS files.

These spreadsheets are in Microsoft Excel format. These files have the extension ".XLS". For example, the Cash Flow Forecast spreadsheet discussed in Chapter 7 is in the file CashFlow.xls. All forms and their filenames are listed below.

To complete a financial planning spreadsheet you must: (1) Open the file in a spreadsheet program that is compatible with XLS files; (2) fill in the needed fields; (3) print it out; (4) rename and save your revised file.

The following are general instructions. However, each spreadsheet program uses different commands to open, format, save, and print documents. Please read your spreadsheet program's manual for specific instructions on performing these tasks.

Step 1: Opening a File

There are three ways to open the spreadsheet files included on the CD-ROM after you have installed them onto your computer:

- **Windows users can open a file by selecting its "shortcut" as follows:** (1) Click the Windows "Start" button; (2) open the "Programs" folder; (3) open the "Publishing Forms" subfolder; (4) click the shortcut to the spreadsheet you want to work with.

- **Both Windows and Macintosh users can open a file directly by double clicking it.** Use My Computer or Windows Explorer (Windows 2000, XP, or Vista) or the Finder (Macintosh) to go to the folder you installed or copied the CD-ROM's files to. Then, double click the specific file you want to open.

- **You can also open a file from within your spreadsheet program.** To do this, you must first start your spreadsheet program. Then, go to the File menu and choose the Open command. This opens a dialog box where you will tell the program (1) the type of file you want to open (*.XLS) and (2) the location and name of the file (you will need to navigate through the directory tree to get to the folder on your hard disk where the CD-ROM's files have been installed). If these directions are unclear you will need to look through the manual for your spreadsheet program—Nolo's technical support department will not be able to help you with the use of your spreadsheet program.

Where Are the Files Installed?

Windows Users
- XLS files are installed by default to a folder named \Publishing Forms in the \Program Files folder of your computer.

Macintosh Users
- XLS files are located in the "Publishing Forms" folder.

Step 2: Entering Information Into the Spreadsheet

Fill in the appropriate information according to the instructions and sample spreadsheets in the book. As you fill in these spreadsheets, numeric calculations are performed automatically. If you do not know how to use your spreadsheet program to enter information into an XLS file, you will need to look through the manual for your spreadsheet program—Nolo's technical support department will not be able to help you with the use of your spreadsheet program.

Step 3: Printing Out the Spreadsheet

Use your spreadsheet program's "Print" command to print out your document. If you do not know how to use your spreadsheet program to print a document, you will need to look through the manual for your spreadsheet program—Nolo's technical support department will not be able to help you with the use of your spreadsheet program.

Step 4: Saving Your Spreadsheet

After filling in the form, use the "Save As" command to save and rename the file. Because all the files are "read only," you will not be able to use the "Save" command. This is for your protection. If you save the file without renaming it, you will overwrite the original financial planning spreadsheet, and you will not be able to create a new document with this file without recopying the original file from the CD-ROM.

If you do not know how to use your spreadsheet program to save a document, you will need to look through the manual for your spreadsheet program—Nolo's technical support department will not be able to help you with the use of your spreadsheet program.

List of Forms Included on the Forms CD-ROM

The following files are in rich text format (RTF):

FILE NAME	FORM TITLE
AdRateCard.rtf	Advertising Rate Card
ArtAgreement.rtf	Artwork Permission Agreement
ArtMemo.rtf	Art Memo
ArtMemoIllustrator.rtf	Art Direction Memo: Illustrator
ArtMemoPhotographer.rtf	Art Direction Memo: Photographer
BoardGuidelines.rtf	Editorial Advisory Board Guidelines
EditorialCalendar.rtf	Editorial Calendar
InsertionOrder.rtf	Insertion Order
IssueSchedule.rtf	Issue Schedule
PhotoAgreement.rtf	Photo Permission Agreement
PhotoWorksheet.rtf	Photo Permission Worksheet
PublicationSpecs.rtf	Publication Specification Sheet

The following files are in portable document format (PDF):

FILE NAME	FORM TITLE
Interview.pdf	Job Interview Questions
PrintChecklist.pdf	Printing Checklist
EmailChecklist.pdf	Email Services Checklist
IRS990.pdf	IRS Form 990
IRS990EZ.pdf	IRS Form 990-EZ
IRSForm990T.pdf	IRS Form 990-T
ISSNApplicationForm.pdf	ISSN Application Form
PSForm3500.pdf	PS Form 3500
PSForm3524.pdf	PS Form 3524
PSForm3526.pdf	PS Form 3526
PSForm3541.pdf	PS Form 3541

The following spreadsheet is in Microsoft Excel Format (XLS):

FILE NAME	FORM TITLE
Budget.xls	Budget Worksheet

Index

C

W

X

m o r e   f r o m

N O L O

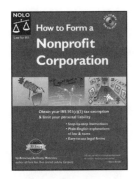

How to Form a Nonprofit Corporation
by Attorney Anthony Mancuso

Book w/CD-ROM

If you want tax-exempt status for your nonprofit organization, this is the book you need. It shows you how to create and operate a nonprofit corporation in your state, obtain federal 501(3)(c) tax exemption, qualify for public charity status, prepare articles of incorporation, create bylaws—and much more.

Provides all the forms you need as tear-outs and on CD-ROM.

$49.99/NNP

Effective Fundraising for Nonprofits
Real-World Strategies That Work
by Attorney Ilona Bray

Getting tax-exempt status is just the first step for a nonprofit—whether it succeeds or fails depends entirely on its ability to raise donations. Turn to this book to get the job done. You'll find out how to work with donors, plan special events, solicit grants, get media coverage, start a side business and more.

Covers IRS rules and regulations, grassroot strategies and dozens of resources.

$24.99/EFFN

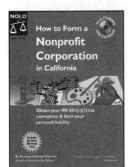

How to Form a Nonprofit Corporation in California
by Attorney Anthony Mancuso

Book w/CD-ROM

This all-in-one guide shows nonprofit groups how to organize as a nonprofit corporation in the Golden State. Line by line, it helps you fill out the federal 501(c)(3) IRS tax-exemption application form. It also helps you get through California's tax-exemption form, and understand the California Nonprofit Integrity Act of 2004.

Provides all the forms you need as tear-outs and on CD-ROM.

$49.99/NON

800-728-3555 or **www.nolo.com**

m o r e   f r o m

N O L O

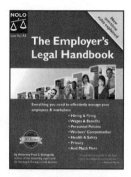

The Employer's Legal Handbook
by Attorney Fred S. Steingold

The most complete guide to your legal rights and responsibilities, *The Employer's Legal Handbook* shows you how to comply with the most recent workplace laws and regulations, run a safe and fair workplace and avoid lawsuits.

$39.99/EMPL

Dealing With Problem Employees
by Attorneys Amy DelPo & Lisa Guerin

This book combines the practical and legal information employers need. Providing a plain-English overview of employment law, it also shows readers how to head off potential problems, recognize who is and isn't a problem employee, avoid legal trouble and much more

$44.99/PROBM

Create Your Own Employee Handbook
by Attorneys Lisa Guerin & Amy DelPo

Book w/CD-ROM

Whether you have ten employees or thousands, this easy-to-use book lets you provide them with a guide to your company's benefits, policies, procedures and more. A CD-ROM allows you to cut-and-paste the policies to create your own handbook instantly.

$49.99/EMHA

800-728-3555 or www.nolo.com

MEET YOUR NEW ATTORNEY

"Loves walking in the rain and drawing up prenuptial agreements."

"Enjoys fine wine and creating living trusts."

"Spends time gardening and doing trademark searches."

Brent
San Francisco

Juliana
Phoenix

Ron
Seattle

Start a great relationship
(you can skip the walks on the beach)

You don't need just any attorney. You need that "special someone" – someone whose personality puts you at ease, whose qualifications match your needs, whose experience can make everything better.

With Nolo's Lawyer Directory, meeting your new attorney is just a click away. Lawyers have created extensive profiles that feature their work histories, credentials, philosophies, fees – and much more.

Check out Nolo's Lawyer Directory to find your attorney – you'll feel as if you've already met, before you ever meet.

Visit us and get a free eBook!
http://lawyers.nolo.com/book

Meet your new attorney **NOLO'S LAWYER DIRECTORY**

The attorneys listed above are fictitious. Any resemblance to an actual attorney is purely coincidental.

Protecting your family
has never been easier

...make your will online *now*

Nolo Now lets you create a legal will from the comfort of your home computer. Complete a quick step-by-step interview, print your document, get witnesses, sign it – and you're done! Best of all, you don't pay until you're ready to click "print."

Nolo Now is simple, straightforward and completely legal. Providing your loved ones with the safety and security of a will is so easy, anyone can do it!

Find out more and get a free eBook!
http://nolonow.nolo.com/book